Mystery of the Church

Mystery of the Church

Paul Haffner

GRACEWING

First published in 2007
by

Gracewing
2, Southern Avenue
Leominster
Herefordshire
HR6 0QF
www.gracewing.co.uk

Second edition 2010, revised and reset.
Third impression 2014, with minor corrections.

ISBN 978 0 85244 133 6

Cover design: Byzantine icon of St Peter and St Paul sustaining the Church.

Contents

Preface

This book started to take shape in the lectures on the theology of the Church which I gave at the Pontifical Institure *Regina Mundi* and the Pontifical Athenaeum Regina *Apostolorum* here in Rome. This text is clearly not the only one to be written on the theology of the Church in recent years. Nevertheless, it attempts to offer a global vision of the main themes in ecclesiology, which although they may have been treated elsewhere, have often been treated in a partial or unilateral way. One specific problem of some post-Conciliar ecclesiology has in fact been the one-sided approach to this study in certain quarters. Sometimes the horizontal aspect of the Church has been exaggerated at the expense of the vertical. Other times, the particular Church has been highlighted to the exclusion of the universal. In any case, the conviction of this book is that the Second Vatican Council certainly represented a milestone in ecclesiology, especially, but not exclusively, in the constitutions *Lumen Gentium, Unitatis Redintegratio* and *Gaudium et Spes*. This does not mean however that Vatican II spoke the last word on this area, or closed the doors on further development in reflection on the Church; far from it, since the post-conciliar years have already indicated interesting steps forward. Also, Vatican II clearly did not intend to break with two thousand years of Church tradition, but rather synthesized that tradition and actualized it for today. Indeed the Second Vatican Council needs to be read and interpreted in the light of that same tradition.

The unfolding of the book follows a simple historical and logical order. The first chapter deals with the divine institution of the Church, and the second treats the essential nature of the Church. The successive four chapters examine the traditional four 'notes of the Church' or her unity, holiness, catholicity and apostolicity. The seventh chapter discusses the Church in relation to salvation. Chapter eight looks at the Church and the world, and finally chapter nine unfolds the eschatological question of the Church and the Kingdom.

This book owes much to many, and here I would like to offer individual thanks to all who helped me in some way with its preparation. Once again at the publishers, Mr. Tom Longford and Jo Whale deserve my gratitude for their constant help and encouragement in the various stages of production. Ben and Heather Akers kindly looked at the text for me and suggested helpful corrections. The book is dedicated to Rt Rev Crispian Hollis, Bishop of Portsmouth, for many reasons. First, he is the bishop of the diocese to which I am attached, and has offered support and encouragement over the years. Second, he has celebrated his ruby anniversary of priestly ordination during the writing of this work, and even more recently celebrated twenty years as a bishop. Third, the diocese of Portsmouth recently marks its 125th birthday. Last, but by no means least, Bishop Crispian has exemplified the practical end of the Mystery of the Church, so it is appropriate that he should be remembered with warmth and affection in these pages.

Rome, 29 June 2007
Solemnity of the Apostles Peter and Paul

Abbreviations

AAS =	*Acta Apostolicae Sedis. Commentarium officiale.* Rome: Vatican Polyglot Press, 1909– .
CCC =	*Catechism of the Catholic Church.* Dublin: Veritas, 1994.
CCL =	*Corpus Christianorum series latina.* Tournai: Brepols, 1954– .
CSEL =	*Corpus Scriptorum Ecclesiasticorum Latinorum.* Wien: 1866– .
DS =	H. Denzinger. *Enchiridion Symbolorum, Definitionum et Declarationum de rebus fidei et morum.* Bilingual edition edited by P. Hünermann. Bologna: EDB, 1995.
ED =	Pontifical Council for Christian Unity, *Ecumenical Directory.* Vatican City: Vatican Polyglot Press, 1993.
EV =	*Enchiridion Vaticanum.* Documenti ufficiali della Chiesa. Bologna: Edizioni Dehoniane.
IG =	*Insegnamenti di Giovanni Paolo II.* Vatican City: Vatican Polyglot Press, 1978–2005.

IP = *Insegnamenti di Paolo VI*. Vatican City: Vatican Polyglot Press, 1963–1978.

OR = *L'Osservatore Romano*, daily Italian edition.

ORE = *L'Osservatore Romano*, weekly English edition.

ND = J. Neuner and J. Dupuis, *The Christian Faith in the Doctrinal Documents of the Catholic Church*. Sixth edition. New York: Alba House, 1996.

PG = J.P. Migne. *Patrologiae cursus completus, series graeca*. 161 vols. Paris: 1857–1866.

PL = J.P. Migne. *Patrologiae cursus completus, series latina*. 221 vols. Paris: 1844–1864.

SC = *Sources Chrétiennes*. Paris: Cerf, 1942– .

1

Origins of the Church

The ways of Christ are holy, and He has built the holy city, that is, the Church, in which He also dwells. For He abides among the saints, and we have become temples of the living God, having Christ within us through the participation of the Holy Spirit. He, therefore, founded a Church, with Himself as its foundation, in which we also, as rich and precious stones, are built into a holy temple, as a dwelling-place for God in the Spirit.

St Cyril of Alexandria, *Commentary on Isaiah*, 4

The Mystery of the Church expresses the divine love with which the Father achieves His salvific will in Christ, by the power of the Holy Spirit, through His holy people.[1] According to St Paul in his letter to the Ephesians, God chose us and 'destined us for adoption to himself through Jesus Christ in accord with the favour of his will, for the praise of the glory of his grace that he granted us in his beloved Son' (Ep 1:4–6).[2] The Mystery of the Church is an essential part of that eternal purpose or plan that the Father accomplished in Christ Jesus our Lord: 'He has let us know the mystery of His purpose, according to His good pleasure which He determined beforehand in Christ, for Him to act upon when the times had run their course: that He would bring everything together under Christ, as Head, everything in the heavens and everything on earth' (Ep 1:9–10; cf. 3:11). This destiny of the human person, chosen and called to be an adopted child of God, concerns not only the individual dimension of the human race, but its community dimension as well. The manifold wisdom of God has now been made known through the Church (Ep 3:10).

In the eternal design of God, the Church constitutes, in Christ and with Christ, an essential part of the universal economy of salvation in which the love of God is expressed. That eternal plan contains the destiny of human beings, who have been created in the image and likeness of God, called to the dignity of children of God and adopted as children of the heavenly Father in Jesus Christ. God conceives, creates and calls to Himself a community of persons. The Christian is predestined in Christ (cf. Ep 1:4, 5), as a member of the Church, which is predestined as the body of the redeemed in Christ.[3] Therefore, in God's eternal design, the Church, as the unity of humanity in Christ the Head, becomes part of a plan which includes all creation. One could say it is a 'cosmic' plan, that of uniting everything in Christ the Head. The Firstborn of all creation becomes the principle of 'recapitulation' for this creation, so that God can be 'all in all' (1 Co 15:28), and Christ is the keystone of the universe. As the living body of those who belong to Him by their response to the vocation of being children of God, the Church is associated with him, as participant and minister, at the centre of the plan of universal redemption.[4] The Church is a Mystery not because it is completely intangible, but in the sense of being in some ways beyond the grasp of human reason, and therefore revealed by Christ. It is both visible and invisible, holy and yet made up of sinners, involved in the present course of history and yet orientated to the life to come. Above all, it is both human and divine, like Jesus Christ its Founder. It is the mystery of a new community of God's people, which includes, in the bond of the communion of saints, in addition to the faithful on earth who follow Christ along the way of the Gospel, those too who are completing their purification in purgatory, and the saints in heaven.[5]

This first chapter considers the historical and ontological origin of the Church. The Church is *called* into being by

God, in a transcendent action; it is not therefore equivalent to a democratic type of vision where the convocation of the people is horizontal and immanent. In the Gospel of Matthew, when Jesus, in response to Peter's confession of faith, announced the establishment of His Church, 'Upon this rock I will build my Church' (Mt 16:18), He employed the expression *mou ten ekklesían*. This word *ekklesía* was used in the Septuagint (the Greek translation of the Bible dating from the second century B.C.) to translate the Hebrew *qahàl* and the corresponding Aramaic *qahalà,* which Jesus probably used in His response to Simon Peter. Both the Hebrew term *qāhāl* and the Greek *ekklesía* mean 'gathering' or 'assembly'. *Ekklesía* is etymologically related to the Greek verb *kalein,* which means 'to call'. In Semitic speech the word meant, in practice, 'assembly' ('called together'), and it was used in the Old Testament to designate the 'community' of the chosen people, especially in the desert (cf. Dt 4:10; Ac 7:38). In Jesus' day, the expression was still being used.[6] Jesus used the term to speak of His messianic community, that new assembly called together through the covenant in His blood, the covenant proclaimed in the Upper Room (cf. Mt 26:28). In both Semitic and Greek usage, the assembly received its character from the will of the one who convoked it and from the purpose for which he called it. Both in Israel and in the ancient Greek city-states *(pòleis)* various assemblies were called, those of a profane nature (political, military or professional), as well as those which were religious and liturgical.[6]

The word 'Church' (in Latin *ecclesia,* from the Greek *ekkalein,* to 'call out of') means a convocation or an assembly. It designates the assemblies of the people, usually for a religious purpose (cf. Ac 19:39). *Ekklesia* is frequently adopted in the Greek Old Testament to render the Hebrew expression *qāhāl* for the assembly of the Chosen People before God, above all for their assembly on Mount Sinai where Israel received the Law and was established by God as His holy people (cf. Ex 19). By calling itself Church, the first community of Christian believers recognized itself as heir to that assembly. In the Church, God is 'calling together' His people from all the ends of the earth. The equivalent Greek term *Kyriake,* from which the English word Church and the German *Kirche* are derived, signifies 'what belongs to the Lord'.[8] As St Cyprian remarked, the Church is drawn into being by the Most Holy Trinity:

> What He has made us by the second birth He wishes us to continue during our infancy, that we who have begun to be children of God may abide in His peace, and that having one spirit we should also have one heart and one mind. Thus God does not accept the sacrifice of one who is in disagreement but commands him to go back from the altar and first be reconciled with his brother, so that God may be placated by the prayers of a peacemaker. Our peace and concord are the greatest possible sacrifice to God—a people united in the unity of the Father, and of the Son, and of the Holy Spirit.[9]

Realism

The realist fabric of God's action in time and space guarantees the perennial value of a discourse on ecclesiology as well as about other theological topics. Realism requires a serious grasp of the various aspects of the being and action of the Church, of her true historical foundation, of her union with Christ, and of her visible character. These mysteries have a bearing on the material world, and this physical aspect must be taken seriously as well. Thus realism defends ecclesial truths against a mythological perspective, or an excessively symbolic view of their nature, which often, in modernist and rationalist circles, tends to water them down. At the same time, a realist perspective defends ecclesiology from dissolving into pious sentimentalism, and instead grounds it solidly in the Word of God and right reason. Similarly, ecclesiology guarantees a realist basis for the whole of theology, since the Church is tied to the reality of the Incarnation, which is itself the base for all realism. The mystery of God the Son coming at a fixed point in time and assuming what he had created adds to a realist appreciation of time and matter. It is no longer possible to escape up the blind alleys of cyclic notions of time, of pantheistic notions of matter, of idealistic notions of reality. All time, all history, all matter, all space, radiate from the moment when God the Son took human flesh.[10]

Old Testament preparation

The Church was prepared and prefigured in the Old Testament, even from the moment of the creation itself, in the primitive covenant with Adam and Eve in which they were elevated to a supernatural state of communion with God and with each other. The words of God in the book of Genesis 'It is not right that the man should be alone,' (Gn 2:18) refer prophetically to the communion which is His Church and to the union of man and wife which is a figure of the union of Christ and His Church. Our first parents were invited to obey the covenant command not to eat the fruit of the tree of the knowledge of good and evil and for that obedience were rewarded with the supernatural life of grace. This covenant was a treaty involving however two unequal partners, God and man.[11] An analogy links the creation covenant with the New and Eternal Covenant in Christ as expressed in the Paschal Mystery: 'Just as Eve was formed from Adam's side as he slept, so also was the Church born from the pierced heart of Christ as He slept in death upon the Cross.'[12]

The profound meaning of the covenant unfolds with the parallel between Adam and Christ and Eve and Our Lady.[13] Christ and Our Lady were predestined from all eternity.[14] Similarly, the Church was *predestined* from all eternity, and thus is not a chance product of history or evolution. This eternal mystery of the Church spans past, present and future, as the eternal plan of God unfolds in time:

> The eternal Father, by a free and hidden plan of His own wisdom and goodness, created the whole world. His plan was to raise men to a participation of the divine life... He planned to assemble in the holy Church all those who would believe in Christ. Already from the beginning of the world the foreshadowing of the Church took place. It was prepared in a remarkable way throughout the history of the people of Israel and by means of the Old Covenant. In the present era of time the Church was constituted and, by the outpouring of the Spirit, was made manifest. At the end of time it will gloriously achieve completion, when, as is read in the Fathers, all the just, from Adam and 'from Abel, the just one, to the last of the elect', will be gathered together with the Father in the universal Church.[15]

The Old Testament speaks of various types of assemblies. However, when it deals with the community of the Chosen People as a whole, it emphasizes the religious and even theocratic nature of those people who have been called together, by explicitly proclaiming that they belong to the one God. For this reason, it considers the entire people of Israel to be the *qāhāl* of Yahweh and calls them such, precisely because they are the Lord's 'special possession, dearer than all other people' (Ex 19:5). It is an altogether special belonging to and relationship with God, based on the covenant made with him and on acceptance of the commandments given to them by intermediaries between God and the people at the moment of their call, which Sacred Scripture designates precisely as 'the day of the assembly,' *yòm haqqahàl* (cf. Dt 9:10; 10:4). This feeling of belonging spans Israel's whole history and endures, in spite of repeated betrayals and the recurrence of crises and defeats. This theological truth continued in history, was expressed by the appeal of the prophets in times of disappointment, like deutero-Isaiah: he encouraged Israel in the name of God, toward the end of the exile, 'Fear not, for I have redeemed you; I have called you by name; you are mine' (Is 43:1). This was an announcement that, in virtue of the Old Covenant, He would soon intervene to free His people.

This covenant with God, the result of His own choice, forges a religious character for the entire people of Israel and a transcendent purpose to their whole history, even though its earthly course experiences good times and bad. This fact explains the biblical language which calls Israel 'the assembly of God,' *qāhāl Elohim* (cf. Neh 13:1), and more frequently *qāhāl Yahweh* (cf. Dt 23:2–4, 9). It is the permanent awareness of a belonging based on the election of Israel by God made in the first person: 'You shall be my special possession, dearer to me than all other people... You shall be to me a kingdom of priests, a holy nation' (Ex 19:5–6).[16] Among the people of the Old Testament, out of great respect for the proper name of God, *qāhāl Yahweh* was read as *qāhāl Adonai,* 'the assembly of the Lord'. For this reason it was also translated in the Septuagint as *ekklesía Kyriou;* we would say 'the Church of the Lord'.[17] The people of the Old Testament were called into union with God through the covenant. While the assembly under the Old Law and then the Church in the New Testament is not essentially a mere social or political reality, but is initiated by God, it does however have social, cultural and political consequences. The people were called through the covenant, which involved being purified and separated from other peoples: 'The Lord then said to Moses, "Go to the people and tell them to sanctify themselves today and tomorrow. They must wash their clothes and be ready for the day after tomorrow; for the day after tomorrow, in the sight of all the people, the Lord will descend on Mount Sinai"'(Ex 19:10–11; cf. 2 Ch 31:18).

After the original covenant with our first parents, God made several other covenants with His chosen people, the first of which was with Noah. God addressed Noah and his sons in these solemn words: 'I am now establishing my covenant with you and with your descendants to come, and with every living creature that was with you: birds, cattle and every wild animal with you; everything that came out of the ark, every living thing on earth. And I shall maintain my covenant with you: that never again shall all living things be destroyed by the waters of a flood, nor shall there ever again be a flood to devastate the earth' (Gn 9:9–11). The sign of this covenant was a rainbow, as a reminder of 'the eternal covenant between God and every living creature on earth, that is, all living things'(Gn 9:16). The fact that this covenant was already termed *eternal,* clearly signifies that it prefigures the eternal New Covenant in Christ. The covenant with Noah also already expressed the characteristics of a relationship between God and His people.

The next step in the progressive revelation of God's covenant took place with Abraham. God invited him to move to a new land: 'Go forth from the land of your kinsfolk… to a land that I will show you. I will make of you a great nation and I will bless you' (Gn 12:1–2). This promise was then confirmed by a covenant (Gn 15:18; 17:1–4) and was solemnly proclaimed after the sacrifice of Isaac. Following God's request, Abraham was ready to sacrifice his only son whom the Lord had given to him and his wife Sarah in their old age. Here God only meant to test his faith, and to prefigure the Sacrifice of Christ His Son, which would seal the New Covenant. In this sacrifice, then, Isaac did not die, but continued living. However, Abraham had consented in his heart to the sacrifice and this sacrifice of the heart, the proof of a magnificent faith, obtained for him the promise of innumerable descendants: 'I swear by myself, declares the Lord, that because you acted as you did in not withholding from me your beloved son, I will bless you abundantly and make your descendants as countless as the stars of the sky and the sands of the seashore' (Gn 22:16–17). The fulfilment of this promise was to take place in various stages. Abraham was destined to become 'the father of all who have faith' (cf. Gn 15:6; Ga 3:6–7; Rm 4:16–17). Our Lady's *Magnificat* echoes the fulfilment of this promise: 'He has come to the help of Israel his servant, mindful of his faithful love-according to the promise he made to our ancestors, of his mercy to Abraham and to his descendants for ever' (Lk 1:54–55).

The first stage of fulfilment was achieved in Egypt where 'the Israelites were fruitful and prolific. They became so numerous and strong that the land was filled with them' (Ex 1:7). By now Abraham's stock had become 'the Israelite people' (Ex 1:9). However, they suffered the humiliating condition of slavery. Faithful to His covenant with Abraham, God called Moses and said, 'I have witnessed the affliction of my people in Egypt and have heard their cry… I have come down to rescue them… Come, now! I will send you… to lead my people, the Israelites, out of Egypt' (Ex 3:7–10). Moses was called to lead that people out of Egypt, but was only God's agent in fulfilling his plan, the instrument of his power. Israel, then, is the people who enjoy God's favour: 'It was not because you are the largest of all nations that the Lord set his heart on you and chose you, for you are really the smallest of all nations. It was because the Lord loved you and because of his fidelity to the oath he had sworn to your fathers' (Dt 7:7–8). The Israelites were not chosen to be the People of God because of their human qualities, but solely by God's initiative.[18]

The divine initiative, the Lord's sovereign choice, assumed the form of a further covenant, which was enacted after the deliverance of Israel from slavery in Egypt. Moses was the mediator of this covenant at the foot of Mount Sinai. When Moses came to the people and related all the words and ordinances of the Lord, they all answered with one voice, 'We will do everything that the Lord has told us.' Moses then wrote down all the words of the Lord and, rising early the next day, he erected at the foot of the mountain an altar and twelve pillars for the twelve tribes of Israel. Then sacrifices were offered and Moses splashed half of the blood of the sacrifice on the altar. Taking the book of the covenant, he read it aloud to the people, once again receiving from those present the promise to obey the words of God. Finally, he sprinkled the people with the other half of the blood (cf. Ex 24:3–8). The Book of Deuteronomy explains the significance of this event: 'Today you are making this agreement with the Lord: he is to be your God and you are to walk in his ways and observe his statutes, commandments and decrees, and to hearken to his voice. Today the Lord is making this agreement with you: you are to be a people peculiarly his own' (Dt 26:17–18). The covenant with God is a special 'promotion' for Israel, who thus becomes 'a people sacred to the Lord [their] God' (cf. Dt 26:19). This means that they belong to God in a reciprocal form: 'Then I will be your God and you shall be my people' (Jr 7:23). God commits Himself to the covenant, and all the infidelities on the people's part at the various stages of their history do not affect God's fidelity to the covenant. This covenant opens the way to the new covenant foretold in the Book of the Prophet Jeremiah: 'But this is the covenant which I will make with the house of Israel after those days, says the Lord. I will place my law within them, and write it upon their hearts' (Jr 31:33).

In virtue of the divine initiative taken in the covenant, a people becomes the People of God, and as such they are holy, that is, sacred to the Lord God: 'For you are a people sacred to the Lord, your God' (Dt 7:6; cf. Dt 26:19). The meaning of this consecration also clarifies the words of Exodus: 'You shall be to me a kingdom of priests, a holy nation' (Ex 19:6). Even though during the course of their history this people would commit many sins, they did not cease being the People of God. For this reason, Moses appealed to the Lord's fidelity to the covenant which he himself had established, and addressed a moving petition to him: 'Destroy not your people, your heritage,' as we read in Deuteronomy (9:26). For His part, God did not cease addressing his word to the Chosen People. He speaks to them many times through the prophets. The principal commandment continues to be to love God above all things: 'You shall love the Lord, your God, with all your heart, with all your soul, and with all your strength' (Dt 6:5). This commandment is joined to the commandment of love for one's neighbour: 'I am the Lord. You shall not defraud or rob your neighbour... Take no revenge and cherish no grudge against your fellow countrymen. You shall love your neighbour as yourself' (Lev 19:13, 18).

A further theme characterizes the biblical texts: the God who made a covenant with Israel wants to be present among His people, present in a special way. During the pilgrimage in the desert this presence was revealed in the meeting tent. The book of Exodus explains, regarding the meeting tent:

> Whenever Moses went out to the tent, the people would all rise and stand at the entrance of their own tents, watching Moses until he entered the tent. As Moses entered the tent, the column of cloud would come down and stand at its entrance while the Lord spoke with Moses. On seeing the column of cloud stand at the entrance of the tent, all the people would rise and worship at the entrance of their own tents. The Lord used to speak to Moses face to face as one man speaks to another (Ex 33:8–11).

The gift of this presence was a special sign of divine election, which is revealed in symbolic ways and as the type of a future reality: God's covenant with his new people in the Church. Later, it was expressed by the temple which King Solomon built in Jerusalem.

The Old Testament covenant featured several constitutive elements. First, by God's choice, His own were set apart and therefore comprised a holy people. In this context, God made promises to His chosen people, and offered them the commandments, which they were required to follow. Among His people, there were priests who were appointed to offer sacrifice to God in the name of His people. The covenant was made visible by signs, and its fundamental formula was: 'I will be your God and You will be my people' (Jr 32:38).

While the Old Covenant was established with the specific people chosen by God, the people of Israel, the Old Testament foretells a future universality which indicates the foundation of the Church. The promise God made to

Abraham: 'All the communities of the earth shall find blessing in you' (Gn 12:3), a promise renewed several times and extended to 'all the nations of the earth' (Gn 18:18), finds its fulfilment only in the Church of Jesus Christ. Further texts specify that this universal blessing would be communicated by the offspring of Abraham (cf. Gn 22:18), Isaac (cf. Gn 26:4) and Jacob (cf. Gn 28:14). The same concept is repeated in other expressions by the prophets, especially in the Book of Isaiah:

> It will happen in the final days that the mountain of the Lord's house will rise higher than the mountains and tower above the heights. Then all the nations will stream to it, many peoples will come to it and say, 'Come, let us go up to the mountain of the Lord, to the house of the God of Jacob that He may teach us his ways so that we may walk in His paths.' For the Law will issue from Zion and the word of the Lord from Jerusalem. Then He will judge between the nations and arbitrate between many peoples (Is 2:2–4).

Isaiah's eschatological banquet is also an indication of the future promised Church, and its final destiny: 'On this mountain, for all peoples, the Lord of Hosts is preparing a banquet of rich food, a banquet of fine wines, of succulent food, of well-strained wines. On this mountain, He has destroyed the veil which used to veil all peoples, the pall enveloping all nations; He has destroyed death for ever' (Is 25:6–8). From Second Isaiah, the text indicates the universality of the Church as 'servant of the Lord': 'I, the Lord, have grasped you by the hand and shaped you; I have made you a covenant of the people and light to the nations' (Is 42:6). The Book of Jonah is also significant when it describes the prophet's mission to Nineveh, which was outside Israel's sphere (cf. Jon 4:10–11). These passages, and others too, lead to an understanding that the Chosen People of the Old Covenant was a foreshadowing of and preparation for the future People of God, which would be universal in extent. Therefore, after Christ's Resurrection, the 'Good News' was first proclaimed to Israel (cf. Ac 2:36; 4:10).[19]

The Old Testament also contains many significant types of the Church. One particularly powerful image is that of the Ark of the Covenant (1 Ch 15:25, 26, 28, 29; 16:6, 16:37; 17:1; 22:19; 28:2, 18). The Letter to the Hebrews points out that this Ark is symbolic for the present age (cfr. Heb 9:9). The Ark contained 'the gold jar containing the manna, Aaron's branch that grew the buds, and the tables of the covenant' (Heb 9:4). These three objects in the Ark are types of the Church of Christ. The gold jar containing the manna, is a prefiguration of the Holy Eucharist. The rod of Aaron which blossomed is a symbolic foreshadowing of the hierarchy. The tables of the ten Commandments of Moses are a typical representation of the Word of Holy Scripture.

The bridal image of the Church is prefigured in the Songs of Songs and in the book of the prophet Hosea. The allegorical interpretation of the Song of Songs is rendered very probable by the prophetic portrayal of the relation between Yahweh and Israel as like that of husband and wife: 'My love is mine and I am his' (Sg 2:16). The permanent union between Christ and His Church is also prefigured in the Song of Songs: 'Set me like a seal on your heart, like a seal on your arm'(Sg 8:6). Yahweh chose Israel for His Spouse, clothing her with gold and silver and rich garments, and made her famous among the nations for her beauty and splendour (Ez 16:3–14; Is 54:6ff.; 62:4f.; Ho 2:19f.). The prophet Jeremiah refers to the love of Israel's betrothal (Jr 2:2). The bridal love also encapsulates the new, universal and everlasting covenant prophesied by Jeremiah (Jr 31:31–34; 32:37–38, 40). The twelve Tribes of Israel (cf. Nm 13:4–15) prefigure the Apostolic College, as a permanent institution in the Church (Rev 21:10–14).

New Testament foundation

The writers of the Greek text of the New Testament followed the Septuagint translation. This fact explains why they call the new People of God (the new Israel) *ekklēsia,* and also why they refer the Church to God. St Paul frequently speaks of the 'Church of God' (cf. 1 Co 1:2; 10:32; 15:9; 2 Co 1:1; Gal 1:13), or the 'churches of God' (cf. 1 Co 11:16; 1 Th 2:14; 2 Th 1:4). By this usage he emphasizes the continuity of the Old and New Testaments, even to the point of calling Christ's Church 'the Israel of God' (Ga 6:16). However, St Paul soon found a way to formulate the realities of the Church founded by Christ, as when Paul speaks of the Church 'in God the Father and the Lord Jesus Christ' (1 Th 1:1), or the 'Church of God in Jesus Christ' (1 Th 2:14). In the Letter to the Romans, he even speaks of the 'churches of Christ' (Rm 16:16) in the plural, having in mind—and keeping his eye on—the local Christian churches, as in Palestine, Asia Minor and Greece.

This progressive development in language is an assurance that in the first Christian communities the newness of Christ's words: 'Upon this rock I will build my Church' (Mt 16:16), gradually becomes clearer. The words of Isaiah's prophecy are now applied to this Church in a new sense with greater depth: 'Fear not, for I have redeemed you; I have called you by name; you are mine' (Is 43:1). This 'divine calling together' is the work of Jesus Christ, the incarnate Son of God; He establishes and builds 'His' Church as a 'calling together of all people in the new covenant.' He chooses a visible foundation for this Church and entrusts to Peter the mandate of governing her. This Church, therefore, belongs to Christ and will always remain His. This is the conviction of the first Christian communities; this is their faith in the Church of Christ.

The terminological and conceptual reading of the New Testament texts, indicates some clear concepts which bear on the meaning of the Church. These ideas can be synthesized in the following assertion: the Church is the new community of individuals, instituted by Christ as a 'calling together' of all those called to be part of the new Israel in order to live the divine life, according to the graces and demands of the covenant established by the sacrifice of the cross. This calling together entails for each one a call which requires a response of faith and cooperation in the purpose of the new community, determined by Him who gives the call: 'It was not you who chose me, but I who chose you and appointed you to go and bear fruit' (Jn 15:16). This is the source of the Church's connatural dynamism, which has an immense field of activity, because it is a calling to belong to Him who wishes to 'sum up all things in Christ' (Eph 1:10).

The purpose of this calling together is to be introduced into divine communion (cf. 1 Jn 1:3). The first step in achieving this goal consists in listening to the Word of God which the Church receives, reads and lives in the light which comes from on high, as a gift of the Holy Spirit, according to the promise Christ made to the apostles: 'The Holy Spirit that the Father will send in my name will teach you everything and remind you of all that I told you' (Jn 14:26). The Church is called and sent to bring the word of Christ and the gift of the Spirit to everyone: to all the people who will be the 'new Israel,' beginning with children, about whom Jesus said: 'Let the children come to me' (Mt 19:14). However, all are called, young and old, and among adults, persons of every condition. As St Paul says, 'There is neither Jew nor Greek, there is neither slave nor freeman, there is neither male nor female; for you are all one in Christ Jesus' (Gal 3:28). Finally, the goal of this calling together involves an eschatological destiny, because the new people are completely oriented toward the heavenly community, as the first Christians knew and felt: 'For here we have no lasting city; we are seeking one which is to come' (Heb 13:14). 'We have our citizenship in heaven; it is from there that we eagerly await the coming of our Saviour, the Lord Jesus Christ' (Ph 3:20).[20]

The word which was used by Jesus in speaking of His Church was the expression *qāhāl*, and this word is associated with the Greek expression *ekklēsia* in the Septuagint.[21] We have seen that in the Old Testament, *qāhāl* signified an assembly or a congregation, often in a Covenant context. The new wine of Jesus' teaching could not be contained within old wineskins, nor could the institutions of the Old Israel contain the spiritual dynamism of the Gospel. Jesus founded His *qāhāl*, which was prepared for in the Old Covenant, but yet was new and distinct from Israel. When it was required to translate Jesus' teaching from Aramaic into Greek, the word *ekklēsia* was already in use among Greek speaking Christians to identify their own community as the New Israel, and at the same time was different from the expression *synagōgē*, which lay too close to the Jewish concept of synagogue. The expression *ekklēsia* indicated the messianic community gathered around Christ (Mt 16:18), which developed as the Christian community expanded. Originally the term indicated the mother Church in Jerusalem (Ac 8:1), later the individual Churches throughout Judaea (Gal 1:22), and then among the pagans (Ac 13:1, Jm 5:14). The word refers to gatherings (1 Co 11:18) and regions (Rm 16:5). It indicates the Church united under God (Ac 20:28), and for various aspects which we consider later on, such as the Church as the Body of Christ, or as the Bride of Christ. The word *ekklēsia* 'stood contemporaneously for the liturgical gathering of Christians, the group of believers in local centres, and the body of believers in all regions'.[22] The continuity and discontinuity between Old Testament and New Testament therefore comes clearly into view, whereby the New and Eternal Covenant replaces the Old.[23] St Paul refers to the inclusion of the Gentiles as a previously unrevealed mystery, because it is based upon the abrogation of the Mosaic law and entails a degree of nearness to the Lord that exceeds the expectations of the Old Covenant.[24]

Christ wished to found a Church and did in fact do so. The economy of salvation is orientated to the establishment of the Church, as the First Vatican Council put it:

> The eternal Shepherd and Guardian of our souls, in order to continue for all time the saving work of redemption, determined to build His holy Church so that in it, as in the house of the living God, all the faithful might be united together in the bond of one

> faith and one charity. Therefore, before He was glorified, He prayed to His Father not for the apostles only, but also for those who were to believe in Him through their word, that they all might be one as the Son Himself and the Father are one.[25]

Instead, the modernists based their thought on Kantian subjectivism and upon an evolutionary concept of truth. The modernist tendency towards a subjectivist and an evolutionary concept of truth coupled with a liberal approach to biblical criticism, led to an attempt to undermine the doctrine of the divine institution and divine and supernatural aspects of the Church. Since one of the fundamental principles of modernism was historical development, this system proposed a development based on purely human and social factors.

Modernism entertains several philosophical antecedents. The first of these is the error of deism, or the idea that, although God created the universe, He left it to run on its own according to natural causes ever afterwards, so that there have never been nor ever will be any divine interventions or supernatural happenings; thus there is only a universal natural religion requiring belief in God and the performance of one's duty, while all positive religion was rejected. The freethinker Herbert of Cherbury (1581–1648), is considered the father both of English deism and of naturalism in religion, and this is not surprising, since his exclusion of any role of God in the history of the world easily led to the suggestion that God does not exist at all. The second error can be termed naturalism, or the notion that everything in the world can be explained from natural causes alone; there is no supernatural reality. The third component is rationalism, or the error that human reason, based upon self-evident principles, is the sole judge of certified knowledge. René Descartes (1596–1650) is recognized to be the father of modern rationalism because of his universal methodical doubt and his method of deduction solely from self-evident principles of human reason. Descartes actually excluded from his universal methodical doubt the truths of faith and morals,[26] and he accepted that man can know with certainty from the light of faith,[27] but the series of biblical critics who followed him in the eighteenth century turned his universal methodical doubt against the text of Sacred Scripture and left no place for a real light of faith either in the production of the Bible or in its interpretation. The fourth error is empiricism, or the notion that all certified knowledge is based upon verification by sense experience and experiment. Immanuel Kant (1724–1804) modified Cartesian reasoning in a theory of knowledge based on the belief that man cannot know external reality, but only his reasoning about what he experiences with his senses. The fifth error, subjectivism, as propounded by Kant, is the idea that man can know only the objects of his own thoughts and experiences (*phenomena*) but he cannot know reality external to his own mind (*noumena*). Georg Wilhelm Friedrich Hegel (1770–1831) modified the static philosophy of Kant with a dynamic philosophy according to which all reality is in constant development. Under Hegel's influence, David Strauss (1808–1874) and Ferdinand Baur (1792–1860) 'developed a higher criticism of the Bible in which its supernatural elements were systematically explained away as products of mythology'.[28] Sixth, there is evolutionism, or the ideology that all reality is evolving as a whole in a vaguely upward direction and there are no immutable realities.

Among the errors of modernism, Pope St Pius X condemned the one which denied that Christ instituted the Church: 'It was far from the mind of Christ to found a Church as a society which would continue on earth for a long course of centuries. On the contrary, in the mind of Christ the kingdom of heaven together with the end of the world was about to come immediately.'[29] These errors reappeared in a kind of neomodernism, espoused for example by H. Küng, L. Boff, and G. Lohfink. Hans Küng, following the existentialist and demythologizing approach of R. Bultmann, states categorically that, during the pre-Easter period, Jesus did not found a Church, but only '*laid the foundations* for the emergence of a post-resurrectuion Church.' Also, Lohfink proposed, erroneously, that the New Testament writers conceived of the Church only as an eschatological Israel, and this idea does not require the 'foundation' of the Church.[30]

Faithful theology has always been clear however that Jesus Christ is both the Foundation and the Founder of His Church. Current theology generally envisages that the foundation of the Church involved a series of well-prepared steps on the part of Christ, its divine Founder. The fact that the institution of the Church is seen as a process does not of course undermine its divine foundation, or weaken the nature of its institution. Rather, it is simply an expression of divine mercy, so that the unfolding of this institution could be received more fruitfully by all. This process in the foundation of the Church can be summarized as follows. First, there is a clear link with the Old Testament prophecy and prefiguration of the Church, since the Old Testament promises and covenant regarding the People of God are presupposed in the preaching of Jesus and retain all of their saving power (Mt 4:17). The mystery of the Church is thus manifest in its very foundation. The Lord Jesus set it on its course by preaching the Good News, that is, the coming of the Kingdom of God, which, for centuries, had been promised in the Scriptures.[31] Next, the Church is already expressed in the great invitation by Jesus to all people to be converted and believe in Him (Mt 4:17). An especially significant moment in the institution of the Church is the calling and institution of the Twelve as an effective sign of future restoration of all of Israel (Mk 3:13–19). These Apostles represent the permanent foundation stones of the Church (Rev 21:10–14). The giving of the new name to Simon Peter, and the special place entrusted to him among the apostles and his mission, namely the foundation of the Papacy is a clear revelation of the nature of the institution of the Church (Mt 16:18). At the same time, the rejection of Jesus on the part of Israel and the separation between the Jewish people and the disciples of Jesus, is an indication of the radical novelty of the Church (Mt 21: 28–46; 23; Jn 6:60f.).

Central to the institution of the Church is the historical fact that Jesus, at the Last Supper, when He instituted the Eucharist, and in His Passion and Death, which was freely taken on, continued to preach the Universal Kingdom (different from the Old Covenant) of God, which consists of the gift of divine life to all people (Jn 14–17). The Last Supper is, in a very real sense, the 'womb' of the Church. There the priesthood is instituted (Jn 17:17–19), extending the dynamic whereby the Father sends the Son (Jn 20:21) and the Son sends the Apostles. (Mt 28:20). The Holy Eucharist is also instituted (Mt 26:26–29 and parallels). The last Supper leads up to Christ's Death and Resurrection, the paschal Mystery, in which the Church was born from the wounded side of Christ. After the Lord's Resurrection, the community of Jesus and His disciples is reconstituted in the power of the Resurrection, and the disciples are introduced into true ecclesial life after Easter (Ac 1:12–14). In this way, the foundation of the Church was laid before Easter, but it was finished only after Easter. Pentecost put the seal on the institution of the Church, because the sending of the Holy Spirit which makes the her a true creature of God, with a universal call (Ac 2:1–41). After Pentecost the disciples of Jesus Christ extended their mission to the nations and constituted the Church among the nations (Ac 13:44–52). In this context, there occurred the definitive rupture between the 'new Israel' and Judaism (Ac 15:13–21 and Ac 7). When Jesus, who had suffered death on the Cross for mankind, had risen, He appeared as the One constituted as Lord, Christ and eternal Priest, and He poured out on His disciples the Spirit promised by the Father. From this source the Church, equipped with the gifts of its Founder and faithfully guarding His precepts of charity, humility and self-sacrifice, receives the mission to proclaim and to spread among all peoples the Kingdom of Christ and of God and to be, on earth, the initial budding forth of that kingdom. While it slowly grows, the Church strains toward the completed Kingdom and, with all its strength, hopes and desires to be united in glory with its King.[32] None of the steps given above, when taken alone, makes up the whole, but when they are all taken together, they show that the foundation of the Church should be understood as an historical process and event. Thus, the Church becomes the continuation of the mission of Christ and His Apostles.[33]

The early moments of Church life are recorded in the Acts of the Apostles: 'These remained faithful to the teaching of the apostles, to the brotherhood, to the breaking of bread and to the prayers' (Ac 2:42). We see that right from the start three main elements of the Church are indissolubly linked, namely ecclesial communion (referred to as the brotherhood, a weak translation of the Greek term *koinonia*), communion of faith (noted as the teaching of the apostles), and sacramental or Eucharistic communion (described as the breaking of bread). In these words, Saint Luke provides a kind of definition of the Church, whose constitutive elements include fidelity to the 'teaching of the Apostles', 'communion', 'the breaking of the bread' and 'prayer'.[34]

Trinitarian Origin of the Church

Having dealt with the historical origin of the Church, we now turn to its ontological origin. This ontological origin, or the origin of the being of the Church is to be compared to the way a fountain is the perpetual source of water. In the first place, the origin of the Church is Trinitarian. The Church is represented within the icon of the Most Holy Trinity.[35] Communion in the Church mirrors the unity within the Most Holy Trinity. Mission within the Church mirrors the eternal begetting of the Son, and the procession of the Holy Spirit from the Father and the Son or through the Son (in the Greek view). In other words, the Church expresses the mystery of the movement from the Trinity to the Trinity in the economy of salvation (known classically as *exitus* and *redditus*). In order to render present and efficacious throughout history what Christ accomplished once and for all in His time on earth, Christ sent from the Father His Holy Spirit, who was to carry on inwardly His saving work and prompt the Church to spread out.[36] The Church thus results from a dual mission: that of the Son who with the Incarnation forms in Himself the Head (Col 1:18; Ep 1:9–10) and that of the Holy Spirit, who on the day of Pentecost, forms the Body.

Christological Origin of the Church

The permanent origin of the Church lies in Christ: not only at its historical birth, but she proceeds from her Lord in the most intimate way, because He continually nourishes and builds her through His Holy Spirit. Christ is the foundation-stone of the Church, 'He is the living stone, rejected by human beings but chosen by God and precious to Him' and His Church consists of 'living stones making a spiritual house as a holy priesthood to offer the spiritual sacrifices made acceptable to God through Jesus Christ' (1 Pt 2:4–5). The Most Holy Eucharist celebrates and actualizes the union between Christ and His Mystical Body. This origin of the Church is based on the Incarnation and Redemptive act. A causal influence of the Eucharist is present at the Church's very origins. By analogy with the Covenant of Mount Sinai, sealed by sacrifice and the sprinkling of blood, the actions and words of Jesus at the Last Supper laid the foundations of the new messianic community, the People of the New Covenant.[37] The celebration of the Eucharist is at the centre of the process of the Church's continued growth. As often as the Sacrifice of the Cross, by which 'Christ our Passover has been sacrificed' (1 Co 5:7), is celebrated on the altar, the work of our redemption is carried out. At the same time in the Sacrifice and the Sacrament of the Eucharist, the unity of the faithful, who form one body in Christ (cf. 1 Co 10:17), is both expressed and effected.[38] In the striking interplay between the Eucharist which builds up the Church, and the Church herself which 'makes' the Eucharist, the primary causality is expressed in the first formula: the Church is able to celebrate and adore the mystery of Christ present in the Eucharist precisely because Christ first gave Himself to her in the sacrifice of the Cross.[39]

Several attempts have been made to establish non-ecclesial or non-institutional forms of Christianity, sometimes in Pentecostal or charismatic circles, or else falsely to oppose the institutional and the charismatic elements within the Church:

> It is certainly fitting to recall this fact at a moment like the present one when it happens that not without sorrow we can hear people—whom we wish to believe are well-intentioned but who are certainly misguided in their attitude—continually claiming to love Christ but without the Church, to listen to Christ but not the Church, to belong to Christ but outside the Church.[40]

The absurdity of this dichotomy is clearly evident in this phrase of the Gospel: 'Anyone who rejects you rejects me' (Lk 10:16). How is it possible to love Christ without loving the Church, if the finest witness to Christ is that of St Paul: 'Christ loved the Church and sacrificed himself for her'? (Ep 5:25). Pope John Paul II also pointed out the danger of this false opposition:

> Many are separating, and even opposing the Church and Christ, when they say, for example, Christ—yes, the Church—no. This opposition is not entirely new, but has been proposed again in certain parts of the contemporary world.[41]

Sometimes this dichotomy arises from a flawed answer to the question whether it is legitimate to include among the divine truths to be believed a human, historical, visible reality such as the Church. It is a reality, which like any human thing, has limitations, imperfections and sinfulness on the part of the persons who belong to every level of her institutional structure: lay people as well as ecclesiastics, even among the pastors of the Church, without anyone being excluded from this sad inheritance of Adam.

Another reason for rejecting the essential union between Christ and His Church is sometimes based on a general principle of rejecting mediation. There are indeed people who, although admitting the existence of God, wish to maintain an exclusively personal contact with him, without allowing any mediation between their own conscience and God. This error arose also in the Protestant Reformation.[42] Instead, Christ and His Church are inseparable.

Pneumatological Origin of the Church

The Church is generated in the power of the Holy Spirit. This creative power of the Spirit is prefigured in the account of the creation at the beginning of the book of Genesis, where He hovered over the waters in the creation (Gn 1:2). Mary, the Mother of God, conceived Christ in her womb by the power of the Holy Spirit. The Church, as New Creation and Mystical Body of Christ comes to birth in the power of the Holy Spirit. Pentecost is indeed considered as the birthday of the Church: 'When Pentecost day came round, they had all met together, when suddenly there came from heaven a sound as of a violent wind which filled the entire house in which they were sitting; and there appeared to them tongues as of fire; these separated and came to rest on the head of each of them. They were all filled with the Holy Spirit and began to speak different languages as the Spirit gave them power to express themselves' (Ac 2:1–4). Through the power of the Holy Spirit, the Church left the womb of the upper room and entered the world. The tongues represent the missionary aspect and universality, of the Church, linked with her Catholicity.[43] The Church becomes in this way an indicator of the presence of the Holy Spirit in our world: 'Where the Church is there also is the Spirit of God; where the Spirit of God is there is also the Church and all grace.'[44] In a profound sense, the Holy Spirit is the Soul of the Church: 'What the soul is to the body, the Spirit is to the Body of Christ which is the Church: the Holy Spirit does in the whole Church what the soul does in all the members of a single body.'[45]

Marian Origin of the Church

Our Lady contributed to the foundation of the Church, through her active cooperation in the Incarnation and Redemption. The Mother of God enjoyed a key position in the life of the early Church as portrayed in the Acts of the Apostles. Mary was present from the beginning of the primitive community (cf. Ac 1:14), while she shared with the disciples and some women believers the prayerful expectation of the Holy Spirit, who was to descend on them. After Pentecost, the Blessed Virgin continued to live in fraternal communion with the Church and took part in the prayers, in listening to the Apostles' teaching, and in the Eucharistic celebration (cf. Ac 2:42). She who had lived in close union with Jesus in the house of Nazareth, now lives in the Church in intimate communion with her Son, present in the Eucharist.

As a member of the first community, Mary the Mother of Jesus was surely respected and venerated by all. All the early Christians understood the pre-eminence of Mary who brought forth the Son of God, the one universal Saviour. Moreover, the virginal character of her Motherhood allows her to witness to the extraordinary contribution to the Church's good offered by the one who, giving up human fruitfulness through docility to the Holy Spirit, puts herself completely at the service of God's kingdom.[46] The Holy Spirit reveals the *Theotokos* and She is the One who in a unique way is the revelation of the Holy Spirit in the Church.[47] In the life of the Mother of God one can distinguish two descents of the Holy Spirit. The first, when by the power of the Holy Spirit, she received the Son of God into her womb in the Incarnation, and the second during the descent of the Holy Spirit upon her and the Apostles at Pentecost. The former had the objective function of Mary's divine maternity, the latter was personal: a realisation in her person of the degree of holiness that corresponded to her unique function within the Church. The words of the crucified Christ on Golgotha: 'Woman, behold your Son'

(Jn 19:26), with which her role as the universal Mother of believers was begun, unfolded new and limitless horizons for her Motherhood. The gift of the Holy Spirit, received at Pentecost through the exercise of this mission, induced her to offer the help of her motherly heart to all who are on their way towards the total fulfilment of God's kingdom. Mary is constituted a pre-eminent and as a wholly unique member of the Church.[48] Mary occupies a place in the Church which is highest after Christ and yet at the same time is also closest to us.[49]

Mary's particular membership of the Church was first highlighted by St Augustine. He places Mary before the Church as member of the body of Christ as part of the Church: 'Mary is part of the Church, a holy member, a quite exceptional member, the supremely wonderful member, but still a member of the whole body.'[50] Then, St Chromatius of Aquileia observed with keen discernment: 'The Church was united… in the Upper Room with Mary the Mother of Jesus and with His brethren. The Church therefore cannot be referred to as such unless it includes Mary the Mother of our Lord, together with His brethren.'[51] As theological reflection deepened, Mary was seen as a model member, in a Trinitarian perspective. For, by her complete adherence to the Father's will, to his Son's redemptive work, and to every prompting of the Holy Spirit, the Virgin Mary is the Church's model of faith and charity. Thus she is the 'exemplary realisation' or type of the Church.[52] She reveals the Church at its origins and in its life today. The figure of Mary constitutes the fundamental reference in the Church. Mary is a mirror placed before the Church, in which the Church is invited to recognize her own identity as well as the dispositions of the heart, the attitudes and the actions which God expects from her.[53]

Mary, the Mother of God, also indicates the eschatological destiny of the Church. She is the eschatological icon of the Church. In her we contemplate what the Church already is on her own 'pilgrimage of faith,' and what she will be in the homeland at the end of her journey. There, in the glory of the Most Holy and Undivided Trinity, in the communion of all the saints, the Church is awaited by the one she venerates as Mother of her Lord and as her own mother. In the meantime the Mother of Jesus, in the glory which she possesses in body and soul in heaven, is the image and beginning of the Church as it is to be perfected in the world to come. Likewise she shines forth on earth until the day of the Lord shall come, a sign of certain hope and comfort to the pilgrim People of God.[54]

Notes

1. See G. Philips, *La Chiesa e il suo mistero* (Milano: Jaca Book, 1975), I, p. 71.
2. See also St Paul to the Romans: 'For those He foreknew He also predestined to be conformed to the image of His Son, so that He might be the firstborn among many brothers' (Rm 8:29).
3. See Pope John Paul II, *Discourse at General Audience* (31 July 1991).
4. See Pope John Paul II, *Discourse at General Audience* (31 July 1991).
5. Pope John Paul II, *Discourse at General Audience* (17 July 1991).
6. In a text from the Qumran community regarding the war of the sons of darkness, the expression *qehál 'El*, 'assembly of God,' is used along with others like it on military insignia (1 QM 5:10).
7. See Pope John Paul II, *Discourse at General Audience* (17 July 1991).
8. See *CCC* 751.
9. St Cyprian, *Treatise on the Lord's Prayer*, 23–24 in *CSEL* 3, 284–285.
10. See St Bonaventure, *Hexaemeron*, Collatio 1, n.10: Christus 'mediator Dei et hominum est, tenens medium in omnibus.'
11. See Gn 1:26–28; 2:15–16, 21.
12. St Ambrose, *Exposition of the Gospel according to Luke*, 2, 85–88 in *CCL* 14, 69–71. See also St John Chrysostom, *Catechesis*

to Catechumens, 3, nn.17–19 in *SC* 50, 176–177; St Thomas Aquinas, *Summa Theologiae* I, q. 92, a. 3.

13. See Rm 5:15: 'There is no comparison between the free gift and the offence. If death came to many through the offence of one man, how much greater an effect the grace of God has had, coming to so many and so plentifully as a free gift through the one man Jesus Christ!' The theme of the parallel between Adam and Christ and Eve and Our Lady is also found in the context of Irenaeus' theme of recapitulation: 'The Lord then was manifestly coming to his own things, and was sustaining them by means of that creation that is supported by himself. He was making a recapitulation of that disobedience that had occurred in connection with a tree, through the obedience that was upon a tree. Furthermore, the original deception was to be done away with—the deception by which that virgin Eve (who was already espoused to a man) was unhappily misled. That this was to be overturned was happily announced through means of the truth by the angel to the Virgin Mary (who was also [espoused] to a man)... So if Eve disobeyed God, yet Mary was persuaded to be obedient to God. In this way, the Virgin Mary might become the advocate of the virgin Eve. And thus, as the human race fell into bondage to death by means of a virgin, so it is rescued by a virgin. Virginal disobedience has been balanced in the opposite scale by virginal obedience. For in the same way, the sin of the first created man received amendment by the correction of the First-Begotten' (St Irenaeus, *Adversus haereses*, Book 5, chapter 19, 1 in *SC* 153, 248–251).
14. See Vatican II, *Lumen Gentium*, 61: 'Predestined from eternity by that decree of divine providence which determined the incarnation of the Word to be the Mother of God, the Blessed Virgin was in this earth the virgin Mother of the Redeemer, and above all others and in a singular way the generous associate and humble handmaid of the Lord. She conceived, brought forth and nourished Christ. She presented Him to the Father in the temple, and was united with Him by compassion as He died on the Cross. In this singular way she cooperated by her obedience, faith, hope and burning charity in the work of the Saviour in giving back supernatural life to souls. Wherefore she is our mother in the order of grace.'

15. Vatican II, *Lumen Gentium*, 2.
16. Pope John Paul II, *Discourse at General Audience* (17 July 1991).
17. See Pope John Paul II, *Discourse at General Audience* (17 July 1991).
18. See Pope John Paul II, *Discourse at General Audience* (30 October 1991).
19. See Pope John Paul II, *Discourse at General Audience* (13 November 1991).
20. Pope John Paul II, *Discourse at General Audience* (17 July 1991).
21. See P. Grech, 'Tradition and Theology in Apostolic Times' in R. C. Fuller, L. Johnson and C. Kearns, *A New Catholic Commentary on Holy Scripture* (London: Nelson 1975), pp. 874–875. Grech remarks (p. 874) that other Aramaic words are not in question as expressions for Church in Aramaic. The word *Kenishta* occurs too late in Rabbinic literature (around 250 AD), while the expression *'ēdāh* is never associated with *ekklēsia* in the Septuagint.
22. *Ibid.*, p. 844.
23. See Heb 8:13; Vatican II, *Lumen Gentium*, 9.
24. See Ep 3:2–13 and S. Grindheim, 'What the OT Prophets Did Not Know: The Mystery of the Church in Eph 3,2–13' in *Biblica* 84 (2003), pp. 531–553.
25. Vatican I, Dogmatic Constitution on the Church, Introduction, in DS 3050.
26. See R. Descartes, 'Reply to the Fourth Set of Objections,' in R. M. Hutchins et al., *The Great Books of the Western World*, vol. 31, p. 162.
27. Cf. Descartes, 'Reply to the Second Set of Objections,' in Hutchins et al., *The Great Books of the Western World*, vol. 31, p. 125.
28. B. Blanshard, 'Rationalism,' in *The Encyclopedia Americana* (1967), vol. 23, p. 230c.
29. Pope St Pius X, *Lamentabili Sane*, n.52 in DS 3452: 'Alienum fuit a mente Christi Ecclesiam constituere veluti societatem super terram per longam saeculorum seriem duraturam; quin immo in mente Christi regnum caeli una cum fine

mundi iamiam adventurum erat.' For the English translation see ND[846/52].

30. See H. Küng, *The Church* (New York: Image Books, 1976), p. 108; G. Lohfink, *Gesù e la Chiesa* in *Corso di teologia fondamentale* (Brescia: 1990), III, pp. 49, 95.
31. See Vatican II, *Lumen Gentium,* 5.
32. *Ibid.*
33. See International Theological Commission, *Selected Themes in Ecclesiology* (1985), 1.4.
34. See Pope Benedict XVI, Encyclical Letter *Deus caritas est,* 20. The Pope adds: 'The element of "communion" (*koinonia*) is not initially defined, but appears concretely in the verses quoted above: it consists in the fact that believers hold all things in common and that among them, there is no longer any distinction between rich and poor (cf. also Ac 4:32–37). As the Church grew, this radical form of material communion could not in fact be preserved. But its essential core remained: within the community of believers there can never be room for a poverty that denies anyone what is needed for a dignified life.'
35. In Andrej Rublev's icon, we see the mysterious story where Abraham receives three visitors as he camps by the oak of Mamre. He serves them a meal. As the conversation progresses he seems to be talking straight to God, as if these 'angels' were in some way a metaphor for the three Persons of the Blessed Trinity. In Rublev's representation of the scene, the three gold-winged figures are seated around a white table on which a golden, chalice-like bowl contains a roasted lamb. In the background of the picture, a house can be seen at the top left and a tree in the centre. Less distinctly, a rocky hill lies in the upper right corner. The composition is a great circle around the table, focussing the attention on the chalice-bowl at the centre, which reminds the viewer inescapably of an altar at the Eucharist. The tree is on the way to the house. The tree represents the Cross of Christ, and the house, the Church. It is the beginning and end of our lives. Its roof is golden. Its door is always open for the traveller. It has a tower, and its window is always open so that the Father can incessantly scan the roads for a glimpse of a returning prodigal son.

36. See Vatican II, *Ad Gentes*, 3–4.
37. See Pope John Paul II, Encyclical Letter *Ecclesia de Eucharistia*, 21.
38. See Vatican II, *Lumen Gentium*, 3.
39. See Pope Benedict XVI, Apostolic Exhortation *Sacramentum Caritatis* (2007), 14.
40. Pope Paul VI, Apostolic Exhortation *Evangelii Nuntiandi*, 16.
41. Pope John Paul II, *Discourse at General Audience* (24 July 1991).
42. See Pope John Paul II, *Discourse at General Audience* (24 July 1991).
43. The catholicity of the Church will be treated in chapter five below.
44. St Irenaeus, *Adversus haereses*, Book 3, chapter 24, 1 in *SC* 211, 474–475: 'Ubi enim Ecclesia, ibi et Spiritus Dei; et ubi Spiritus Dei, illic Ecclesia et omnis gratia.'
45. St Augustine, *Sermon 267*, 4, 4 in *PL* 38, 1231.
46. Cf. Pope John Paul II, *Discourse at General Audience* (30 July 1997), 4.
47. Cf. A. Schmemann, 'Mary and the Holy Spirit' in *The Virgin Mary. The Celebration of Faith. Sermons*, Vol. 3 (Crestwood, NY: 1995), p. 72.
48. See Vatican II, *Lumen Gentium*, 53.
49. See Pope Paul VI, *Allocution to the Council* (4 December 1963) in *AAS* 56 (1964), p. 37. See also Vatican II, *Lumen Gentium*, 54.
50. St Augustine, *Sermon 25*, 7 in *PL* 46, 938: 'Maria portio est ecclesia, sanctum membrum, excellens membrum, supereminens membrum, sed tamen totius corporis membrum.'
51. St Chromatius of Aquileia, *Sermon 30*, 1 in *SC* 164, p. 134.
52. See *CCC* 994, and also Vatican II, *Lumen Gentium*, 53, 63.
53. See Congregation for the Doctrine of the Faith, *Letter to the Bishops of the Catholic Church on the Collaboration of Men and Women in the Church and in the World* (2004), 15.
54. See P. Haffner, *The Mystery of Mary* (Leominster: Gracewing, 2004), pp. 232, 265–266. See *CCC* 972 and also Vatican II, *Lumen Gentium*, 68–69, and 2 Pt 3:10.

2

Nature of the Church

> *For the Church is lofty and conspicuous, and well known to all men in every place. It is also lofty in another sense; for her thoughts have nothing earthly, but she is above all that is earthly, and with the eyes of the understanding, looks upon, as far as it is possible, the glory of God, and glories in doctrines truly exalted, concerning God. Therefore, with justice may the house of God be called a mountain by the understanding, and it is perfectly visible, as being raised upon the hills; and one may say of it, and with great cause, what as a notable illustration was uttered by the mouth of the Saviour: 'A city placed upon a hill cannot be hidden.'*
>
> St Cyril of Alexandria, *Commentary on Isaiah*, 1

In order to understand better her activity, the first step is to consider the nature of the Church. Clearly, the nature of the Church is the key to understanding her actions, because being precedes action, which again constitutes a realist approach to ecclesiology.[1] An idea of the nature of the Church is conveyed by studying the names and images which are used to describe her reality.

Proper names

Proper names are a literal description of the Church, as has been seen in the historical development of the name 'Church' in the Old and New Testaments.[2] In her historical reality and theological mystery the Church was prepared in the People of God of the Old Covenant. Although designated by the term *qāhāl* (or assembly) adopted in the Old Testament, it is clear from the New Testament that the Church is the People of God established in a new way through Christ and in virtue of the Holy Spirit.[3]

> God... does not make men holy and save them merely as individuals, without bond or link between one another. Rather has it pleased Him to bring men together as one people, a people which acknowledges Him in truth and serves Him in holiness. He therefore chose the race of Israel as a people unto Himself. With it He set up a covenant. Step by step He taught and prepared this people, making known in its history both Himself and the decree of His will and making it holy unto Himself.[4]

The idea of the Church as the New People of God is already expressed by St Peter to the first Christian communities: 'Once you were "no people," but now you are God's people' (1 Pt 2:10). St Paul affirmed: 'For we are the temple of the living God, as God said: "I will live with them and move among them, and I will be their God and they shall be my people"' (2 Co 6:16). All this clearly shows that from the beginning the Church was conscious of the continuity and, at the same time, the newness of her own reality as the People of God.

The Church is the People of God of the New Covenant, the nucleus of the new humanity which has been called in its entirety to be part of the new people:

> That messianic people, although it does not actually include all men, and at times may look like a small flock, is nonetheless a lasting and sure seed of unity, hope and salvation for the whole human race.

> Established by Christ as a communion of life, charity and truth, it is also used by Him as an instrument for the redemption of all, and is sent forth into the whole world as the light of the world and the salt of the earth (cf. Mt 5:13–16).[5]

This concept of the Church is thus linked to her universality which will be treated later.[6]

The People of God is marked out by characteristics that make it a people also in a human sense in analogy with other peoples.[7] Nevertheless, the New People of God is clearly distinguished from all other religious, ethnic, political, or cultural groups found in history: it is the People of God. God took the initiative, He 'loved us first' (1 Jn 4:19) and so acquired a people for Himself from those who previously were not a people: 'a chosen race, a royal priesthood, a holy nation' (1 Pt 2:9). A person becomes a member of this people not by a physical birth, but by faith in Christ, and Baptism. This People has for its Head Jesus the Christ (the anointed, the Messiah). Because the same anointing, the Holy Spirit, flows from the Head into the body, this is 'the messianic people'. The status of this people lies in the dignity and freedom of the sons of God, in whose hearts the Holy Spirit dwells as in a temple. Its law is the new commandment to love as Christ loved us (Cf. Jn 13:34), which is the 'new' law of the Holy Spirit. Its mission is to be salt of the earth and light of the world (Cf. Mt 5:13–16). This people is 'a most sure seed of unity, hope, and salvation for the whole human race'. Finally, its destiny 'is the Kingdom of God which has been begun by God Himself on earth and which must be further extended until it has been brought to perfection by Him at the end of time'.[8]

The concept of the Church as the People of God is a necessary one, as the Church is indeed a Priestly, Prophetic, and Kingly People. However, the concept on its own is not sufficient. The expression 'People of God' is not in itself clear, and requires further theological elaboration to avoid misunderstanding. In particular, the fact that it is specifically the People of God we are considering, excludes the idea of people understood in a purely biological, racial, cultural, political or ideological sense of the word.[9] Thus the people proceeds 'from above' from God, from His election, His covenant. Moreover, the Second Vatican Council was careful not merely to restate the Old Testament idea of people of God, but rather spoke of the *New* People of God.[10] Thus it is necessary to conceive of the Church as the People of God, but at the same time, not sufficient. Nicolas, following Congar, notes that the notion of People of God is insufficient for the following reasons. First, it does not shed sufficient light upon the relation between Christ and His Church. Second, on its own it fails to give enough clarity to the hierarchical structure of the Church. Finally it does not make sufficiently clear that Church is already in some way the Kingdom. In order to clarify the concept of the 'New People of God', it would be necessary to consider this expression in the light of the sacramentality of the Church.[11]

The letters of Paul express the concept of the Church as a mystery. To start with, the Apostle proclaims Christ 'according to the revelation of the mystery kept secret for long ages but now manifested' (Rm 16:25–26). 'The mystery hidden from ages and from generations past, but now manifested to His holy ones, to whom God chose to make known the riches of the glory of this mystery among the Gentiles; it is Christ in you, the hope of glory' (Col 1:26–27). This is the mystery revealed to comfort hearts, to give instruction in love, to achieve a full understanding of the richness which it contains (cf. Col 2:2). At the same time the Apostle asks the Colossians to pray 'that God may open a door to us for the word, to speak of the mystery of Christ,' hoping for himself 'that I may make it clear, as I must speak' (Col 4:3–4).

This divine mystery, the mystery of the salvation of humanity in Christ, is brought about by God's initiative for the benefit of human beings. As St Paul writes in his letter to the Ephesians: 'This mystery, as it is now revealed in the Spirit to His holy apostles and prophets, was unknown to humanity in previous generations: that the gentiles now have the same inheritance and form the same Body and enjoy the same promise in Christ Jesus through the gospel. I have been made the servant of that gospel by a gift of grace from God who gave it to me by the workings of His power. ' (Ep 3:5–7).

The Church is a divine mystery because the divine design (or plan) for humanity's salvation is realized in her, namely, 'the mystery of the kingdom of God' revealed in the word and very life of Christ. This mystery was revealed by Jesus first of all to the apostles: 'The mystery of the kingdom of God has been granted to you. But to those outside everything comes in parables' (Mk 4:11). Therefore, the eternal initiative of the Father, who conceives the saving plan which was revealed to humanity and accomplished in Christ, is the foundation of the Church's mystery. In the Church, through the work of the Holy Spirit, the mystery is shared with human beings, beginning with the apostles. By this sharing in the mystery of Christ, the Church is the body of Christ. The Pauline image and concept of body of Christ express at the same time the truth of the Church's mystery and the truth of her visible character in the world and the history of humanity.

The Greek word *mysterion* was rendered in Latin as *sacramentum*. In the Latin Church the term *sacramentum* has acquired the more specific meaning of designating the seven sacraments. According to the teaching of the Council of Trent, a sacrament 'is a sign of a sacred reality and the visible expression of invisible grace'.[12] Obviously, this definition can only refer to the Church in an analogical sense, and so it does not suffice to express what the Church is. She is a sign, but not only a sign; in herself she is also the fruit of redemption. The sacraments are means of sanctification; the Church, instead, is the assembly of the persons sanctified; thus, she constitutes the purpose of the saving action (cf. Ep 5:25–27). With these clarifications, the term 'sacrament' can be applied to the Church. The Church is indeed the sign of the salvation accomplished by Christ and meant for all human beings through the work of the Holy Spirit. The sign is visible; the Church, as the community of God's people, has a visible character. The sign is also efficacious, inasmuch as belonging to the Church obtains for people union with Christ and all the graces necessary for salvation.

In 1937, Yves Congar began to formulate his ecclesiology in sacramental terms. Around the same time, the Belgian theologian Emile Mersch wrote of the Church as prolonging the humanity of Christ, and therefore as the sacrament par excellence. Twenty-five years later, Henri de Lubac insisted on the necessary distinction between Christ and the Church, but claimed nevertheless that the Church perpetuated the work of the Son of God on earth. As the 'prolongation of the humanity of Christ' the Church was understood to participate in and contribute to the accomplishment of salvation. The German Jesuit Otto Semmelroth brought this concept of the Church to its preconciliar fruition in the 1950s.[13] Citing Pope Pius XII's 1943 encyclical *Mystici corporis*, which described Christ as the instrument of God still at work in the life of the church (the *incarnati Verbi instrumentum*), Semmelroth portrayed the saving action of God as located in the present in the life of the Church, which possesses the divine reality in such a real and objective way, that whoever is in contact with it comes into communion with the divine reality. This, of course, is an instrumental (*ex opere operato*) understanding of the Church as sacrament in which the Church, as a causal instrument, mediates God's salvation to the world. The Second Vatican Council fully assumed the concept of the Church as sacrament: 'The Church is in Christ like a sacrament or as a sign and instrument both of a very closely knit union with God and of the unity of the whole human race.'[14] The vision of the Church as sacrament helps to link effectively the visible and invisible elements in the Church. At the same time it helps us to see how the Church is indefectible. The concept of *ex opere operato* in sacramental theology shows how the sacrament has its efficacy independent of the worthiness or the holiness of the minister. Hence the Church is efficacious despite the weakness of her human members, and is holy despite their sinfulness. The union between Christ and His Church which is permanent and eternal, can be seen as a kind of fundamental sacramental character which marks the Church, setting her aside as Christ's Bride and Mystical Body.

The idea of *communion* (*koinonia*), is very suitable for expressing the core of the Mystery of the Church.[15] Indeed the concept of communion lies at the heart of the way that the Church understands herself, insofar as it is the Mystery of the personal union of each human being with the divine Trinity and with the rest of mankind, initiated with the faith.[16] Communion, having begun as a reality in the Church on earth, is directed towards its eschatological fulfilment in the heavenly Church.[17] If this idea of communion, which is not a univocal concept, is to serve as a key to ecclesiology, it has to be understood within the teaching of the Bible and the patristic tradition, in which communion always involves a double dimension: the *vertical* (communion with God) and the *horizontal* (communion among men). It should also be pointed out that the notion of ecclesial communion is a deeper reality than a mere feeling of community or 'togetherness'. As has been stated elsewhere, the tendency today is to regard this dimension in a purely empirical or emotional way, rather than the organic and ontological way in which it should be seen. Ecclesial and Eucharistic communion then risks becoming a celebration of the 'togetherness' of the people, rather than a gathering together of His People by God the Father, through His Son in the power of the Holy Spirit.[18] It is essential to the Christian understanding of *communion* that it be recognised above all as a gift from God, as a fruit of God's initiative carried out in the Incarnation and the Paschal Mystery.[19]

Images of the Church

Human language requires a recourse to many images in order to adequately express the mystery of the Church, as it is human and divine. These various images, representations and analogies only indicate partial aspects of the whole reality.[20] In the Old Testament the revelation of the Kingdom is often conveyed by means of metaphors. In the same way the inner nature of the Church is illustrated in different images taken either from tending sheep or cultivating the land, from building or even from family life and betrothals.[21]

Historical Images

Israel is a prefiguration of the Church in various ways. Jerusalem is an image of the Church as the city and as the house of God:

> I rejoiced when I heard them say:
> 'Let us go to God's house.'
> And now our feet are standing
> within your gates, O Jerusalem.
> Jerusalem is built as a city
> strongly compact.
> It is there that the tribes go up,
> the tribes of the Lord (Ps 122:1–4).

Jerusalem was the home of the Temple and the Ark of the Covenant, and it is precisely this link with the covenant which renders the city an effective image of the Church (1 K 8:1–13). The Old Testament also indicates the prophecy of the Church as a house set on a mountain for all peoples to approach:

> As for foreigners who adhere to the Lord to serve him, to love the Lord's name and become his servants, all who observe the Sabbath, not profaning it, and cling to my covenant: these I shall lead to my holy mountain and make them joyful in my house of prayer. Their burnt offerings and sacrifices will be accepted on my altar, for my house will be called a house of prayer for all peoples (Is 56:6–7).

Jacob's ladder is another image of the Church found in the Old Testament (Gn 28:10–18). Jacob, fleeing from the wrath of his brother, lay down to sleep with a stone for a pillow. During the night he dreamed that he saw a ladder or stairway reaching up into the heavens upon which were angels ascending and descending. At the head of the ladder was God the Father confirming the blessing upon him and promising to protect him on his journey. Above all, God promised that his descendants would be as plentiful as the dust on the ground, spreading out to west and east, to north and south. All peoples on earth will bless themselves by Jacob and his descendants. This clearly represents not only the Old Covenant, but also the New Covenant with the New People of God. Jacob called the place Bethel (house of God). St Augustine wrote that Jacob's ladder represented the Church, and the angels the patriarch saw ascending and descending upon it represented the evangelists or preachers of the Gospel, those who ascended into the heavens, to contemplate the beauty and knowledge of Christ and then descended again to give spiritual milk to the children in Christ.[22]

The Old Testament records that Yahweh instructed Moses and the Israelites to built a 'sacred Tent' and an 'Ark'. This sacred Tent was to be a place where God would be among his people, while the Ark was to house the tables of the Decalogue: 'The people must make a sacred Tent for me, so that I may live among them... Make a box out of acacia wood...Then put in the Box the two stone tablets that I will give you, on which the commandments are written' (Ex 25:8–16; 40). This 'Ark' is referred to in various ways in the Old Testament: the Ark of the Testament (Ex 30:26); the Ark of the Covenant of the Lord (Nb 10: 33), the Ark of the Covenant (Jos 3:6), the Ark of God (1 K 4:6). The Ark was a sign of the covenant, a reminder of the special relationship that existed between God and Israel. Being the most sacred religious symbol of the Israelites, they placed it in the 'Holy of Holies' in the tabernacle during their sojourn in the desert. Made from acacia wood, the Ark of the Covenant measured two cubits and a half in length, a cubit and a half in breadth, and a cubit and a half in height. Outside and inside, it was overlaid with gold, while a golden crown or rim ran around it. At the four corners, four golden rings had been placed through which were passed two poles of acacia wood which allowed the Ark to be carried. The Ark had a cover of pure gold called a 'propitiatory' which contained two sculptured cherubim facing each other—their wings spread out over the entire cover (cf. Ex 25:10–22). It is worth noting that this is the only exception in the Old Testament to the law forbidding the Israelites to make graven or carved images. This is all the more surprising since the Ark, which was kept behind the veil in the sanctuary, also contained other sacred objects of Israel such as Aaron's rod and a golden vessel containing a gomer of manna on which God had fed the Israelites during their desert wanderings (cf. Ex 16: 32–35). While the Ark is an image of Christ, it also represents His Church, in the sense of being the house of God and Christ.

Women in the Old Testament are also images of the Church of Christ, in the sense of being Bride and Mother. Sarah, as the Mother of nations is an image of the fertility and fecundity of the Church: 'Furthermore God said to Abraham, "As regards your wife Sarai, you must not call her Sarai, but Sarah. I shall bless her and moreover give you a son by her. I shall bless her and she will become nations: kings of peoples will issue from her"' (Gn 17:15–16). God's gift of fecundity to Rachel is also an image of the Church: 'Then God remembered Rachel; he heard her and opened her womb. She conceived and gave birth to a son, and said, "God has taken away my disgrace!"' (Gn 30:22–23). The blessing conferred on Hannah is also an image of the fecundity of the Church: 'Yahweh visited Hannah; she conceived and gave birth to three sons and two daughters' (1 S 2:21). Ruth's faithfulness, as expressed in a Covenant formula is an image of the fidelity of the Church: 'Wherever you go, I shall go, wherever you live, I shall live. Your people will be my people, and your God will be my God' (Rt 1:16). Judith's confidence in God is an image of the Church which is the honour of all peoples:

> On coming to her house, they blessed her with one accord, saying: You are the glory of Jerusalem! You are the great pride of Israel! You are the highest honour of our race! By doing all this with your own hand you have deserved well of Israel, and God has approved what you have done. May you be blessed by the Lord Almighty in all the days to come! And the people all said, 'Amen!' (Jdt 15:9–10).

Esther is an image of the Church at prayer: 'My Lord, our King, the Only One, come to my help, for I am alone and have no helper but you' (Est 4:17l). The spouse in the Song of Songs is an image of the Church as the Bride of Christ, and has been seen as such by many Fathers and Doctors. The Bride is described as a garden enclosed, and a sealed fountain (Sg 4:12). The image of the New and Eternal Covenant is echoed in the words of the Bridegroom: 'Set me like a seal on your heart, like a seal on your arm. For love is strong as Death, passion as relentless as Sheol. The flash of it is a flash of fire, a flame of the Lord Himself' (Sg 8:6).

The widow of Zarephath (1 K 17:9) is a prefiguration of the Church. She fed the prophet Elijah, and the Lord said: 'Jar of meal shall not be spent, jug of oil shall not be emptied, before the day when Yahweh sends rain on the face of the earth' (1 K 17:14). The guarantee of these earthly gifts of food foreshadows the fact that, through the Church, heavenly sacraments will never fail.[23] Similarly, in the New Testament, the widow who put two small coins into the temple treasury, also represents the Church in a mystical manner, since 'she in her poverty has put in everything she possessed, all she had to live on' (Mk 12:44). The Church renders to God her total self, and is a widow to the world. For some Fathers the coins represent the two Testaments, or else faith and grace.[24]

Several women from the New Testament are also images of the Church. First, Elizabeth is an image of the Church's faith, not least when she exclaims to her cousin Mary: 'Yes, blessed is she who believed that the promise made her by the Lord would be fulfilled' (Lk 1:45). Mary Magdalen is an image of conversion and witness to the Resurrection 'Having risen in the morning on the first day of the week, He appeared first to Mary of Magdala from whom He had cast out seven devils' (Mk 16:9). Above all Our Blessed Lady is the perfect image and model of the Church:

> The Church indeed, contemplating her hidden sanctity, imitating her charity and faithfully fulfilling the Father's will, by receiving the word of God in faith becomes herself a mother. By her preaching she brings forth to a new and immortal life the sons who are born to her in baptism, conceived of the Holy Spirit and born of God. She herself is a virgin, who keeps the faith given to her by her Spouse whole and entire. Imitating the mother of her Lord, and by the power of the Holy Spirit, she keeps with virginal purity an entire faith, a firm hope and a sincere charity.[25]

Indeed, Mary is an 'outstanding model' because her perfection surpasses that of all the other members of the Church. The Second Vatican Council states that Mary carries out this role 'in faith and in charity'.[26] Without forgetting that Christ is the first model, the Council suggests in this way that there are interior dispositions proper to the model realized in Mary, which help the Christian to establish an authentic relationship with Christ. In fact, by looking at Mary, the believer learns to live in deeper communion with Christ, to adhere to Him with a living faith and to place his trust and his hope in Him, loving Him with his whole being.[27]

Natural images

Various other images are taken from creation, from family life, from agriculture, from the home, buildings, and seafaring. Many of these are expressed in the parables of Jesus. His parables and His teaching on His Kingdom make it clear that the Church is an organic and social entity, with a visible hierarchical organization, aiming at bringing all peoples into such an attitude of mind and heart that the just claims of God His Father are recognized and honoured on earth, and hereafter in the heavenly kingdom in which alone Christ's ideal will be perfectly achieved. On earth the kingdom of heaven is likened to a man that sowed good seed in his field, but while everybody was asleep his enemy came and sowed weeds among the wheat (Mt 13:24); again it is 'like a dragnet that is cast in the sea and brings in a haul of all kinds of fish'(Mt 13:47); again it is likened to ten virgins—the wise and the foolish.

The Church is likened to a sheepfold whose one and indispensable door is Christ (Jn 10:1–10). It is a flock of which God Himself foretold He would be the shepherd, (Cf. Is 40:11; Ex 34:10–11) and whose sheep, although ruled by human shepherds are nevertheless continuously led and nourished by Christ Himself, the Good Shepherd and the Prince of the shepherds, who gave His life for the sheep. The Church is a field to be cultivated, the village of God (1 Co 3:9). On that land the ancient olive tree grows whose holy roots were the Prophets and in which the reconciliation of Jews and Gentiles has been brought about and will be brought about (Rm 11: 13–26). That land, like a choice vineyard, has been planted by the heavenly Vinedresser (Is 5:1–10; Mt 21: 33–43):

> When a farmer sets out to till the ground he has to take proper tools and clothing for work in the fields: so when Christ, the heavenly King and the true Husbandman, came to humanity laid waste by sin, He clothed Himself in a body and carried the Cross as His implement and cultivated the deserted soul. He pulled up the thorns and thistles of evil spirits and tore up the weeds of sin. With fire He burnt up all the harvest of its sins. When thus He had tilled the ground of its soul with the wooden plough of His Cross, He planted in it a lovely garden of the Spirit; a garden which brings forth for God as its Master the sweetest and most delightful fruits of every sort.[28]

The image of the Church as the Vine and branches (Jn 15:1–17) readily lends itself not only to the idea of communion within the Church, but also to the intrinsic Eucharistic aspect. The true Vine is Christ who gives life and the power to bear abundant fruit to the branches, that is, to us, who through the Church remain in Christ without Whom we can do nothing.

Many images refer to the Church as the building of God, which then becomes His Temple (See Ps 121; Ez 43:1–2, 4–7; 47:1–12; Ac 7: 48–50; 1 Co 3:9–11, 16–17). The Greek expression *hieron* meaning 'temple area, holy ground' is adopted 74 times in the New Testament, while the word *naos* signifying 'temple building or sanctuary' is found 45 times. Whereas *hieron* designates the totality of the holy space, *naos* refers to the sanctuary within the Temple area where God dwells. In the New Testament, the temple generally referring to the building for worship in Jerusalem. The church, as the locus of the abiding presence of the Spirit, is described as God's field and God's building (1 Co 3:9; 1 Pt 2:5). Paul uses 'Temple of God' as a metaphor for the Christian community in that they are the sanctuary where the Spirit dwells (1 Co 3:16–17; 2 Co 6:16).

The Lord Himself compared Himself to the stone which the builders rejected, but which was made into the cornerstone (Mt 21:42; cf. Ac 4:11; 1 Pt 2: 7; Ps. 117:22). When Jesus recounted the parable of the house built on rock, He proposed a clear message of the Church:

> Everyone who comes to me and listens to my words and acts on them—I will show you what such a person is like. Such a person is like the man who, when he built a house, dug, and dug deep, and laid the foundations on rock; when the river was in flood it bore down on that house but could not shake it, it was so well built (Lk 6:47–48).

On this foundation the Church is built by the apostles, (cf. 1 Co 3:11) and from it the Church receives durability and consolidation. St Paul refers to the Church as the building of God (1 Co 3: 9). This edifice has many names to describe it: the house of God (1 Tm 3:15) in which His family dwells; the household of God in the Spirit (Ep 2: 19–22.); the dwelling place of God among men (Rev 21: 3). From the image of the Church as the dwelling of God is developed the picture of the Church as His holy temple. This Temple, symbolized in places of worship built out of stone, is praised by the Holy Fathers and, not without reason, is compared in the liturgy to the Holy City, the New Jerusalem.[29] As living stones we are built into the Church here on earth (1 Pt 2:5). The image is closely linked with that of Bride, when St John contemplates this Holy City coming down from heaven at the renewal of the world as a bride made ready and adorned for her husband (Rev 21:16). The fact that the Church is the Temple of the Holy Spirit relates also to the bridal image of the Church whereby 'what the soul is to the human body, the Holy Spirit is to the Body of Christ, which is the Church'.[30]

A further historical Old Testament image of the Church which is fulfilled in the New Testament is that of Noah's ark (Gn 6:12–19; 7:23). St John Chrysostom proposed in this context:

> The ark cannot suffer shipwreck, because it has the Lord of all at its helm. The Church is therefore like the ark and Noah symbolizes Christ, and the dove the Holy Spirit. And just as the ark saves those within her amidst the waves of the sea, so also the Church saves all who are going astray.[31]

Later St Gregory of Tours also extolled this image of the Church: 'Do not doubt that this ark is the model of Mother Church. The Church crosses the waves and reefs of this earthly existence and saves us from the evils that threaten us, carrying us in her maternal womb, and surrounding us with a holy embrace.'[32] Then, St Thomas Aquinas also adopted this image, linking it with salvation within the Church: 'No one ought to be indifferent to the Church, or allow himself to be cut off and expelled from it; for there is but one Church in which men are saved, just as outside of the ark of Noah no one could be saved.'[33]

In the New Testament, Noah's ark becomes the barque of Peter, tossed about but remaining safe (see Mt 14:22–33 and parallels). Pope Pius XII recalled this image, saying that our heavenly Father guides 'the barque of the Catholic Church in the teeth of a raging tempest.'[34] Pope Benedict XVI further developed this picture:

> The barque of the Church is forever being buffeted by the wind of ideologies that penetrate it with their waters, seemingly condemning it to sink. And yet, precisely in the Church's suffering, Christ is victorious. [...] He stays on His boat, the ship of the Church. Thus even in the ministry of Peter there is revealed the weakness of what comes from man, but also the strength of God.[35]

This image of the Church as a ship is one which is helpful for describing salvation through the Church.[36]

Another New Testament image of the Church is that of the lampstand. Christ has designated holy Church the lampstand, over which the word of God sheds light through preaching, and illumines with the rays of truth whoever is in this house which is the world, and fills the minds of all men with divine knowledge.

> This word is most unwilling to be kept under a bushel; it wills to be set in a high place, upon the sublime beauty of the Church. For while the word was hidden under the bushel, that is, under the letter of the law, it deprived all men of eternal light. For then it could not give spiritual contemplation to men striving to strip themselves of a sensuality that is illusory, capable only of deceit, and able to perceive only decadent bodies like their own. But the word wills to be set upon a lampstand, the Church, where rational worship is offered in the spirit, that it may enlighten all men. For the letter, when it is not spiritually understood, bears a carnal sense only, which restricts its expression and does

> not allow the real force of what is written to reach the hearer's mind. Let us, then, not light the lamp by contemplation and action, only to put it under a bushel—that lamp, I mean, which is the enlightening word of knowledge—lest we be condemned for restricting by the letter the incomprehensible power of wisdom. Rather let us place it upon the lampstand of holy Church, on the heights of true contemplation, where it may kindle for all men the light of divine teaching.[37]

Mystical Body of Christ

A key New Testament description of the Church which is more than just an image is that of the Mystical Body of Christ. The intimate communion which the Church enjoys with Jesus was expressed in the image of the vine and branches: 'Abide in me, and I in you… I am the vine, you are the branches' (Jn 15:4–5). Christ proclaimed a real communion between His own body and ours: 'He who eats my flesh and drinks my blood abides in me, and I in him' (Jn 6:56). When His visible presence was taken from them, Jesus did not leave His disciples like orphans. He promised to remain with them until the end of time; He sent them His Spirit (Cf. Jn 14:18; 20:22; Mt 28:20; Ac 2:33). As a result communion with Jesus has become, in a way, more intense: 'By communicating His Spirit, Christ mystically constitutes as His body those brothers of His who are called together from every nation.'[38] St Paul then proposed the image of the Church as Christ's Mystical Body especially in his letters to the Ephesians and to the Colossians. The Pauline texts indicate Christ as 'the Head of the Church; which is His Body, the fullness of Him who is filled, all in all' (Ep 1:22–23; Cfr Col 1:18). Also in the well-known text to the Corinthians St Paul elaborated his ecclesiological vision:

> For as with the human body which is a unity although it has many parts—all the parts of the body, though many, still making up one single body—so it is with Christ. We were baptized into one body in a single

> Spirit, Jews as well as Greeks, slaves as well as free men, and we were all given the same Spirit to drink. And indeed the body consists not of one member but of many. Now Christ's body is yourselves, each of you with a part to play in the whole. And those whom God has appointed in the Church are, first apostles, secondly prophets, thirdly teachers; after them, miraculous powers, then gifts of healing, helpful acts, guidance, various kinds of tongues. (1 Co 12:12–14, 27–28).

The Apostolic Fathers further elaborated this picture. For example, the *Didaché* linked the Eucharistic Body of Christ with His Mystical Body: 'As this broken Bread was scattered over the hills, and then, when gathered, became one, so may your Church be gathered from the ends of the earth into your Kingdom.'[39] More explicitly, Pope St Clement I wrote to the Corinthians: 'Why do we divide and tear to pieces the members of Christ, and raise up strife against our own body, and why have we reached such a height of madness as to forget that we are members one of another?'[40] St Irenaeus is familiar with the idea that the Churches scattered throughout the world form a unique community; and that communion corresponds to a mystical reality, for the Church is the grouping of the adopted sons of God, the body of which Christ is the Head, simply 'the great and glorious body of Christ,' which Gnostics divide and seek to destroy.[41] St Irenaeus develops further the link between Christ's Mystical Body and His Eucharistic Body in the context of recapitulation:

> When the chalice we mix and the bread we bake receive the word of God, the Eucharistic elements become the body and blood of Christ, by which our bodies live and grow. How then can it be said that flesh belonging to the Lord's own body and nourished by His body and blood is incapable of receiving God's gift of eternal life? Saint Paul says in his letter to the Ephesians that we are members of His body, of His flesh and bones. He is not speaking of some spiritual and incorporeal kind of man,

> for spirits do not have flesh and bones. He is speaking of a real human body composed of flesh, sinews and bones, nourished by the chalice of Christ's blood and receiving growth from the bread which is His body.[42]

For Tertullian, all the faithful are members of one and the same body, the Church is in all those members, and the Church is Jesus Christ.[43] St Ambrose proposed our close union with Christ as the basis and motive of the charity we have for one another, since we form only one Body, of which He is the Head.[44] St Augustine further elaborated the concept of the Church as the Body of Christ. The Church is the Body of Christ and the Holy Spirit is the soul of that Body; for the Holy Spirit does in the Church all that the soul does in all the members of one body; hence the Holy Spirit is for the body of Jesus, which is the Church, what the soul is for the human body. Therefore if we wish to live in the Holy Spirit, if we wish to remain united to Him, we must preserve charity, love truth, desire unity, and persevere in the Catholic faith; for just as a member amputated from the body is no longer vivified by the soul, so he who has ceased to belong to the Church no longer receives the life of the Holy Spirit.[45] St Augustine sometimes fused two pictures of the Church, that of bride and that of city or dwelling, and so links the somatic and political models of the Church:

> All together we make up the members and the Body of Christ; not only when we are gathered in this place, but when we are scattered throughout the world; not only those who are living today, but also all those who have existed since the time of Abel, and will exist until the end of the world. Whatever just person lives their life, whether we generate or are generated, all together we form the one Body of Christ... This Church which is a now a pilgrim here on earth, will be joined to the one in heaven, where the angels are citizens... And these two form but one Church, the City of the great King.[46]

St Thomas Aquinas also taught that the Church was the Body of Christ and the Temple of the Holy Spirit: 'We see that in a man there are one soul and one body; and of his body there are many members. So also the Catholic Church is one body and has different members. The soul which animates this body is the Holy Spirit.'[47]

This picture of the Church as a body indicates the intimate bond between Christ and His Church. Not only is she gathered around Him; she is united in Him, in His Body. Three aspects of the Church as the Body of Christ are to be more specifically noted: the unity of all her members with each other as a result of their union with Christ; Christ as the Head of the Body; and the Church as the Bride of Christ.

Christians who respond to God's word and become members of Christ's Body, become intimately united with Him: 'In that body the life of Christ is communicated to those who believe, and who, through the sacraments, are united in a hidden and real way to Christ in His Passion and glorification.'[48] This is especially true of Baptism, which unites us to Christ's Death and Resurrection, and the Eucharist, by which 'really sharing in the body of the Lord, …we are taken up into communion with Him and with one another.'[49] The unity of the Body of Christ does not eliminate the diversity of its members: 'In the building up of Christ's Body there is engaged a diversity of members and functions. There is only one Spirit who, according to his own richness and the needs of the ministries, gives his different gifts for the welfare of the Church.'[50] The unity of the Mystical Body produces and stimulates charity among the faithful: 'From this it follows that if one member suffers anything, all the members suffer with him, and if one member is honoured, all the members together rejoice.'[51] Finally, the unity of the Mystical Body triumphs over all human divisions: 'For as many of you as were baptized into Christ have put on Christ. There is neither Jew nor Greek, there is neither slave nor free, there is neither male nor female; for you are all one in Christ Jesus' (Ga 3:27–28).

Christ 'is the Head of the Body, the Church' (Col 1:18). He is the principle of creation and redemption. Raised to the Father's glory, 'in everything He is pre-eminent,' (Col 1:18) especially in the Church, through whom He extends His reign over all things. Christ unites us with His Passover: all His members must strive to resemble Him, 'until Christ be formed' in them (Ga 4:19). 'For this reason we…are taken up into the mysteries of His life, …associated with His sufferings as the body with its head, suffering with Him, that with Him we may be glorified.'[52] Christ provides for our growth: to make us grow towards Him, our Head (Cf. Col 2:19; Ep 4:11–16). He provides in His Body, the Church, the gifts and assistance by which we help one another along the way of salvation.

Christ and His Church thus together make up the 'whole Christ' (*Christus totus*). The Church is one with Christ. In the words of St Augustine: 'Marvel and rejoice: we have become Christ. For if He is the Head, we are the members; He and we together are the whole man… The fullness of Christ then is the Head and the members. But what does head and members mean? Christ and the Church.'[53] Our Redeemer has shown himself to be one person with the holy Church whom He has taken to Himself.[54] According to the Angelic Doctor, Head and members form as it were one and the same mystical person.[55]

In St John's Gospel, it is stated that Christ is so full of grace and truth that we receive from His inexhaustible fullness (John 1:14–16). These words of the disciple whom Jesus loved also demonstrate why Christ our Lord should be declared in a very particular way Head of His Mystical Body. Pope Pius XII elaborated further on this mystery:

> As the nerves extend from the head to all parts of the human body and give them power to feel and to move, in like manner our Saviour communicates strength and power to His Church so that the things of God are understood more clearly and are more eagerly desired by the faithful. From Him streams into the body of the Church all the light with which

> those who believe are divinely illumined, and all the grace by which they are made holy as He is holy.[56]

Bride of Christ

The doctrine of the Church as bride of Christ 'is rooted in the biblical reality of the creation of the human being as male and female'.[57] At the same time the reverse is also true, namely that the doctrine of the distinction and relation between male and female is anchored in the mystery of the Church. This is highlighted in the Song of Songs, which uses human love between a man and a woman as an image of God's love for His people or Christ's love for His Church. In a certain sense, the kiss imparted by the bridegroom to the bride in the Song of Songs (Sg 1:2) is symbolic of the new Creation. It is highly significant that the kiss is given right at the beginning of the Song in a type of analogy with the start of the book of Genesis (see Gn 2:7) and thus represents a new inbreathing of life into redeemed humanity. St Gregory of Nyssa observed the similarity between the kiss exchanged between the man and his spouse in the Song of Songs and the gratuitous and life-giving action of the Word and the Holy Spirit upon the soul.[58]

The bridal image of the Church is prefigured in the Old Testament (for example Sg 8:6–7, Ho 2–3) and revealed in the New Testament (Ep 5:25–27, 32). The Church, called 'that Jerusalem which is above' is also called 'our mother'(Ga 4:26; cf. Rev 12:17). It is described as the spotless spouse of the spotless Lamb, (Rev 19:7; 21:2,9; 22:17) whom Christ 'loved and for whom He delivered Himself up that He might sanctify her' (Ep 5:26), whom He unites to Himself by an unbreakable covenant, and whom He unceasingly 'nourishes and cherishes'(Ep 5: 29), and whom, once purified, He willed to be cleansed and joined to Himself, subject to Him in love and fidelity, (cf. Ep 5:24) and whom, finally, He filled with heavenly gifts for all eternity, in order that we may know the love of God and of Christ for us, a love which surpasses all knowledge (cf. Ep 3:19).

The Fathers reflected on the image of the Church in the Scriptures. Concerning the passage from the Song of Songs: 'I am the Flower of the field and the Lily of the valleys; as the lily among the thorns, so is my neighbour among the daughters' (Sg 2:1–2), Origen wrote:

> It seems that He, who is at once the Bridegroom and Word and Wisdom, says these words about Himself and the Bride to His friends and companions. But according to the kind of interpretation that we have proposed to follow, Christ is to be understood as speaking in this way with reference to the Church, and to be calling Himself 'the Flower of the field and the Lily of the Valleys.' We call a 'field' a level piece of ground that is under cultivation and is tilled by farmers; valleys, on the other hand, rather suggest stony and uncultivated places. So we can take the field as meaning that people which was cultivated by the Prophets and the Law, and the stony, untilled valley as the Gentiles' place... So we will take His saying, 'as the lily among thorns, so is my neighbour among the daughters,' as denoting the Church of the Gentiles...because she has come forth among the infidels and unbelievers, as from among thorns.[59]

St Cyprian adopts the image of the Church as the Bride of Christ insisting on her unicity: 'The Bride of Christ cannot be defiled. She is inviolate and chaste. She knows but one home, and with a chaste modesty She guards the sanctity of one bedchamber. It is She that keeps us for God, She that seals for the kingdom the sons whom She bore. Whoever is separated from the Church and is joined to an adulteress is separated from the promises of the Church; nor will he that forsakes the Church of Christ attain to the rewards of Christ. He is an alien, a worldling, and an enemy.'[60]

St Gregory of Nyssa also considers the bridal image in order to provide a model of communion within the Church:

> But if perfect love casts out fear, as Scripture says, fear being transformed into love, then whatever

> attains to salvation will be found to constitute a unity. All its elements will be gathered up into one by being grafted on to the one Good, in the perfect unity which is typified by the dove. This we learn from the words that follow: 'My dove is one, my perfect one.' And the same is declared even more clearly in the Gospel in the words of Our Lord, when He proclaims to His disciples that they should all become one by being grafted on to the one and only Good; so that through the unity of the Holy Spirit, as the Apostle says, bound together by the bond of peace, they should all become one Body and one Spirit.[61]

The Church, journeys in a foreign land while on earth, away from the Lord (cf. 2 Co 5: 6), and so is living in exile. It seeks and experiences those things which are above, where Christ is seated at the right-hand of God, where the life of the Church is hidden with Christ in God until it appears in glory with its Spouse (cf. Col 3:1–4.) St Bernard links the image of the Church as Bride with her exile and her eschatological fulfilment: 'Bride of Christ! You are dark, but beautiful, O daughter of Jerusalem: even though the effort and the pain of this long exile disfigures you, nevertheless you are adorned with heavenly beauty.'[62]

Related to the image of the Church as Bride is that of the Church as family. The Church is God's family in the world. The teaching of St Paul is very emphatic in this regard: 'So then, as we have opportunity, let us do good to all, and especially to those who are of the household of faith' (Ga 6:10). In this family no one ought to go without the necessities of life. Yet at the same time *caritas* and *agape* extend beyond the frontiers of the Church. The parable of the Good Samaritan remains as a standard which imposes universal love towards the needy whom we encounter 'by chance' (cf. Lk 10:31), whoever they may be. Without in any way detracting from this commandment of universal love, the Church also has a specific responsibility: within her family no member should suffer through being in need.[63] The various images and pictures of the Church that have been discussed shed light on some fundamental characteristics of her nature which are now examined.

The Church as visible and invisible

Christ, who is both Divine and human, instituted, established and continually sustains here on earth His holy Church, which reflects Her Founder, and is a visible organization 'through which He communicates truth and grace to all men.'[64] The Church is thus at the same time a 'society structured with hierarchical organs and the Mystical Body of Christ', a visible society and a spiritual community, 'the earthly Church and the Church endowed with heavenly riches.'[65] These dimensions together constitute one complex reality which is essentially 'both human and divine, visible but endowed with invisible realities, zealous in action and dedicated to contemplation, present in the world, but as a pilgrim, so constituted that in her the human is directed toward and subordinated to the divine, the visible to the invisible, action to contemplation, and this present world to that city yet to come, the object of our quest.'[66]

One consequence is that ecclesial communion is at the same time both invisible and visible. As an invisible reality, it is the communion of each human being with the Father through Christ in the Holy Spirit, and with the others who are fellow sharers in the divine nature (cf. 2 Pt 1: 4), in the passion of Christ (cf. 2 Co 1: 7), in the same faith (cf. Ep 4:13; Phm 6), in the same spirit (cf. Ph 2:1.). In the Church on earth, there is an intimate relationship between this invisible communion and the visible communion in the teaching of the Apostles, in the sacraments and in the hierarchical order. By means of these divine gifts, which are very visible realities, Christ carries out in different ways in history His prophetical, priestly and kingly *function* for the salvation of mankind.[67] This link between the invisible and visible elements of ecclesial communion constitutes the Church as the *sacrament* of salvation.

The negation of the visible character of the Church of Christ, and of its hierarchical constitution, has generally come from the heritage of the Reformers and also those who exaggerate the charisms of the Church at the expense of her institutional aspects. On the other hand, those currents which tend to over stress the social aspects of the Church have maybe seen the visible side of the Church, but neglected her mystical nature. Nevertheless, it is in and through the Church that Jesus Christ has willed to effect the salvation of mankind. From the beginning that Church has been a complex entity, and its history is filled with incidents in which men have concentrated upon some one essential element of its constitution to the exclusion of another equally essential element, and have sometimes drifted into heresy. The Church has its visible and its invisible elements, its individual and its social claims, its natural and its supernatural activities, its adaptability to the needs of the times, while it is uncompromising in vindicating that which it holds from Christ and for Christ.

The development of the doctrine of the visible Church and of the authority of its visible head upon earth has been very marked. The persistent rejection of these revealed truths demanded their reiterated assertion and their vigorous defence. No thinking man can overlook the fact of Catholicism: there stands in the midst of the world a body of people with a worldwide organization, and a carefully graded hierarchy, with a well-defined far-reaching process of teaching, law-making, and jurisdiction. The First Vatican Council explained how this visible aspect of the Church also constitutes a demonstration of her credibility:

> God, through His only begotten Son, founded the Church, and He endowed His institution with clear notes to the end that she might be recognised by all as the guardian and teacher of the revealed word. To the Catholic Church alone belong all those things, so many and so marvellous, which have been divinely ordained to make for the manifest credibility of the Christian faith. What is more, the Church herself

> by reason of her astonishing propagation, her outstanding holiness and her inexhaustible fertility in every kind of goodness, by her catholic unity and her unconquerable stability, is a kind of great and perpetual motive of credibility and an incontrovertible evidence of her own divine mission.[68]

In this teaching, the interplay between visible elements and invisible elements is shown in bold relief; and so it has been from the days of Our Lord Himself. His parables and His teaching on His Kingdom make it clear that it is an organic and social entity, with an external hierarchical organization, aiming at bringing all peoples into such an attitude of mind and heart that the just claims of God His Father are recognized and honoured on earth, and hereafter in the heavenly kingdom in which alone Christ's plan will be perfectly achieved.

Now it was precisely the visible organized body of men that Saul the persecutor knew, when he approved of the death of Stephen, a deacon of the organized Church, and when he 'began doing great harm to the church; he went from house to house arresting both men and women and sending them to prison' (Ac 8:3). In later years he recalls that he was 'a persecutor of the Church' (Ph 3:6). He considered himself the least of the apostles and not really fit to be called an apostle, because he had been persecuting the Church of God (cf. 1 Co 15:9).

Christ has willed that His Church should be the sacrament of salvation for all peoples. He might have willed otherwise: He might have dealt with individual people as though no other individual people existed, by direct and immediate action, without taking into account the actions, the reactions, and the interactions of people upon one another; without the realities underlying the Mystical Body; He might have ensured the preservation of his doctrine by direct revelation to individuals; He might have willed that His followers should have been unknown in this world and known only to Him, linked without knowing it in the invisible, mysterious life of grace—with no external sign of communion.

However that was not His will. He has taken into account the normal workings of our nature and He has elevated them to the supernatural order. Our individuality is respected, our social nature is respected too. The human person is essentially a contingent and therefore dependent being: dependent upon others for his life and his preservation, yearning for the company and the help of others. This is also reflected in the life of grace: the personal love of Our Lord for each one of us does not deprive us of the supernatural help, support, and sympathy of those with whom we are united in Christ, in His Church. Under the headship of the successor of Peter, the Church founded by Christ teaches, safeguards and sanctifies its members, and their coordinated, directed prayers and efforts combine to achieve the purpose for which Christ founded His Church—by mutual help and intercession and example.

Man is a sense-bound creature and the appeal of sense is continuous. Our Lord has taken our nature into consideration. The merely invisible we can accept on His authority. However, He has given us a visible Church, with recognizable doctrines, laws and means of sanctification, in which man is at home. We accept Our Lord's gift to us with gratitude and strive to avail ourselves of the visible and invisible character. He has willed that as individuals we should be united with Him by sanctifying grace, and that at the same time we should be united to one another within a unique communion, an unparalleled solidarity, which is the reality designated as the Mystical Body of Christ. He has further willed that all the members of His Mystical Body should be members of the visible, organized hierarchical society to which He has given the power of teaching, ruling, and sanctifying. That visible Church is to be the unique indefectible Church which is to last until the end of time, and in its unity to extend all over the world.

The analogy of body and soul is applied to the Church of Christ, and is helpful in emphasizing the relative importance of the visible and invisible elements of the Church. Our Lord wills that all should have life and should have it more abundantly: we have that life when we form part of the Mystical Body of Christ by supernatural charity. All the merely external elements of Church membership will be insufficient unless the purpose of that external organization is achieved: life-giving union with Christ. It is for that purpose above all that the visible Church exists.

The study of the Church as communion is an antidote to the nominalist concept of a simple association of believers who have been redeemed.[69] In this latter sense, the Church would not have a strong link with Christ the Risen One. The Church would not be an ontological form of existence, and would no longer be seen in terms of the will of her Founder, but merely in terms of the 'needs' of her members. Much of Protestant theology, following the road of nominalism, conceives the Church in this manner, as a moral union rather than an ontological one.[70]

The Church as institutional and charismatic

All of creation is hierarchical, so it is not surprising that the Church mirrors in her own way the hierarchy which is found in the various parts of the created order, the animate, the human and the angelic orders. The hierarchy of the Church is intimately linked with her apostolicity.[71] The union between the hierarchical and charismatic elements in the Church is closer and more organic than many realise, as Joseph Ratzinger pointed out:

> After all, what are the fundamental institutional factors in the Church, the permanent organization that gives the Church its distinctive shape? The answer is, of course, sacramental office in its different degrees: bishop, priest, deacon... That this structural element of the Church, which is the only permanent one, is a sacrament, means that it must be perpetually recreated by God. It is not at the Church's disposal, it is not simply there, and the Church cannot set it up on its own initiative. It

> comes into being only secondarily through a call on the part of the Church. It is created primarily by God's call to this man, which is to say, only charismatically-pneumatologically.[72]

The institutional and charismatic aspects of the Church are complementary, and should never be seen in contrast or tension, as some recent authors like Hans Küng or Leonardo Boff have tried to propose. Even Lubac seems to suggest a tension between the institutional and the sacramental:

> The only real Church, the Church which is the Body of Christ, is not merely that strongly hierarchical and disciplined society whose divine origin has to be maintained, whose organization has to be upheld against all denial and revolt. That is an incomplete notion and but a partial cure for the separatist, individualist tendency of the notion to which it is opposed; a partial cure because it works only from without by way of authority, instead of effective union. If Christ is the sacrament of God, the Church is for us the sacrament of Christ; she represents him, in the full and ancient meaning of the term; she really makes him present.[73]

In the overly charismatic approach to ecclesiology, the danger is seeking the gifts of God rather than the God of gifts. At the same time, one should not think that 'this ordered or "organic" structure of the body of the Church contains only hierarchical elements and with them is complete; or, as an opposite opinion holds, that it is composed only of those who enjoy charismatic gifts—though members gifted with miraculous powers will never be lacking in the Church'.[74] Charisms are graces of the Holy Spirit, and whether extraordinary or simple, directly or indirectly benefit the Church, ordered as they are to her building up; they can also be for the temporal good of humankind.[75] These gifts should be accepted with gratitude by the person who receives them and by all members of the Church as well. They are a wonderfully rich grace for the entire Body of Christ, provided they really are genuine gifts of the Holy Spirit and are used in full obedience to the authentic promptings of this same Spirit, that is, in keeping with charity, the true measure of all charisms (cf. 1 Co 13).[76] This raises the question of the discernment of charisms. No charism is exempt from being referred and submitted to the Church's hierarchy, whose office is 'not indeed to extinguish the Spirit, but to test all things and hold fast to what is good,' so that all the diverse and complementary charisms work together 'for the common good'.[77]

Communion and mission

Another 'binomial' describing the Church is that of communion and mission. While communion has been already seen above in this chapter, considering these two aspects of ecclesial reality together is very opportune. God the Holy Trinity, Father, Son and Spirit, defines what communion means and the Church is the invitation to share in that unique set of relationships which characterises the divine life. This communion finds its origins in God and at its heart we find relationship, community and communication. The Church is thus a communion between God and His people whom He has chosen, and between the brotherhood and sisterhood which is ours. 'More and more we are conscious of living in a fragmented world and one which has lost any strong sense of communion—or rather, a world in which communion is to be found among football supporters and clubs of like-minded people, rather than in the rich and varied and multi-faceted 'band of brothers and sisters' which makes up the community of Christ's disciples.'[78] Communion within the Church is established in the Word of God and in the sacraments which are the wonderful and mysterious ways in which God communicates with us and makes it possible for us to communicate with one another, which then leads to mission. At the heart of mission is the sharing of our experience of God.[79]

In the Old Testament, the words of the Prophet Zechariah express the link between communion and mission: 'In those days, ten men from nations of every language will take a Jew by the sleeve and say: we want to go with you, since we have learned that God is with you' (Zc 8:23). Those words prophesy a vision of the Church as a communion, which is so compelling and so attractive that others are irresistibly drawn to it. It speaks of a communion which is inextricably bound up with mission. From the New Testament, the last words which the Lord spoke to His disciples just before the Ascension express communion and mission in the Church: 'Go, therefore, make disciples of all nations; baptise them in the name of the Father and of the Son and of the Holy Spirit, and teach them to observe all the commands I gave you. And look, I am with you always; yes, to the end of time' (Mt 28: 19–20).[80] St Peter and St Paul are the exemplars of this twofold reality in the Church. While St Peter expresses and symbolizes ecclesial unity, St Paul represents her missionary aspect. It should be remembered that there can be no mission without communion, and at the same time, ecclesial communion of itself leads to mission. In this way, the Church lives out the words of St Augustine: 'Receive what you are, become what you receive.'[81] The next chapter will shed further light on this concept as it deals with the unity of the Church.

Notes

1. See St Thomas Aquinas, *Summa Theologiae*, I, q. 51, a. 2; I, q. 77, a. 3 and I, q. 80, a. 2 as examples of a few instances of the axiom *agere sequitur esse*.
2. See chapter one, pp. 3–4, 6–7, 13–16 above.
3. See Pope John Paul II, *Discourse at General Audience* (6 November 1991).
4. Vatican II, *Lumen Gentium*, 9.
5. *Ibid.*
6. See chapter five, pp. 121–125, 129–132 below.
7. See *CCC* 782.
8. Vatican II, *Lumen Gentium*, 9.

9. See International Theological Commission, *Selected themes in Ecclesiology* (1985), 2.2.
10. See Vatican II, *Lumen Gentium*, 9.
11. See J.-H. Nicolas, *La Chiesa e i Sacramenti*, vol. II of *Sintesi Dogmatica. Dalla Trinità alla Trinità* (Città del Vaticano: LEV, 1992), pp. 33–34.
12. Council of Trent, Thirteenth Session, *Decree on the Most Holy Eucharist*, chapter 3 in DS 1639.
13. Y. Congar, *Un peuple messianique* (Paris: Cerf, 1975), p. 62. Congar cites the following article of Semmelroth, 'Die Kirche als "sichtbare Gestalt der unsichtbaren Gnade"' in *Scholastik* 18 (1953), pp. 23–29.
14. Vatican II, *Lumen Gentium*, 1.
15. See Congregation for the Doctrine of the Faith, Letter *Communionis Notio* to the Bishops of the Catholic Church on some aspects of the Church understood as Communion, 1. This document also points out that 'some approaches to ecclesiology suffer from a clearly inadequate awareness of the Church as a mystery of communion, especially insofar as they have not sufficiently integrated the concept of communion with the concepts of People of God and of the Body of Christ, and have not given due importance to the relationship between the Church as communion and the Church as sacrament.'
16. See Pope John Paul II, *Address to the Bishops of the United States of America*, (16 September 1987), 1, and 1 Jn 1:3.
17. Vatican II, *Lumen Gentium*, 48.
18. See P. Haffner, *The Sacramental Mystery* (Leominster: Gracewing, 2008), p. 123.
19. See Congregation for the Doctrine of the Faith, *Communionis Notio*, 3.
20. See International Theological Commission, *Selected themes in Ecclesiology* (1985), 2.1.
21. See Vatican II, *Lumen Gentium*, 6.
22. See St Augustine, *Treatise on Saint John*, 7, 23 in *CCL* 36, 80–81; see also 2 Co 12:2.
23. See Saint Ambrose, *Concerning widows*, chapter 3, 17 in *PL* 16, 240.

24. See *ibid.*, chapter 5, 29 in *PL* 16, 243.
25. Vatican II, *Lumen Gentium*, 64.
26. Vatican II, *Lumen Gentium*, 53.
27. See Pope John Paul II, *Discourse at General Audience* (6 August 1997), 4.
28. St Macarius, *Homily 28*, Part 3 in *PG* 34, 711–712.
29. Cfr. Origen, *On Matthew's Gospel*, 16, 21 in *PG* 13, 1443; Tertullian, *Against the Marcionites*, 3, 7 in *PL* 2, 357.
30. St Augustine, *Sermon 267*, 4 in *PL* 38, 1231.
31. St John Chrysostom, *Homily on Lazarus*, 6, 7 in *PG* 48, 1037.
32. St Gregory of Tours, *Historia Francorum*, I, 4 in *PL* 71, 164.
33. St Thomas Aquinas, *On the Apostles Creed*, a.9.
34. Pope Pius XII, Encyclical *Mystici Corporis*, 6.
35. Pope Benedict XVI, *Homily for Solemnity of St Peter and St Paul* (29 June 2006).
36. This topic will be addressed in chapter seven below.
37. Saint Maximus the Confessor, *Inquiry addressed to Thalassius*, Q. 63 in PG 90, 667–670.
38. Vatican II, *Lumen Gentium*, 7.
39. *Didaché*, 9, 4 in *SC* 248, 176–177.
40. Pope St Clement I, *First Letter to the Corinthians*, 46, 6–7 in *PG* 1, 303.
41. St Irenaeus, *Adversus haereses*, Book 4, chapter 33, 7 in *SC* 100, 816–817.
42. St Irenaeus, *Adversus haereses*, Book 5, chapter 2, 3 in *SC* 153, 34–37.
43. See Tertullian, *De Paenitentia*, 10 in *CCL* 1, 337.
44. See St Ambrose, *Letter 76*, 12 in *PL* 16, 1262.
45. See St Augustine, *Sermon 267* in *PL* 38, 1231, and see p. 24 above.
46. St Augustine, *Sermon 341*, 9, 11 in *PL* 39, 1499–1500.
47. St Thomas Aquinas, *On the Apostles Creed*, a. 9.
48. Vatican II, *Lumen Gentium*, 7.
49. *Ibid.*; cf. Rm 6:4–5; 1 Co 12:13.
50. Vatican II, *Lumen Gentium*, 7.

51. *Ibid.*; cf. 1 Co 12:26.
52. Vatican II, *Lumen Gentium*, 7; cf. Ph 3:21; Rm 8:17.
53. St Augustine, *On St. John's Gospel*, 21, 8 in *PL* 35, 1568.
54. See Pope St Gregory the Great, *Moralia in Job*, praefatio, 14 in PL 75, 525.
55. St Thomas Aquinas, *Summa Theologiae*, III, q. 48, a. 2.
56. Pope Pius XII, Encyclical *Mystici Corporis*, 49.
57. Pope John Paul II, Apostolic Letter *Mulieris Dignitatem*, 23.2.
58. See St Gregory of Nyssa, *Sermon 2 on the Song of Songs* in *PG* 44, 785–786.
59. Origen, *Commentary on the Song of Songs*, Book 3, 4, 1–2 and 5 in SC 376, 516–519.
60. St Cyprian, *De Ecclesiae catholicae unitate*, 6 in *SC* 500, 186–189.
61. St Gregory of Nyssa, *Sermon 15 on the Song of Songs* in *PG* 44, 1115–1118.
62. St Bernard, *Sermon 27 on the Song of Songs*, 14. See Sg 1:5.
63. See Pope Benedict XVI, *Deus caritas est*, 25.
64. Vatican II, *Lumen Gentium*, 8.
65. *Ibid.*
66. Vatican II, *Sacrosanctum Concilium*, 2. Cf. Heb 13:14.
67. See Congregation for the Doctrine of the Faith, *Communionis Notio*, 4. Cf. Vatican II, *Lumen Gentium*, 25–27.
68. Vatican I, Dogmatic Constitution *De Fide*, 3.
69. For the concept of nominalism see my work *The Mystery of Reason* (Leominster: Gracewing, 2001), pp. 13, 113. William of Ockham (1280–1349), a Franciscan philosopher and theologian is usually associated with nominalism. Ockham linked with his tendency towards simplification a certain scepticism, or a distrust of the ability of the human mind to reach certitude in the most important areas of philosophy. In the process of simplification he rejected the distinction between essence and existence, and protested against the Thomistic doctrine of active and passive intellect. His scepticism appeared in his denial that human reason can prove either the immortality of the soul or the existence, unity, and infinity of God. These truths, Ockham proposed, are known to us by Revelation alone. In ethics he was a voluntarist,

maintaining that all distinction between right and wrong depends on the will of God. William's best known contribution to Scholastic philosophy is his theory of universals, which is a modified form of nominalism, more closely allied to conceptualism than to nominalism of the extreme type. The universal, he says, has no existence in the world of reality. Real things are known to us by intuitive knowledge, and not by abstraction. The universal is the object of abstractive knowledge. Therefore, the universal concept has for its object, not a reality existing in the world outside us, but an internal representation which is a product of the understanding itself and which stands in the mind, for the things to which the mind attributes it. Universals signify individual things and stand for them in propositions. For Ockham, only individual things exist, and by the very fact of a thing's existence it is individual. The nominalist spirit was inclined to analysis rather than to synthesis, and to criticism rather than to speculation.

70. Cfr. K. Brockmueller, *Christentum am Morgen des Atomzeitalters* (Frankfurt am Main: Knecht, 1955), p. 116.
71. See chapter six below.
72. J. Ratzinger 'The Theological Locus of Ecclesial Movements' in *Communio* 25 (Fall 1998), p. 482.
73. H. de Lubac, *Catholicism: Christ and the Common Destiny of Man* (San Francisco: Ignatius Press, 1988), p. 76.
74. Pope Pius XII, Encyclical *Mystici Corporis*, 17.
75. See *CCC* 799.
76. See *CCC* 800.
77. See *CCC* 801. See also Vatican II, *Lumen Gentium*,12, 30; Pope John Paul II, *Christifideles Laici*, 24; 1 Th 5:12, 19–21; 1 Co 12:7.
78. See Bishop C. Hollis, 'Signs of Hope: A Journey of Faith into Communion and Mission' in *The Pastoral Review* 2/1 (January 2006), p. 34.
79. See Bishop C. Hollis, *A Church for the Twenty-First Century* (1997); see Idem, *Growing together in Christ* (2004), 10–16.
80. Bishop C. Hollis, *Growing together in Christ* (2004), 19–22.
81. St Augustine, *Sermon 272* in *PL* 38, 1247–1248.

3

The Church is One

Separate a ray of the sun from its body of light, its unity does not allow a division of light; break a branch from a tree; when broken, it will not be able to bud; cut off the stream from its fountain, and that which is cut off dries up. Thus also the Church, shining with the light of the Lord, sheds forth her rays over the whole world, yet it is one light which is everywhere diffused, nor is the unity of the body separated. Her fruitful abundance spreads her branches over the whole world. She broadly expands her rivers, liberally flowing, yet her Head is one, her source one; and she is one mother, plentiful in the results of fruitfulness: from her womb we are born, by her milk we are nourished, by her spirit we are animated.

St Cyprian, *On the Unity of the Church*, 5

The unity of the Church is the first of her traditional four *marks*. In the Niceno-Constantinopolitan Creed affirmed by the First Council of Constantinople (381), these four marks are solemnly proclaimed, as belief in the One, Holy, Catholic and Apostolic Church.[1] It is of course true that some authors have indicated further items, like St Robert Bellarmine (1542–1621) who spoke of fifteen marks of the Church.[2] Nevertheless, these various marks can be reduced to the traditional four which the Church proclaims in the Creed. The four marks under consideration are not so to speak simply moral marks or temporary signs, they are rather part of her being. The Church is indefectible in her unity, sanctity, catholicity and apostolicity: they will never be found wanting, never be lost. Indefectibility corresponds to charity which can never fail in the Church as a whole. Infallibility corresponds to the gift of faith which will also never be lost, since 'the gates of hell can not prevail against her' (see Mt 16:18).

Basis for unity

The unity of the Church is prefigured and prophesied in the Old Testament. When the Lord commanded Abram, 'Leave your country, your kindred and your father's house for a country which I shall show you; and I shall make you a great nation' (Gn 12:1–2), God promised all the families of the earth would be blessed: this promise is fulfilled in the Church. The prophet Daniel foretold that all peoples, nations and languages shall serve the kingdom of God. Again, this unity is found in the Catholic Church (Da 7:14). The Church which Jesus Christ established was to be distinguished by its unity. Jesus affirms that a kingdom divided against itself is laid waste and will not stand (Mt. 12:25; Mk 3:25; Lk 11:17). To Simon Peter, Jesus replies 'I will build my Church' (Mt 16:18). Here the word Church is used in the singular, so there is only one Church built upon one Rock with one teaching authority. Jesus stated there must only be one flock and one shepherd (Jn 10:16), indicating once again the unity of the Church. Jesus prays that His followers may be perfectly one as He is one with the Father (Jn 17:11,21,23). The oneness of Jesus with the Father is perfect. Thus, the unity Jesus prays for must imply the unity of the Church. Jesus states that the visible unity of the Church would be a sign that He was sent by God (Jn 17:21). He teaches that the unity of the Church is what bears witness to Him and the reality of who He is and what He came to do for us. There is only one Church that is universally united, and only the unity of the Catholic Church truly bears witness to the reality that Jesus Christ was sent by the Father.

St Paul writes that Christians must live in harmony with one another (Rm 15:5). However, this can only be realized if there is one Church with one body of faith. This can only happen by the charity of the Holy Spirit who dwells within the Church. The Apostle prays for no dissensions and disagreements among Christians, who should be of the same mind and the same judgment (1 Co 1:10). He offers the image of the Church as one Body, implying a visible unity (Ep 1:22–23; 5:23–32; Col 1:18,24). The Church is one body, one Spirit, one faith and one baptism: this requires doctrinal unity (Ep 4:3–5). Christ is the Head of the one body, the Church. He is not the Head of many bodies or many sects (Col 1:18). St Paul states that the Church is the Bride of Christ (Ep 5:25); Jesus has only one Bride, not many. St Peter exhorts the Church to have unity of spirit (1 Pt 3:8): this is impossible unless there is a central teaching authority given to us by God.

The early Church Fathers deepened the Church's understanding of its unity. The inner spiritual unity which permeates the Church finds expression in a common confession of faith by the entire body of the Church, participation in the same sacraments; and submission to the same canons and ecclesiastical decrees. In one of his many epistles, St Cyprian writes: 'Christ established one Church, even though it is divided throughout the entire world into many parts. It is the same with the unity of the bishops, who, although many, constitute a unity due to the identity of their conviction.'[3] Elsewhere, he expresses a similar opinion: 'We ought firmly to hold and assert this unity, especially those of us that are bishops who preside in the Church, that we may also prove the episcopate itself to be one and undivided… The episcopate is one, each part of which is held by each one for the whole.'[4] According to St Irenaeus:

> The overseers of the Church, to whom all the world is entrusted, vigilantly guard apostolic tradition, witnessing to us that all keep one and the same faith, that all profess the same Father, that all accept the same purpose of the incarnate economy, the same spiritual gifts; they make use of the same laws in

> the administration of the Church and in the execution of other ecclesiastical ministries; they await the same coming of the Lord.[5]

Finally, in his epistle for the deposition of Arius, St Athanasius remarks 'The Catholic Church is one body, in compliance with the commandment in holy scripture to preserve a bond of concord and peace...'[6]

In other societies, the bond of unity is almost always defined by the composite will of the members, freely joined together to form a moral entity that may be changed or corrected, entered or left according to personal preference and depending on the juridical structure of the organization. Ecclesial unity is also to be distinguished from an artificial forced appearance of togetherness, as seen in a totalitarian state, where a despotic leader or system forces people together. Nor is Church unity to be conceived as mere community sentiment or feeling, where social or psychological pressure forms the bond between the people. Indeed the bond uniting members of the Church transcends mutual human attraction or repulsion, and comes from above, as a grace which redeems, heals and perfects fallen human nature. In this sense, within the Church, 'there can be neither Jew nor Greek, there can be neither slave nor freeman, there can be neither male nor female' not because these distinctions cease to exist, but rather are no longer a source of division because the Church is 'one in Christ Jesus' (Ga 3:28). The Church was called into being by the Holy Trinity and founded by the Son of God: its constitution is therefore immutable and independent of the ebb and flow of human caprice. Membership is not a matter of whim but determined as a condition of salvation. Consequently the unity of the Church lies in the order of being, and so she is not simply a mystical or moral association, because her origin, stability and unity are derived immediately from the will of God.

In other institutions, the essence of unity is something that is extrinsic to the individual members. It is a kind of psychological construct which does not substantially affect their character as people. As social beings, they need to belong to some society, but without the necessity of specifying which organization or what form the society must take and least of all with no essential change in their personality effected by membership. By contrast, adherence to the Church means partaking in Christ Himself, with consequent changes in the souls of each member that are truly ontological, or in the order of being. Those who belong to the Church, animated by the Spirit of God, are inherently different from those who do not belong. They become, in the words of Jesus Christ, branches of the Vine which is Himself; or, according to St Paul, the eyes, hands and feet of that mysterious Body of which Christ is the Head.

The divine and human elements in the Church create and require her unity. She comes from the Triune God, the One and the True, the Source of all true unity, and participates in the oneness of the life of the Godhead. Thus, the Church is one because of her source: 'the highest exemplar and source of this mystery is the unity, in the Trinity of Persons, of one God, the Father and the Son in the Holy Spirit.'[7] The Church is one because of Christ her Founder. She is one in the image of His hypostatic union, and in the unity wrought by His redemptive act, for 'the Word made flesh, the prince of peace, reconciled all men to God by the cross,... restoring the unity of all in one people and one body'.[8] The Church is one because of her 'soul': 'It is the Holy Spirit, dwelling in those who believe and pervading and ruling over the entire Church, who brings about that wonderful communion of the faithful and joins them together so intimately in Christ that he is the principle of the Church's unity.'[9]

John Adam Möhler (1796–1838), approached ecclesiology in the context of Romanticism, a reaction against the arid intellectualism of the Enlightenment. His principle of unity within the Church is the action of the Holy Spirit: 'The Church exists through a life directly and continually moved by the divine Spirit, and is maintained and continued by the loving mutual exchange of believers.'[10] For Möhler Church unity is twofold in character: a unity of spirit and a unity of body. This mystical unity is effected by the Holy Spirit who binds all the faithful in one communion; He also guarantees the mental unity of doctrine, or the comprehensive expression of the Christian mind in opposition to the manifold forms of heresy, and finally assures unity in multiplicity, which is the preservation of individuality within the unity of all the faithful. In a later work, *Symbolik,* Möhler complemented this pneumatological approach with Christological and sacramental considerations. In this work, the Church, once characterised by him as the family of believers who have the fullness of the Spirit, is now described as the one visible community of believers that is the extension in space and time of the body of Jesus. To put it in a different way, the Church is the continuation of the Incarnation of the Word of God.[11]

On the human side, the unity of mankind, the whole of which is intended to be incorporated into the Mystical Body, demands a Church that is manifestly one and undivided. Moreover, the fact that there is no approach to God save through Christ, who is the 'one mediator between God and men' (1 Tm 2:5), reinforces the need for unity. He is the only Door to God's sheepfold (Jn 10:1); we cannot hope to please the Father except in so far as He sees us in His Son. The great richness of human diversity is not opposed to the Church's unity. Yet sin and the burden of its consequences constantly threaten the gift of her oneness. Therefore the Apostle has to exhort Christians to 'maintain the unity of the Spirit in the bond of peace' (Ep 4:3).

The unity within the Church is visibly expressed, so that the inward reality is signified in its outward sign. In this sense the unity of the Church is sacramental. The visible unity is expressed in the charity which 'binds everything together in perfect harmony' (Col 3:14). Jesus says a city set on a hill cannot be hidden (Mt 5:14), and this can be understood in reference to the Church.[12] The Church is not merely an invisible and spiritual presence, but a single, visible and universal body through the Eucharist: it is an extension of the Incarnation. The unity of the pilgrim Church is also assured by other visible bonds of communion: like the profession of one faith and one baptism received from the Apostles (Ep 4:5), the common celebration of divine worship (1 Co 10:17), especially of the sacraments, apostolic succession through the sacrament of Holy Orders, maintaining the fraternal concord of God's family.[13] In particular, the unity of the Church is expressed in the person of St Peter's successor: 'The sole Church of Christ [is that] which our Saviour, after His Resurrection, entrusted to Peter's pastoral care, commissioning him and the other apostles to extend and rule it… This Church, constituted and organized as a society in the present world, subsists in the Catholic Church, which is governed by the successor of Peter and by the bishops in communion with him.'[14] Christ placed Blessed Peter over the other apostles, and 'instituted in him a permanent and visible source and foundation of unity of faith and communion'.[15]

The Eucharist builds the unity of the Church. Saint Paul refers to this unifying power of participation in the banquet of the Eucharist when he writes to the Corinthians: 'The bread which we break, is it not a communion in the body of Christ? Because there is one bread, we who are many are one body, for we all partake of the one bread' (1 Co 10:16–17). Saint John Chrysostom's commentary on these words is profound and perceptive:

> For what is the bread? It is the body of Christ. And what do those who receive it become? The Body of Christ, not many bodies but one body. For as bread is completely one, though made of up many grains of wheat, and these, albeit unseen, remain nonetheless present, in such a way that their difference is not apparent since they have been made a perfect whole, so too are we mutually joined to one another and together united with Christ.[16]

The Eucharist is constitutive of the Church's being and activity. This is why Christian antiquity used the same words, *Corpus Christi*, to designate Christ's body born of the Virgin Mary, His eucharistic body and His ecclesial body. The Lord Jesus, by offering Himself in sacrifice for us, in His gift effectively indicated the mystery of the Church. It is significant that the Second Eucharistic Prayer, invoking the Paraclete, formulates its prayer for the unity of the Church as follows: 'may all of us who share in the body and blood of Christ be brought together in unity by the Holy Spirit.' The sacrament of the Eucharist expresses and effects the unity of the faithful within ecclesial communion. The Eucharist is thus found at the root of the Church as a mystery of communion.[17] Indeed, the Eucharistic sacrifice of Christ is 'the supreme sacramental manifestation of communion in the Church'.[18] The unity of ecclesial communion is concretely manifested in the Christian communities and is renewed at the celebration of the Eucharist, which unites them and differentiates them in the particular Churches, 'in and from which the one and only Catholic Church comes into being'.[19] Indeed, 'the oneness and indivisibility of the eucharistic body of the Lord implies the oneness of his Mystical Body, which is the one and indivisible Church. From the eucharistic centre arises the necessary openness of every celebrating community, of every particular Church. By allowing itself to be drawn into the open arms of the Lord, it achieves insertion into his one and undivided body.'[20] Consequently, in the celebration of the Eucharist, the individual members of the faithful find themselves in their Church, the Church of Christ. From this eucharistic perspective, adequately understood, ecclesial communion is seen to be Catholic by its very nature.[21]

The image of the Church as the Body of Christ is to proclaim her unity, her undividedness: 'We, being many, are one body in Christ' (Rm 12:5). This oneness is not simply a unity of ideals and aspirations, the unity of the Church was not a prospect set before her to be realized in the remote future; it was an intimate mark of her constitution from the beginning. The unity promised by Christ was that proper to the society of His faith, the performance of one act of worship, the acceptance of one system of government. The figure of the Church as the Bride of Christ stresses that she is one and unique, as many Patristic authors pointed out, saying that there is only one Body of Christ, and only one Bride of Christ (see Ep 4:4–5). In a particularly incisive fashion, St Cyprian wrote: 'The Bride of Christ cannot be defiled. She is inviolate and chaste. She knows but one home, and with a chaste modesty She guards the sanctity of one bedchamber.'[22] The unity of the Church is therefore more profound than simple uniformity. This unity is ontological, not simply moral; it can never be lost.[23]

The unity of the Church is not to be seen in a type of dialectic tension with the diversity which it contains. The Church's unity indeed guarantees her diversity. The universality of the Church involves and implies, on the one hand, a most solid unity, and on the other, a plurality and a diversification, which do not obstruct unity, but rather confer upon it the character of communion.[24] This plurality refers both to the diversity of ministries, charisms, and forms of life and apostolate within each particular Church, and to the diversity of traditions in liturgy and culture among the various particular Churches.[25] Thus so-called inculturation must express the communion of faith which the Church reveals.

Fostering a unity that does not obstruct diversity, and acknowledging and fostering a diversity that does not obstruct unity but rather enriches it, is a fundamental task of the Roman Pontiff for the whole Church,[26] and also of each Bishop in the particular Church entrusted to his pastoral ministry.[27] However, the construction and protection of this unity, whereby diversity confers the character of communion, is also a task of everyone in the Church, because all are called to build it up and preserve it each day, above all by means of that charity which is 'the bond of perfection' (Col 3:14).[28]

Many institutions, movements and religious communities established by Papal Authority for specific tasks in the Church contribute to ecclesial communion precisely through this unity in diversity. They belong as such to the universal Church, though their members are also members of the particular Churches where they live and work. The manner of belonging to the particular Churches, with its own particular flexibility, takes different juridical forms. However, this does not erode the unity of the particular Church founded on the Bishop; rather, it helps endow this unity with the interior diversity which is a feature of communion.[29]

The subsistence of the Church

In the Second Vatican Council, on two occasions, the expression was used that the Church of Christ (and its unity) subsists in the Catholic Church.[30] The expression subsists (*subsistit in*) has seen many different interpretations since the time of the Council, not all of them sound or correct. The actual meaning of the Latin *subsistere* signifies 'to exist' or 'to be', and more specifically to 'remain standing' to 'stand still', 'resist' and 'remain'. Thus 'subsistence' refers to the perduring, historical continuity and the permanence of all the elements instituted by Christ in the Catholic Church, in which the Church of Christ is concretely found on this earth. The use of this expression, which indicates the full identity of the Church of Christ with the Catholic Church, does not change the doctrine on the Church. Rather, it stems from and brings out more clearly the fact that there are numerous elements of sanctification and of truth which are found outside her structure, but which as gifts properly belonging to the Church of Christ, impel towards Catholic unity.[31] The person who proposed the use of the expression *subsistit* in the document *Lumen Gentium* was the Jesuit, Fr Sebastian Tromp. One of his overall priorities at the Council was to achieve a condemnation of indifferentism and, consequently, a declaration of absolute identity between the Catholic Church and the Church of Christ.

Adopting the expression '*subsistit in*', the Second Vatican Council sought to harmonize two doctrinal statements. On the one hand, that the Church of Christ, despite the divisions which exist among Christians, continues to exist fully only in the Catholic Church. On the other hand, outside her structure, several elements of sanctification and truth are to be found, namely in those Churches and ecclesial communities which are not yet in full communion with the Catholic Church. However, concerning these realities, it needs to be stated that 'they derive their efficacy from the very fullness of grace and truth entrusted to the Catholic Church'.[32] The expression *subsistit* signifies that Christ's Church truly exists and not in pieces, like a patchwork. She is not an unattainable utopia but a concrete reality. The Lord guarantees the Church's existence despite all the human errors and sins found in her earthly members. The term *subsistit* implies that there is also an ecclesial reality outside the Catholic community, and this challenge is a strong incentive to pursue unity.[33]

Wounds to unity

While the essential unity of the Church of Christ can never be lost, it can be wounded or obscured. The lack of unity among Christians is certainly a wound for the Church; not in the sense that she is deprived of her unity, but 'in that it hinders the complete fulfilment of her universality in history'.[34] As the Apostle remarked concerning the Mystical Body of Christ: 'If one member suffer any thing, all the members suffer with it: or if one member glory, all the members rejoice with it' (1 Co 12:26). The historical fact of divisions within the Church has been noted since the time of St Paul's letters to the Corinthians:

> In this one and only Church of God from its very beginnings there arose certain rifts, which the Apostle strongly censures as damnable. But in subsequent centuries much more serious dissensions appeared and large communities became separated from full communion with the Catholic Church—for which, often enough, men of both sides were to blame.[35]

These ruptures that wound the unity of Christ's Body, can be classified according to three main categories: heresy, apostasy, and schism. Heresy and apostasy offend against the communion of faith, schism against hierarchical communion. These offences do not occur without human sin: where there are sins, there are also divisions, schisms, heresies, and disputes.[36] Where there is virtue, however, there also are harmony and unity, from which arise the one heart and one soul of all believers.[37]

Those Christians, who after historical separations have taken place, are born into separated Churches or communities, cannot be charged with the sin of the separation; the Catholic Church accepts them with respect and affection as brothers: 'All who have been justified by faith in Baptism are incorporated into Christ; they therefore have a right to be called Christians, and with good reason are accepted as brothers in the Lord by the children of the Catholic Church.'[38] Outside the visible confines of the Catholic Church are found 'many elements of sanctification and of truth'.[39] These include 'the written Word of God; the life of grace; faith, hope, and charity, with the other interior gifts of the Holy Spirit, as well as visible elements'.[40]

There exists a single Church of Christ, which subsists in the Catholic Church, governed by the Successor of Peter and by the Bishops in communion with him.[41] It would therefore be quite false to imagine that the Church of Christ is 'nothing more than a collection—divided, yet in some way one—of Churches and ecclesial communities'. It would also be an error to hold that 'today the Church of Christ nowhere really exists, and must be considered only as a goal which all Churches and ecclesial communities must strive to reach'.[42] In fact, 'the elements of this already-given Church exist, joined together in their fullness in the Catholic Church and, without this fullness, in the other communities'.[43] The Churches and communities separated from the Catholic Church, though they suffer from defects, have 'by no means been deprived of significance and importance in the mystery of salvation'. The Spirit of

Christ has not refrained from using them as means of salvation 'which derive their efficacy from the very fullness of grace and truth entrusted to the Catholic Church'.[44]

The Churches which, while not existing in perfect communion with the Catholic Church, remain united to her by means of the closest bonds, that is, by apostolic succession and a valid Eucharist, are true particular Churches.[45] Therefore, the Church of Christ is present and operative also in these Churches, even though they lack full communion with the Catholic Church, since they do not accept the Catholic doctrine of the Primacy of Peter, which, according to the will of God, the Bishop of Rome objectively possesses and exercises over the entire Church.[46]

A first group of Churches consists of those Christians who separated from full communion as a result of Christological heresies. In historical order, the Nestorian crisis provoked the first split. The Assyrian Church was split from the Catholic Church (the undivided Church of the East and West prior to the Great Schism of 1054) as a result of the Nestorian heresy in 431. Nestorius, a pupil of Theodore of Mopsuestia and bishop of Constantinople, was condemned because he refused to call the Virgin Mary Mother of God (*Theotokos* in Greek), but only call her Mother of Christ. This error was a result of his Christology in which he divided Christ into two persons. Nestorius was condemned at the Council of Ephesus in 431. In the Syriac-speaking world, Theodore of Mopsuestia was held in very high esteem, and the condemnation of his pupil Nestorius was not received well, so that his followers were given refuge. The Persian kings, who were at constant war with the Roman Empire, saw the opportunity to assure the loyalty of their Christian subjects and supported the Nestorian schism by granting protection to Nestorians (462), and allowing the transfer of the theological school of Edessa to the Persian city of Nisibis when the Roman emperor closed it for its Nestorian tendencies (489). The Assyrian Church of the East continued to support Nestorius and refused to denounce him as a heretic, and so it has been regarded as Nestorian, to distinguish it from other ancient Eastern churches. It effectively only accepted the teaching of the first two Ecumenical Councils, the First Council of Nicaea, the First Council of Constantinople. The Assyrian Church produced many zealous missionaries, who travelled and preached throughout Persia and Central and East Asia in the seventh and eighth centuries. Also during this time many Nestorian scholars, having escaped the Byzantines, settled in Gundishapur, Persia and Muharraq in Bahrain, bringing with them many ancient Greco-Roman philosophical, scientific, and literary texts. Nestorian Christianity reached China by 635, and its relics can still be seen in Chinese cities such as Xi'an. About the same time Nestorian Christianity penetrated into Mongolia, eventually reaching as far as Korea. The Nestorian Stele, set up on 7 January 781 at the then-capital of Chang'an, describes the introduction of Christianity into China from Persia in the reign of Tang Taizong. It is of particular interest to note that, within Islamic territories, the Nestorian Church was granted a Charter of Protection by the Caliph of Bagdad in 1138.[47] The Nestorian Churches specifically include the Holy Apostolic Catholic Assyrian Church of the East (or Assyrian Orthodox Church) and the Chaldean Syrian Church of the East (in India). On 11th November 1994, an historic meeting took place in the Vatican between Pope John Paul II and Assyrian Patriarch Mar Dinkha IV, in which a Common Christological Declaration was signed. This text affirmed that 'the divinity and humanity are united in the person of the same and unique Son of God and Lord Jesus Christ, who is the object of a single adoration'.[48]

The next group of Churches in historical order to separate from full communion are termed the Old Oriental Churches, or Oriental Orthodox Churches. Despite similar names, Oriental Orthodox Churches are distinct from the Churches that collectively refer to themselves as Eastern Orthodoxy. The Old Oriental Churches recognize only the first three ecumenical councils—the First Council of Nicaea, the First Council of Constantinople and the Council of Ephesus—and reject the dogmatic definitions of the Council of Chalcedon. These Churches broke away precisely because they did not accept the Council of Chalcedon (AD 451), and are therefore monophysite in origin. The separation resulted in part from the refusal of Dioscorus, the Patriarch of Alexandria, to accept the Christological dogmas promulgated by the Council of Chalcedon, which held that Jesus Christ has two natures, one divine and one human. For the hierarchs who would lead the Oriental Orthodox there was insufficient stress on the fact that the two natures are inseparable and united: this was tantamount to accepting a Nestorian-flavoured terminology, according their definition of Christology, which was founded in the Alexandrine school of theology that advocated a formula which stressed unity of the Incarnation over all other considerations. These Churches came to include the Armenian Apostolic Church, the Coptic Orthodox Church, the Ethiopian Orthodox Church, the Eritrean Orthodox Church, the Indian Orthodox Church (Malankara Syrian) and the Syrian Orthodox Church (Jacobite Syrian). The Antiochian Catholic Church in America is theologically aligned with these Churches, but is not in full communion with them, primarily because it ordains women and does not impose celibacy on its bishops. It cannot therefore be seen as enjoying Apostolic Succession.

In the late twentieth century, the Chalcedonian schism was not seen with the same relevance any more, and from several meetings between the Pope and the Patriarchs of the Oriental Orthodox, reconciling declarations emerged:

> The confusions and schisms that occurred between their Churches in the later centuries, they realize today, in no way affect or touch the substance of their faith, since these arose only because of differences in terminology and culture and in the various formulae adopted by different theological schools to express the same matter. Accordingly, we find today no real basis for the sad divisions and schisms that subsequently arose between us concerning the

> doctrine of Incarnation. In words and life we confess the true doctrine concerning Christ our Lord, notwithstanding the differences in interpretation of such a doctrine which arose at the time of the Council of Chalcedon.[49]

The next series of Churches to be considered is by far the greatest numerically in terms of faithful adherents, and is the Eastern Orthodox Church. It accepts the canons of the first seven ecumenical councils held between the fourth and the eighth centuries. The term Orthodox (ορθόδοξος) is Greek, meaning correct in worship or belief, and is derived from the combination of ορθός (correct, straight, without deviation) and either δόξα (glory or worship) or δοκείν (to teach). Later still, as the Church expanded to all continents and people geographical designators, such as Greek, Russian, and so forth became common and were used in part to indicate which autocephalous group govern that particular congregation and the predominant language used. In 1054, the Great Schism took place between Rome and Constantinople, which led to separation of the Church of the West, the Roman Catholic Church, and the Eastern Orthodox Church. There were doctrinal issues like the Filioque clause and the authority of the Pope involved in the split, but these were exacerbated by cultural and linguistic differences between Latins and Greeks. Prior to that, the Eastern and Western halves of the Church had frequently been in conflict, particularly during periods of iconoclasm and the Photian schism.

The final breach is often considered to have arisen after the capture and sacking of Constantinople by the Fourth Crusade in 1204. In 2004, Pope John Paul II extended a formal apology for the sacking of Constantinople in 1204; this apology was formally accepted by Patriarch Bartholomew of Constantinople. The various Patriarchates and autocephalous and autonomous churches of the Orthodox Church are distinct in terms of administration and local culture, but for the most part exist in full communion with one another, with a few exceptions.[50] In addition there are various other Eastern Orthodox Churches, in varying degrees of standing and communion with the Greater Eastern Orthodox Communion. The Church itself uses a number of terms very specifically to distinguish certain movements within its current structure. Because of the adoption by part of the church of the Gregorian calendar the terms New Calendarist and Old Calendarist are occasionally used to distinguish between those parts of the Church that use the newly introduced Gregorian calendar and the original Orthodox calendar. The term 'True' or 'Genuine' is sometimes added to emphasize a traditionalist status. Likewise the terms 'Moderate' and 'Radical' are used to distinguish those traditionalists who are acting within canonical boundaries and those who have voluntarily broken ties with the rest of the church.

There are a number of Churches claiming to be Catholic, yet they have broken communion with Rome, at a time much later than the Great Schism. These include the American Catholic Church in the United States, the Ancient Apostolic Communion, the Brazilian Catholic Apostolic Church, the Celtic Catholic Church, the Mariavite Church, the Old Catholic Church, the Philippine Independent Church, Chinese Patriotic Catholic Association, and the Polish National Catholic Church. The Apostolic Succession of these groups needs to be examined on an individual basis, as in some cases their practices have led to a loss of this Succession. An example is found in the case of some Old Catholic Churches who have more recently ordained women priests and bishops.[51]

On the other hand, those realities which have not preserved the valid Episcopate and the genuine and integral substance of the Eucharistic mystery, are not Churches in the proper sense; they are known as ecclesial communities. Those who are baptized in these communities are incorporated in Christ and thus are in a certain communion, albeit imperfect, with the Church. Baptism, by its nature, tends and urges toward the full development of life in Christ, through the integral profession of faith, the Eucharist, and full communion in the Church.[52]

Among these ecclesial communities would lie those realities which separated from the Catholic Church before the Reformation, but later assumed its outlook and status. These are late-Medieval groups that Protestants have identified as their spiritual forebears. In some respects, however, their beliefs were distinct from sixteenth-century Protestantism. These would include the Hussites (now extinct), the Wycliffites and Lollards (now extinct) and the Waldensians. Next, there are those Christian communities which arose directly out of the Reformation like the Lutherans, the Anglicans (or Episcopalians), the Presbyterian and Reformed Churches (which follow Calvinist theology). After the Reformation, there was a second wave of reform, under which can be considered the Reformed and Congregationalist Churches, and the Anabaptists. From the Congregationalist came the Baptists. From the latter, sprung such realities as the Abecedarians (now extinct), the Amish, the Hutterites, and the Mennonites. Out of Anglicanism developed Methodism, and also the Quakers or Society of Friends. Although, historically speaking, the Society of Friends can be listed as a Protestant denomination, this is sometimes contested and many Quakers today consider their faith to be a distinct, non-Protestant form of Christianity. Other post-Reformation realities include the Brethren and the Pentecostals.

The elements of sacramental life thus vary according to whether one is speaking of a Church which is endowed with Apostolic Succession, and a valid sacramental system, or of an ecclesial community which generally enjoys valid baptism and marriage among its own members and those of other Christian denominations which recognize their canonical form. Christ's Spirit uses these Churches and ecclesial communities as means of salvation, whose power derives from the fullness of grace and truth that Christ has entrusted to the Catholic Church. All these blessings come from Christ and lead to Him, and are in themselves calls to 'Catholic unity'.[53]

Foundations of Catholic ecumenism

The expression ecumenism derives from the Greek term *oikoumene* which denotes a 'common household' or 'inhabited home'. In a broader sense the expression signifies the whole inhabited world. Historically, the word ecumenism has taken on various meanings, which have often been rather vague and woolly. In the cultural sense it meant the Greco-Roman civilization. In a political sense, from the first century BC, it came to denote the Roman Empire, not so much in a geographical sense, of the extensions of the lands which came into it, but rather in terms of the sum of the peoples who made up this great Empire. In a Christian sense, the term began to be adopted from the fourth century onwards and was synonymous with 'universal'. It then came to designate the Universal Church, or the totality of the Church spread across the globe.

In our days, while keeping its etymological roots in terms of a 'common household' and the 'Universal Church' the expression has acquired the specific meaning of the movement to foster the unity of the Church. The Second Vatican Council saw the ecumenical movement in terms of the 'initiatives and activities planned and undertaken, according to the various needs of the Church and as opportunities offer, to promote Christian unity'.[54] Ecumenism is neither irenicism nor syncretism. The same Council pointed out that 'nothing is so foreign to the spirit of ecumenism as a false irenicism which harms the purity of Catholic doctrine and obscures its genuine and certain meaning'.[55] By *false irenicism* is meant erroneous and distorted enthusiasm for reconciliation at all costs and a related false sense of optimism. *Syncretism* mixes together with Christian theology elements which may be alien and even opposed to it.[56] Thus the goal of ecumenism is not to establish a mix of Christian religions all linked together for purely pragmatic reasons, in which each part subsists according to its own ethos. Nor is the notion acceptable that the Church of Christ exists nowhere yet, but is only a goal, in which all the Christian confessions today would be subsumed into some new reality hitherto unknown. This would offend the once and for all foundation of the one Church by Jesus Christ. Nor does ecumenism seek to set up a more or less imprecise federation of Churches, with some points in common, and sustained by mutual collaboration, rather like the United States of America or the European Union. Finally, ecumenism does not aim to create a super Church, in order to embrace all the various denominations of Christianity together in peaceful community, working together in charity.

The desire for Christian unity is based on the work of the Holy Spirit:

> But the Lord of Ages wisely and patiently follows out the plan of grace on our behalf, sinners that we are. In recent times more than ever before, He has been rousing divided Christians to remorse over their divisions and to a longing for unity. Everywhere large numbers have felt the impulse of this grace, and among our separated brethren also there increases from day to day the movement, fostered by the grace of the Holy Spirit, for the restoration of unity among all Christians. This movement toward unity is called 'ecumenical.' Those belong to it who invoke the Triune God and confess Jesus as Lord and Saviour, doing this not merely as individuals but also as corporate bodies. For almost everyone regards the body in which he has heard the Gospel as his Church and indeed, God's Church. All however, though in different ways, long for the one visible Church of God, a Church truly universal and set forth into the world that the world may be converted to the Gospel and so be saved, to the glory of God.[57]

The Church of Christ can never lose the unity bestowed on her by Christ; rather it is hoped that it will continue to increase until the end of time.[58] Thus we may talk of perfect unity already existing in the Church and unity to be perfected. The gift of unity which Christ always gives His

Church entails a response, so the Church must always pray and work to maintain, reinforce, and perfect this gift. This is why Jesus Himself prayed at the hour of His Passion, and does not cease praying to His Father, for the unity of His disciples: 'That they may all be one. As You, Father, are in Me and I am in You, may they also be one in Us, … so that the world may know that You have sent Me' (Jn 17:21; cf. Heb 7:25). The desire to recover the unity of all Christians is a gift of Christ and a call of the Holy Spirit.[59] Concern for achieving unity 'involves the whole Church, faithful and clergy alike.'[60] Nevertheless, this holy objective of the reconciliation of all Christians in the unity of the one and only Church of Christ, clearly transcends human powers and gifts. That is why hope rests 'in the prayer of Christ for the Church, in the love of the Father for us, and in the power of the Holy Spirit'.[61]

Ecumenism requires certain efforts, attitudes and tools, in order to further Christian Unity. First, a permanent renewal of the Church in greater fidelity to her vocation, as the driving-force of the movement towards unity.[62] Next a genuine conversion of heart is needed, as the faithful 'try to live holier lives according to the Gospel',[63] for it is the unfaithfulness of the members to Christ's gift which causes divisions.[64] Prayer in common is most important, because 'change of heart and holiness of life, along with public and private prayer for the unity of Christians, should be regarded as the soul of the whole ecumenical movement, and merits the name "spiritual ecumenism"'.[65] Another key aid towards Christian unity is fraternal knowledge of each other, among the various denominations.[66] This knowledge requires ecumenical formation of the faithful and especially of priests.[67] Dialogue among theologians and meetings among Christians of the different churches and communities has taken place over the years and has been helpful in bringing Christians closer together.[68] The *rapprochement* among Christians has enabled mutual collaboration in various areas of service to mankind.[69] Ecumenical activity at its deepest level is an expression of the holiness of the Church which we now consider.

Notes

1. See *Symbolum Constantipolitanum,* in DS 150. The expression is: 'Εἰς μίαν, ἁγίαν, καθολικὴν καὶ ἀποστολικὴν Ἐκκλησίαν.'
2. The fifteen marks which St Robert Bellarmine proposed were: 1) The Church's Name, Catholic, universal, and world wide, and not confined to any particular nation or people. 2) Antiquity, in tracing her ancestry directly to Jesus Christ. 3) Constant Duration, in lasting substantially unchanged for so many centuries. 4) Extensiveness, in the number of her loyal members. 5) Episcopal Succession of her Bishops, from the first Apostles at the Last Supper to the present hierarchy. 6) Doctrinal Agreement of her doctrine with the teaching of the ancient Church. 7) Union of her members among themselves, and with their visible head, the Roman Pontiff. 8) Holiness of doctrine in reflecting the sanctity of God. 9) Efficacy of doctrine in its power to sanctify believers, and inspire them to great moral achievement. 10) Holiness of Life of the Church's representative writers and defenders. 11) The glory of Miracles, worked in the Church and under the Church's auspices. 12) The gift of Prophecy found among the Church's saints and spokesmen. 13) The Opposition that the Church arouses among those who attack her on the very grounds that Christ was opposed by His enemies. 14) The Unhappy End of those who fight against her. 15) The Temporal Peace and Earthly Happiness of those who live by the Church's teaching and defend her interests.
3. St Cyprian, *Epistula 10 ad Antonianum,* 24 in *PL* 3, 790.
4. St Cyprian, *De Ecclesiae catholicae unitate,* 5 in *SC* 500, 182–185.
5. St Irenaeus, *Adversus haereses,* Book 5, chapter 20, 1 in *SC* 153, 254–255.
6. St Athanasius, *Letter to St. Alexander of Alexandria on the deposition of Arius,* 1 in *PG* 18, 571–572.
7. Vatican II, *Unitatis Redintegratio,* 2.5. See CCC 812.
8. Vatican II, *Gaudium et Spes,* 78.3. See CCC 812.

9. Vatican II, *Unitatis Redintegratio*, 2.2.
10. J. A. Möhler, *Unity in the Church or the Principle of Catholicism* (Washington, DC: Catholic University of America Press, 1996), p. 93. This is a translation of *Die Einheit in der Kirche oder das Prinzip des Katholizismus, dargestellt im Geiste der Kirchenvater der drei ersten Jahrhunderte* (Köln & Olten: Hegner, 1957).
11. J. A. Möhler, *Symbolik: oder Darstellung der dogmatischen Gegensätze der Katholiken und Protestanten nach ihren öffentlichen Bekenntnissschriften* (Mainz: Kupferberg, 1900).
12. See St Cyril of Alexandria, *Commentary on Isaiah,* Book 1, Oration 2 in *PG* 70, 67–70: 'For the church is lofty and conspicuous, and well known to all men in every place. It is also lofty in another sense; for her thoughts have nothing earthly, but she is above all that is earthly, and with the eyes of the understanding, looks upon, as far as it is possible, the glory of God, and glories in doctrines truly exalted, concerning God ... Therefore, the house of God may rightly be called a mountain by the understanding, and it is perfectly visible, as being raised upon the hills; and one may say of it, and with great cause, what as a notable illustration was uttered by the mouth of the Saviour: "A city placed upon a hill cannot be hidden."'
13. See Vatican II, *Unitatis Redintegratio,* 2; Idem, *Lumen Gentium,* 14; *CIC* 205.
14. Vatican II, *Lumen Gentium,* 8.2.
15. Vatican II, *Lumen Gentium,* 18.2. Cfr. Vatican I, Session IV, *Pastor Aeternus*.
16. St John Chrysostom, *In Epistolam I ad Corinthios Homiliae,* 24, 2 in *PG* 61, 200; cf. *Didaché,* 9, 4 in *SC* 248, 176–177.
17. Cf. St Thomas Aquinas, *Summa Theologiae,* III, q. 80, a. 4.
18. Pope John Paul II, Encyclical *Ecclesia de Eucaristia,* 38.
19. Vatican II, *Lumen Gentium,* 23: 'in quibus et ex quibus una et unica Ecclesia catholica exsistit.'
20. Congregation for the Doctrine of the Faith, *Communionis Notio* (28 May 1992), 11.
21. See Pope Benedict XVI, Apostolic Exhortation *Sacramentum caritatis,* 15.

22. St Cyprian, *De Ecclesiae catholicae unitate,* 6 in *SC* 500, 186–189, and see p. 55 above.
23. Vatican II, *Unitatis Redintegratio,* 4.3.
24. See Pope John Paul II, *Discourse at General Audience* (27 September 1989), 2.
25. See Vatican II, *Lumen Gentium,* 23.
26. See *ibid.,* 13.
27. Cf. Vatican II, *Christus Dominus,* 8.
28. See St Thomas Aquinas, *Exposition on the Symbol of the Apostles,* a. 9: 'The Church is one (…) through the unity of charity, because all are joined in the love of God, and among themselves in mutual love.'
29. See Congregation for the Doctrine of the Faith, *Communionis notio,* 16.
30. See Vatican II, *Lumen Gentium,* 8: 'the one Church of Christ … subsists in the Catholic Church, which is governed by the successor of Peter and by the Bishops in communion with him, although many elements of sanctification and of truth are found outside of its visible structure.' See Idem, *Unitatis Redintegratio,* 4: 'We believe that this unity subsists in the Catholic Church as something she can never lose, and we hope that it will continue to increase until the end of time.'
31. See Congregation for the Doctrine of the Faith, *Responses to some Questions regarding certain aspects of the Doctrine on the Church* (29 June 2007), 2; cf. Vatican II, *Lumen Gentium,* 8.2. See also, A. von Teuffenbach, *Die Bedeutung des subsistit in (LG 8). Zum Selbstverständnis der katholischen Kirche* (München: Herbert Utz Verlag, 2002).
32. See Congregation for the Doctrine of the Faith, *Dominus Iesus,* 16. See also Vatican II, *Unitatis Redintegratio,* 3.
33. See Cardinal J. Ratzinger, 'Answers to main objections against *Dominus Iesus*'. Interview in *Frankfurter Allgemeine Zeitung* (22 September 2000).
34. Congregation for the Doctrine of the Faith, *Communionis Notio,* 17; cf. Vatican II, *Unitatis Redintegratio,* 4.
35. Vatican II, *Unitatis Redintegratio,* 3.1.
36. Cf. *CIC,* can. 751.

37. See *CCC* 817 and Origen, *Homily on Ezekiel*, 9, 1, in *PG* 13, 732.
38. Vatican II, *Unitatis Redintegratio*, 3.1.
39. Vatican II, *Lumen Gentium*, 8.2.
40. Vatican II, *Unitatis Redintegratio*, 3.2; cf. *Lumen Gentium*, 15.
41. Cf. Congregation for the Doctrine of the Faith, *Mysterium Ecclesiae*, 1.
42. Congregation for the Doctrine of the Faith, *Mysterium Ecclesiae*, 1.
43. Pope John Paul II, Encyclical Letter *Ut unum sint*, 14.
44. Vatican II, *Unitatis Redintegratio*, 3.
45. Cf. Vatican II, *Unitatis Redintegratio*, 14, 15; Congregation for the Doctrine of the Faith, *Communionis Notio*, 17.
46. Cf. Vatican I, Constitution *Pastor Aeternus* in DS 3053–3064; Vatican II, *Lumen Gentium*, 22.
47. See A. Mingana (ed.), 'A Charter of Protection granted to the Nestorian Church in A.D. 1138 by Muktafi II, Caliph of Baghdad' in *The Bulletin of the John Rylands Library* 10/1 (1926).
48. *Common Christological Declaration between the Catholic Church and the Assyrian Church of the East* (11 November 1994).
49. *Common Declaration of Pope John Paul II and HH Mar Ignatius Zakka I Iwas* (23 June 1984).
50. Among the exceptions were the lack of relations between the Russian Orthodox Church Outside Russia (ROCOR) and the Moscow Patriarchate (the Orthodox Church of Russia) dating from the 1920s and due to the subjection of the latter to the hostile Soviet regime. This has recently been resolved.
51. At a German Diocesan Synod of 1994, all restrictions for women's admittance to the threefold ministry were removed in the Diocese of the Old Catholics in Germany. The first female priests were 'ordained' on Whitmonday in 1995.
52. See Vatican II, *Unitatis Redintegratio*, 3, 22. Congregation for the Doctrine of the Faith, *Communionis Notio*, 17.
53. See *CCC* 819 and Vatican II, *Unitatis Redintegratio*, 3; *Lumen Gentium*, 8.
54. Vatican II, *Unitatis Redintegratio*, 4.

55. *Ibid.*, 11.
56. See P. Haffner, *The Mystery of Reason* (Leominster: Gracewing, 2002), p. 237.
57. Vatican II, *Unitatis Redintegratio*, 1.
58. See Vatican II, *Unitatis Redintegratio*, 4.3.
59. See *CCC* 819 and Vatican II, *Unitatis Redintegratio*, 1.
60. Cf. Vatican II, *Unitatis Redintegratio*, 5.
61. Cf. *ibid.*, 24.2. See CCC 822.
62. Cf. Vatican II, *Unitatis Redintegratio*, 6.
63. Vatican II, *Unitatis Redintegratio*, 7.3.
64. Vatican II, *Unitatis Redintegratio*, 7.3.
65. Vatican II, *Unitatis Redintegratio*, 8.1.
66. Cf. *ibid.*, 9.
67. Cf. *ibid.*, 10.
68. Cf. Vatican II, *Unitatis Redintegratio*, 4; 9; 11.
69. Cf. *ibid.*, 12.

4

The Church is Holy

The Church believes that she is the manifestation of that newness and that supernature which come in with the Kingdom of God, the manifestation of holiness. She is the new supernatural reality brought by Christ into the world and arrayed in the garment of the transitory; she is the divine truth and grace presented under earthly veils.

Karl Adam, *The Spirit of Catholicism*

The call to holiness belongs to the very essence of God's covenant with the people of Israel in the Old Testament: 'For I am God and not man, the Holy One present among you' (Hos 11:9). God, who in His essence is supreme holiness, the Thrice Holy (cf. Is 6:3), draws near to human beings, His Chosen People, so that they may share in the radiance of this holiness. From the beginning the call to holiness, and indeed, communion in the holiness of God Himself, was written into God's covenant with man: 'You shall be to me a kingdom of priests, a holy nation' (Ex 19:6). In this text from Exodus, communion in the holiness of God Himself and the priestly nature of the chosen people are connected. It is an early revelation of the holiness of the priesthood, which would be fulfilled definitively in the new covenant, through the Blood of Christ, when that 'worship in Spirit and truth' would begin which Jesus spoke of in Sychar during His conversation with the Samaritan woman (cf. Jn 4:24).[1]

Foundations of holiness

The Lord Jesus Christ achieved the holiness of His Church through the work of His earthly ministry and His Redemptive Sacrifice on the Cross: 'Christ loved the Church and sacrificed Himself for her to make her holy by washing her in cleansing water with a form of words, so that when He took the Church to Himself she would be glorious, with no speck or wrinkle or anything like that, but holy and faultless' (Ep 5:25–27). The Church is therefore holy through her Head, the Lord Jesus Christ. She is also holy through the presence in her of the Holy Spirit and His grace-giving gifts, communicated in the Holy Eucharist and other sacred rites of the Church: 'For where the Church is, there is the Spirit of God; and where the Spirit of God is, there is the Church, and every kind of grace; but the Spirit is truth.'[2] The Church is thus 'a chosen race, a kingdom of priests, a holy nation' which God has called 'out of the darkness into His wonderful light' (1 Pt 2:9). Her holiness is thus based on the fact that she has been called out of darkness, and also drawn into union with God, the source of all holiness.

The Church is holy above all through her union with the Heavenly Church. At the same time, the very body of the Church on earth is holy: 'When the first-fruits are made holy, so is the whole batch; and if the root is holy, so are the branches' (Rm 11:16). Those who believe in Christ are 'temples of God, temples of the Holy Spirit' (1 Co 3:16; 6:19). In the true Church there have always been, there always are, and there always will be people of great holiness and with special gifts of grace—martyrs, virgins, ascetics, holy monks and nuns, Popes, bishops, priests and deacons, married people. The Church has an uncounted choir of departed ones of all times and peoples. She has manifestations of the extraordinary gifts of the Holy Spirit, both visible and hidden from the eyes of the world.

The Church is holy by its calling, or its purpose. It is holy also by its fruits: its members are set free from sin and dedicated to the service of God, their gain will be sanctification and their end will be eternal life, as the Apostle Paul teaches (Rm 6:22). Similarly, the Church is holy through its pure, infallible teaching of faith: The Church of the living God is, according to the word of God, the pillar and ground of the truth (1 Tm 3:15). This teaching is unchanging, it is the same as was given to it in the beginning as the teaching of God, in the deposit of Revelation. The unchanging nature of the Church's holiness is described by some Fathers as her eternal youth: 'Do not leave the Church, for there is nothing mightier than She; She will never grow old and will always bloom; thus the Scriptures, showing Her durability and stability, calls Her a mountain.'[3]

Signs of holiness

The Church of Christ is holy both in an interior way and an external way. This interior and exterior holiness is prefigured in the psalms: she is clothed with splendour, her robes embroidered with pearls set in gold (Ps 45:14). The interior sanctity cannot be seen; but the exterior signs can serve as an indication of her holiness, because the Church is by nature sacramental, whereby exterior signs point to an interior grace. With these signs, God makes His Church known. The Church is in some ways a hidden mystery, 'a garden enclosed, a promised bride, and a sealed fountain' (see Ct 4:12). Yet, as the Spouse says in the Song of Songs: 'Your lips, my promised bride, distil wild honey. Honey and milk are under your tongue; and the scent of your garments is like the scent of Lebanon' (Ct 4:11). The exterior signs of the holiness of the Church are like these odours and perfumes, which the seeker can follow and find the true Church.

One sign of the holiness of the Church is found in her miracles. Before Our Lord ascended into heaven, He promised that the Church should be filled with miracles: 'Go out to the whole world; proclaim the gospel to all creation. Whoever believes and is baptised will be saved; whoever does not believe will be condemned. These are the signs that will be associated with believers: in My Name they will cast out devils; they will have the gift of tongues; they will pick up snakes in their hands and be unharmed should they drink deadly poison; they will lay their hands on the sick, who will recover' (Mk 16:15–18). Jesus did not say that only the Apostles would work these miracles, but simply, those who believe. He does not say that every believer in particular would work miracles, but that those who believe will be followed by these signs. Christ does not say it was solely for the Apostolic period that miracles will follow those that believe. Our Lord, then, speaks to the Apostles only, but not for the Apostles only; He speaks of the Church, without limitation of time.

The reason why the power of miracles was left in the Church was as a sign and an encouragement indicating her holiness. She needed it most at the beginning perhaps; now that the holy plant of the faith has taken firm and good root, one need not water it so often; but, all the same, to wish to have the effect altogether taken away as the rationalists and modernists propose, with the necessity and cause remaining intact, is poor philosophy. Indeed the Church has never been without miracles in all of her history, ranging from those performed by her greatest saints to those happening in the daily lives of her weakest members.

There is of course a need to distinguish and discern the true miracle from a false one. This process of discernment is required to see whether the sign comes from God, from human powers not yet fully understood, or from the evil one. A classic example is given in the Old Testament. Moses and Aaron were granted miraculous powers in order to try and convince Pharaoh to let the Jewish people go (Ex 7:8–13). The fact that Aaron was able to turn his staff into a serpent did not convince Pharaoh, since his own magicians were able to do the same by their witchcraft. It is however significant that when Pharaoh's magicians turned their staffs into serpents, 'Aaron's staff swallowed up the staffs of the magicians' (Ex 7:12), as if to indicate that God's miraculous power is infinitely greater than that of any other force, be it human or diabolical.

One aspect of the miraculous in the life of the Church is the gift of prophecy, consisting in the certain knowledge which the human understanding has of things, without any experience or any natural reasoning, by supernatural inspiration. The prophet Joel foretold that in the last days, God would shall pour out His spirit on all humanity: 'Your sons and daughters shall prophesy, your old people shall dream dreams, and your young people see visions. Even on the slaves, men and women, shall I pour out my spirit in those days' (Jl 3:1–2). St Peter interprets this to be the time of the Church (Ac 2:16–20). Our Lord would pour out His Holy Spirit upon His servants, and they would prophesy. The gift of prophecy then is to be continually endowed to the Church, where the servants of God are, and where He always pours out His Holy Spirit. Jesus Christ, ascending on high, led captivity captive, He gave gifts to men. Some indeed He made apostles, and some prophets, and others evangelists, and others pastors and teachers (see Ep 4:8–13). The apostolic, evangelical, pastoral and teaching spirit is always in the Church, and why shall the spirit of prophecy also not be left in her? It is a perfume of the garments of the Bride.

Another clear sign of holiness in the Church is the practise of the perfection of Christian life. In the Gospels, a rich young man protested that he had observed the commandments of God from his tender youth. Our Lord, who sees everything, looking upon him loved him, and He gave him this counsel: 'If you wish to be perfect, go and sell your possessions and give the money to the poor, and you will have treasure in heaven; then come, follow me' (Mt 19:21; cf. Mk 10:21). Our Lord also promised to St Peter and his companions, who had left everything to follow Christ: 'In truth I tell you, when everything is made new again and the Son of Man is seated on his throne of glory, you yourselves will sit on twelve thrones to judge the twelve tribes of Israel. And everyone who has left houses, brothers, sisters, father, mother, children or land for the sake of My Name will receive a hundred times as much, and also inherit eternal life' Mt 19:28–29). The Son of Man Himself left an example of this: 'Foxes have holes and the birds of the air have nests, but the Son of Man has nowhere to lay His Head'(Lk 9:58). Christ was poor to make us rich. He and His disciples lived on alms, says St Luke, for Joanna the wife of Herod's steward Chuza, Susanna, and many others provided for them out of their own resources (see Lk 8:3). When Christ sent His Apostles to preach, He taught them that they should carry nothing on their journey save a staff only, that they should take no purse with them, no haversack, no sandals, that they should be shod with sandals and not be furnished with two coats (see Lk 10:4). These instructions are not absolute commands, they were special counsels, indicating Christian perfection. This poverty for the sake of the Kingdom did not imply that God's creation was evil in any way, but rather that the created good of this world should be seen in the light of its Creator.

The holiness of the Church is also manifested in celibacy or virginity for the sake of the Kingdom. Old Testament prophecy foretold the value of virginity: 'No eunuch should say, "Look, I am a dried-up tree." For the Lord says this: "To the eunuchs who observe my Sabbaths and choose to do my good pleasure and cling to my covenant, I shall give them in my house and within my walls a monument and a name better than sons and daughters; I shall give them an everlasting name that will never be effaced"' (Is 56:3–5). Jesus Christ brought this prophecy to its fulfilment saying: 'There are eunuchs born so from their mother's womb, there are eunuchs made so by human agency and there are eunuchs who have made themselves so for the sake of the kingdom of Heaven. Let anyone accept this who can' (Mt 19:12). St Paul illustrated the link between virginity and poverty for the sake of the Kingdom:

> What I mean, brothers, is that the time has become limited, and from now on, those who have spouses should live as though they had none; and those who mourn as though they were not mourning; those who enjoy life as though they did not enjoy it; those

> who have been buying property as though they had no possessions; and those who are involved with the world as though they were people not engrossed in it. Because this world as we know it is passing away. I should like you to have your minds free from all worry. The unmarried man gives his mind to the Lord's affairs and to how he can please the Lord; but the man who is married gives his mind to the affairs of this world and to how he can please his wife, and he is divided in mind (1 Co 7:29–33).

Again, virginity for the sake of the Kingdom cannot signify that marriage is to be rejected, but rather that God Himself must come first, as He who instituted marriage.

Celibacy and virginity cannot be reduced merely to a canonical or pragmatic requirement in the Church, but is rather part of the very constitution of the Church as Virgin and Mother, sealed as she is with the image of Mary her type. Virginity is therefore founded on a theocentric vision of the Lord being our portion of inheritance and cup (see Ps 15:5).[4]

The final evangelical counsel, that of obedience, is prefigured in the Old Testament. In that context, the Rechabites are greatly praised by the prophet Jeremiah, because they obeyed their father Jonadab in difficult and extraordinary things where, in fact, he had no authority to oblige them: neither they nor any of their families were to drink wine, they were not to sow, not to plant, not to have vineyards, not to build (Jr 35: 6–7). Fathers surely may not so tightly bind the hands of their posterity, unless the latter voluntarily consent to this. The Rechabites however, are praised and blessed by God in approval of this voluntary obedience, by which they had offered themselves with an extraordinary and more perfect renunciation.

Obedience is above all illustrated by the Lord's example. First He shows obedience to His Father, also to His Mother, to St Joseph, to Caesar (to whom He pays tax), and to all creatures in His Passion. For the love of us, He humbled Himself, becoming obedient unto death, even the death on the Cross (Ph 2:8). He taught the lesson of humility, when He said that 'the Son of Man came not to be served but to serve, and to give his life as a ransom for many' (Mt 20:28). Jesus came among us as One who serves (Lk 22:26). He invited the Church to shoulder His yoke and learn from Him, who is gentle and humble in heart (Mt 11:29). Jesus invited the Church to follow His example: 'If anyone wants to be a follower of mine, let him renounce himself and take up his cross every day and follow Me' (Lk 9:23).

He who keeps the commandments denies himself sufficiently for salvation; to humble oneself in order to be exalted is quite enough but still there remains another obedience, humility and self-abnegation, to which the examples and instructions of Our Lord invite us. He would have us learn humility from Him, and He humbled Himself, not only to those whose inferior He was, in so far as He was wearing the form of a servant, but also to His actual inferiors. He desires then, that as He abased Himself, never indeed against His duty but beyond duty, we also should voluntarily obey all creatures for love of Him: He would have us renounce ourselves, after His example. He renounced His own will so decisively that He submitted to the Sacrifice of the Cross, and has served His disciples and servants. He said to His Apostles after washing their feet at the Last Supper 'You call me Master and Lord, and rightly; so I am. If I, then, the Lord and Master, have washed your feet, you must wash each other's feet. I have given you an example so that you may copy what I have done to you' (Jn 13:13–15). The message is that the Church recognises in His words a sweet invitation to a voluntary submission and obedience towards those to whom otherwise we have no obligation, not resting, however lightly, on our own will and judgment, but rather the members of the Church are subjects and slaves of God, and of men for the love of the same God. Obedience should not be seen as an arbitrary or Stoic command merely to strengthen human character, but rather as a participation in God's economy of salvation whereby Jesus said: 'I shall no longer call you servants, because a servant does not know the master's business; I call you friends, because I have made known to you everything I have learnt from My Father' (Jn 15:15).

Our Lord has entrusted to the Church these examples and instructions on poverty, chastity, and obedience. These evangelical counsels are gifts which Christ has left His Church as a sign and instrument of her holiness. From the beginning, the Bride of Christ has put into practice these counsels. St Mary (sister of St Martha) and St John were icons of the religious life which is always a feature of the Church. The Apostles instituted two forms of life; the one according to commandment, the other according to counsel. The model of the perfection of life followed upon the counsel of the Apostles and subsequently, a countless number of Christians have followed the life of perfection as history clearly recounts.

Our Lord had no sooner ascended into heaven then many of the first Christians sold their goods and brought the money to the feet of the Apostles: 'And all who shared the faith owned everything in common; they sold their goods and possessions and distributed the proceeds among themselves according to what each one needed' (Ac 2:44–45). St Peter, putting in practice the gift of evangelical poverty, addressed the cripple which he was to heal: 'I have neither silver nor gold, but I will give you what I have: in the Name of Jesus Christ the Nazarene, walk!' (Ac 3:6).

St Paul kept virginity or celibacy as did St John and St James. St Paul encouraged those widows who had received the gift of celibacy to persevere in it: 'A woman who is really widowed and left on her own has set her hope on God and perseveres night and day in petitions and prayer' (1 Tm 5:5). St Epiphanius, St Jerome, and several other Fathers, understood this passage to refer to widows vowed to Christ as the heavenly Spouse. From that time onward, the counsel of voluntary virginity or celibacy was practised in the Church. Obedience was a counsel which imitated the obedience of Christ Himself, but also bolstered up the other counsels of chastity and poverty. It followed the spirit of St

Paul's words: 'You are not your own' (1 Co 6:19); and again 'All things are yours, and you are Christ's, and Christ is God's' (1 Co 3:22, 23).

In this way, religious life developed within the Church. The first expression was in the form of Christian virgins who professed a life distinguished from the ordinary life by its tendency to perfection; continence and sometimes the renunciation of riches, attached them specially to Christ.[5] In the deserts of Egypt, the monastic life first took root. During the persecution of Decius (around 250 AD) Paul of Thebes and other Christians sought refuge there from their tormentors. Next, St Anthony was won by the words of Jesus in the Gospel: 'If you wish to be perfect, go and sell your possessions and give the money to the poor, and you will have treasure in heaven; then come, follow me' (Mt 19:21). Anthony had disciples, and instituted monastic villages, in which seekers after perfection, living retired from the world, found comfort and encouragement in the example of brothers following the same profession. St Pachomius, a contemporary of St Anthony, brought all his monks together under one roof, thus founding the cenobitic life. Later, in the East, St Basil encouraged the monastic life as having one great advantage over the solitary life, namely the opportunity which it offers for practising charity to one's neighbour. He discouraged excessive mortifications into which vanity and even pride may enter, and permitted his monks to undertake the education of children.

St Augustine, in the common life which he led with the clergy of Hippo, furnished a first outline of canonical life. He instituted monasteries of nuns, and wrote for them in 427 a letter which became the rule known by the name of St Augustine. St Columbanus, an Irish monk (d. 615), left a very demanding monastic rule in Ireland. St Benedict is perhaps the best known founder of Western monasticism; he was inspired by the principles of St Basil for monastic life as well as by the writings of St Augustine and Cassian in writing his rule, which from the eighth to the twelfth century regulated, it may be said, the whole religious life of the West.

With the advent of the Middle Ages, further examples of the religious life emerged and flourished. The Congregation of Cluny was founded by St Odo (abbot from 927 to 942) which, in the twelfth century grouped more than 200 monasteries under the authority of the abbot of the principal monastery; St Bernard was the leading light of the Congregation of Cîteaux, of the eleventh century, to which the Trappists belong. In order to combine the cenobitic and eremitic life, St Romuald (d. 1027) founded the Camaldolese Order, and St John Gualbert (d. 1073) the Congregation of Vallombrosa. From the eleventh century also (1084) date the Carthusians, who needed no reform to maintain them in their pristine fervour.

At the end of the twelfth and the beginning of the thirteenth century churchmen were reproached for their love of riches, and for the laxity of their lives. The mendicant orders established by St Dominic and St Francis offered on the contrary the edifying spectacle of fervent religious. The followers of Dominic and Francis were forbidden the possession of wealth or revenues, even in common. The mendicant orders are marked by two characteristics: poverty, practised in common; and the mixed life, that is the union of contemplation with the work of the sacred ministry. Since 1245, the Carmelites, transplanted from Asia into Europe, have formed a third mendicant order.

The military orders date from the twelfth century, and while observing all the essential obligations of religious life, they had for their object the defence of the cause of Christ by force of arms; among these were the Knights of Malta, formerly called the Equestrian Order of St John of Jerusalem (1118), the Order of Teutonic Knights (1190), the Order of Knights Templars (1118), suppressed by Clement V at the Council of Vienne (1312), at the urgent request of the King of France, Philip the Fair. It became necessary to ransom captives from the hands of the enemies of Christendom, and this noble work was undertaken from the thirteenth century by further new religious orders: the Trinitarians (Order of the Most Holy Trinity), founded by St John de Matha and St Felix of Valois, and the Mercedarians (Order of Our Lady of the Redemption of Captives) founded by St Peter Nolasco. The hospitaller orders were founded as specially devoted to the relief of disease and sickness. The Cellite Brothers were approved by Pope Pius II in 1459; the Brothers Hospitallers of St Anthony were approved by Honorius III in 1218. The most famous, the Order of Brothers of St John of God, dates from 1572.

After the Middle Ages, there arose a new phenomenon, that of the Clerks Regular. These are priests first of all: they have no peculiarity of costume; they undertake all duties suitable to priests, and attend to all the spiritual necessities of their neighbour, especially the education of the young. Being clerks and not canons, they escaped at the same time the inconvenience of having a title of honour and of being bound to any particular church; many of them take a vow not only not to seek for ecclesiastical dignities, but even not to accept them. The first of these were the Theatines, founded in 1524 by St Cajetan and Cardinal Peter Caraffa, later Pope Paul IV. Several institutions of clerks regular, notably the Society of Jesus, make profession also of poverty in common and are thus at the same time clerks regular and mendicant orders.

New orders and forms of religious life have emerged right until the present day. Further expressions of holiness are the new religious movements, fruit of the gifts of the Holy Spirit in these last recent years. Cardinal Ratzinger wrote how it seemed that

> after the great blossoming of the Council, frost was creeping instead of springtime, and that exhaustion was replacing dynamism. Had not the Church in fact become worn-out and dispirited after so many debates and so much searching for new structures?... But suddenly here was something that no one had planned. Here the Holy Spirit himself had, so to speak, taken the floor. The faith was reawak-

> ening precisely among the young, who embraced it without ifs, ands, or buts, without escape hatches and loopholes, and who experienced it in its totality as a precious, life-giving gift.[6]

As regards movements within the Church, these are basically of two kinds, one being contemplative, and the other active. The contemplative movement consists in a looking towards God in prayer, while the active involves more of a relationship with the world. The analogy of Christians as the soul of the world is an ancient image in this regard.[7] In discerning the fruits of how a particular movement contributes to the holiness of the Church, several questions should be asked. One is whether they are a positive response to the needs of the time. Second, whether they can be evaluated adopting the analogy of past movements with a parallel spirituality. Third, whether their spirituality is one which perfects Christian life, thus following the axiom that grace perfects nature. Or, do they rather run counter to nature, tending to destroy or ignore it?[8]

This great history of religious life shows how the teaching of Our Lord, His instructions and counsels of chastity, poverty, and obedience laid down in His Scriptures have borne fruit for the holiness of the Church in every age. The Church has always put in practice these things at all times and in every season; this then is part of her nature: and what would be the use of so many exhortations if they were not to be put in practice? The true Church therefore should shine in the perfection of the Christian life; not so that everybody in the Church is bound to follow it. It is enough that it be found in some notable members and parts, to be a beacon to all the rest. All these orders, like heavenly bees, work in and compose, with the rest of Christianity, the honey of the Gospel, some by preaching, others by writing, others again by prayer, meditation and contemplation; yet others by teaching, others by the care of the poor, the oppressed, the sick and the dying, others by the administration of the sacraments.

Of course holiness and perfection is not only to be sought and found in the religious life, but in all dimensions of the Christian state, as St Francis de Sales pointed out:

> When God created the world He commanded each tree to bear fruit after its kind; and even so He bids Christians,—the living trees of His Church,—to bring forth fruits of devotion, each one according to his kind and vocation. A different exercise of devotion is required of each—the noble, the artisan, the servant, the prince, the maiden and the wife; and furthermore such practice must be modified according to the strength, the calling, and the duties of each individual. Would it be fitting that a Bishop should seek to lead the solitary life of a Carthusian? And if the father of a family were as regardless in making provision for the future as a Capuchin, if the artisan spent the day in church like a Religious, if the Religious involved himself in all manner of business on his neighbour's behalf as a Bishop is called upon to do, would not such a devotion be ridiculous, ill-regulated, and intolerable?... It is an error, nay more, a very heresy, to seek to banish the devout life from the soldier's guardroom, the mechanic's workshop, the prince's court, or the domestic hearth.[9]

The lay members of the Church constitute a holy priesthood to offer the spiritual sacrifices made acceptable to God through Jesus Christ, a chosen race, a kingdom of priests, a holy nation (see 1 Pt 2:5,9). Through their Baptism, the lay faithful participate in the threefold mission of Christ as Priest, Prophet and King. This aspect has always formed part of the living tradition of the Church, as St Augustine illustrated:

> David was anointed king. In those days only a king and a priest were anointed. These two persons prefigured the one and only Priest and King who was to come, Christ (the name 'Christ' means 'anointed'). Not only has our Head been anointed but we, His body, have also been anointed... therefore anointing comes to all Christians, even though in Old

> Testament times it belonged only to two persons. Clearly we are the Body of Christ because we are all 'anointed' and in Him are 'anointed ones'... In a certain way, then, it thus happens that with Head and Body the whole Christ is formed.[10]

The universal call to holiness is not a simple moral exhortation, but an undeniable requirement arising from the mystery of the Church: she is the choice Vine, whose branches live and grow with the same holy and life-giving energies that come from Christ; she is the Mystical Body, whose members share in the same life of holiness of the Head who is Christ; she is the Beloved Spouse of the Lord Jesus, who delivered Himself up for her sanctification (cf. Ep 5:25 ff.). The Spirit that sanctified the human nature of Jesus in Mary's virginal womb (cf. Lk 1:35) is the same Spirit that is abiding and working in the Church to communicate to her the holiness of the Son of God made Man.[11] The vocation to holiness is recognized and lived by the lay faithful, first of all as an undeniable and demanding obligation and as a shining example of the infinite love of the Father that has regenerated them in His own life of holiness... Holiness, is a fundamental presupposition and an irreplaceable condition for everyone in fulfilling the mission of salvation within the Church. The Church's holiness is the hidden source and the infallible measure of the works of the apostolate and of the missionary effort.[12]

The supreme sign of the holiness of the Church is the love which she manifests inwardly and outwardly. Charity then, more than any other virtue binds us closely to Christ and His Church. Many children of the Church, on fire with this heavenly flame, have rejoiced to suffer insults for Christ, and to face and overcome the hardest trials, even at the cost of their lives and the shedding of their blood.[13] The Spirit transforms the heart of the ecclesial community, so that it becomes a witness before the world to the love of the Father, who wishes to make humanity a single family in His Son. The entire activity of the Church is an expression of a love that seeks the integral good of man: it seeks his evangelization through Word and Sacrament, an undertaking that is often heroic in the way it is acted out in history; and it seeks to promote man in the various arenas of life and human activity.[14]

The profound nature of the Church's holiness is expressed in her three-fold responsibility: of proclaiming the word of God (*kerygma-martyria*), celebrating the sacraments (*leitourgia*), and exercising the ministry of charity (*diakonia*). For the Church, charity is a part of her nature, an indispensable expression of her very being.[15]

Holy and composed of sinners

The holiness of the Church is not darkened by the intrusion of the world, or by the sinfulness of her members. Everything sinful and worldly which intrudes into the Church's sphere remains foreign to it and is destined to be sifted out and destroyed, like weeds at reaping time. The opinion that the Church consists only of righteous and holy people without sin is inconsistent with the direct teaching of Christ and His Apostles. The Saviour compares His Church with a field in which the wheat grows together with the darnel (Mt 13:24–30), and again, with a net which draws out of the water both good fish and bad (Mt 13:47–50). In the Church there are both good servants and bad ones (Mt 18:23–35), wise virgins and foolish (Mt 25:1–13). The members of the Catholic Church are all the faithful, and only the faithful, that is, those who undoubtedly confess the pure faith in Christ the Saviour (the faith received from Christ Himself, from the Apostles, from Tradition and Scripture), even though certain of them might have submitted to various sins and failings. The Church judges them, calls them to repentance, and leads them on the path of truth and life. Despite the fact that the members of the Church are subject to sins, they remain and are acknowledged as members of the Catholic Church as long as they do not become apostates and as long as they hold fast to communion of faith, to hierarchical communion and sacramental communion.

However, there is a boundary beyond which sinners become like dead members, and are cut off from the body of the Church, either by a visible action of Church authority or by the invisible act of divine judgment. Thus, those do not belong to the Church who are atheists or apostates from the Christian faith, those who are sinners soiled by a conscious stubbornness and lack of repentance for their sins. Also among those who do not belong to the Church are heretics who have corrupted the fundamental dogmas of the faith, and schismatics who out of self-will have separated themselves from the Church.

Indeed some theologians would say that the existence of sinfulness among the members of the Church while it obscures her beauty, actually proves that she is divinely instituted, because she has managed to survive:

> How helpless, then, seems the cause of Christ! One degraded priest, one passionate or selfish child has Him at his mercy, and betrays Him over and over again. History is full of such sins, and, as each sin is consummated, the cause seems lost. Again and again Christ has been so betrayed, and again and again the world has uttered its comment, 'He cannot keep His friends; He cannot save Himself. Surely He cannot be the Son of God!' Every apostate that has ever lived has been one more incarnate argument against Him; every scandalous Catholic life has furnished a thousand disproofs of His Divinity, and yet Christ lives and is adored; yet His Church with all the sins of her members is accepted as Divine. In fact, these betrayals are worked up into the fabric of God's redemptive Plan. 'For the Son of Man must be betrayed into the hands of sinners… and after three days He shall rise again.' Can any Church be less than Divine which has produced, and has survived, so many Judases?[16]

Casta Meretrix

St Ambrose adopted the expression 'chaste prostitute' only once, in his meditation on Rahab, the woman of Jericho who is mentioned in the book of Joshua. Concretely, Ambrose says that the Church 'as a type was a prostitute, but as a mystery is the Church, united now to the Gentiles by the sharing of the sacraments'.[17] The 'typical' use of Rahab, a contradictory character, to whom was attributed both an unworthy profession and a praiseworthy and providential action, was already a classic in Christian literature. St Matthew's Gospel had recalled her in the genealogy of Jesus Christ (Mt 1:5). The Letter to the Hebrews had featured her as an example of the faith which saves (Heb 11:31). St James, concerned with other aspects of theology, had emphasised her justification obtained through works, namely through the good deed that she did for the Hebrew scouts (Jm 2:25). Clement of Rome, almost as though trying to synthesise and reconcile the two texts, had written: 'Through her faith and her hospitality, Rahab the prostitute was saved.'[18]

After Clement, who dwells a long time on the episode of Joshua 2:1–21, reading it in the light of the Redemption worked by Christ, a clear and definite ecclesiological interpretation of the figure of Rahab is clearly delineated, from Justin to Irenaeus, to Origen, to Cyprian. Indeed, it was partly through reflection upon the 'house of the prostitute', the only house in Jericho which preserved its occupants from death, that the famous principle emerged of *extra Ecclesiam nulla salus*. Origen remarked that the name Rahab means breadth (*latitudo*) and this idea can be applied to the Church: 'No one could be deceived in this regard, no one could be mistaken: outside of this house, that is to say outside of the Church, there is no salvation.'[19] St Cyprian also considered Rahab in relation to the Church: 'Do you think that you can live if you detach yourself from the Church, building yourself other houses and different dwelling places, when Rahab, prototype of the Church, was told that anyone who left the door of her house would be guilty?'[20]

The concept of the Church as the *Casta Meretrix* acquired renewed relevance in the context of the Great Jubilee 2000. Much has been made of the 'Confession of sins and asking for forgiveness' by Pope John Paul II on 12th March 2000, in which he asked forgiveness for mistakes made by Church members. Clearly, the distinction must be made between the Church, which is the Mystical Body of Christ and spouse of Jesus, and its members. Whereas the latter are sinful human beings who can do great wrong, even in the name of the Church, the Church itself is sinless. Some scholars who argue, wrongly, that the Church is sinful have contended that the Church Fathers, through the use of the phrase *Casta Meretrix* or 'chaste prostitute', believed the Church to be sinful. In his study of the ecclesiology of St Ambrose, Cardinal Giacomo Biffi, retired Archbishop of Bologna, responded to this assertion.[21] He argues that the only Church Father to use the phrase was St Ambrose, and then only once. Looking at the phrase in its context, St Ambrose was using it to highlight the Church's holiness and sinlessness: the Church is a 'chaste whore, since many lovers frequent her because of the attractions of love; yet she is free from the contamination of sin'.[22] Cardinal Biffi focuses particularly upon St Ambrose's use of the image of the Church as the Bride of Christ, found in the New Testament. He argues that, given the Church's relationship to Christ, particularly in His mission of redemption, 'it is necessary for anyone who is persuaded, under the guidance of the Word of God, that all salvation and all sanctification issue into the world from the Church, to believe in her beauty and her sanctity'.[23] The Church, argues the Cardinal, sanctifies sinful people and in a certain sense, shoulders responsibility for the sinner. Nevertheless, it is her sons and daughters who are sinful, not Mother Church. As St Albert the Great proposed, the sanctity of the Church consecrated by the power of the Holy Spirit is never diminished (*numquam fallit in Ecclesia*), even if sometimes this sanctity is lost in the individual Christian (*sed nonnunquam fallit in persona*).[24]

In recent years, another error in describing the presence of sinfulness within the Church has been through the Lutheran adage, *justus simul et peccator,* justified and yet still a sinner.[25] This expression cannot be used for the individual Christian, still less does it apply to the Church as a whole. Lutherans hold that the justified person remains a sinner because concupiscence is not eliminated by baptism, and they hold that concupiscence is sin. In their view the justified person is therefore both righteous and a sinner. When Lutherans say that concupiscence makes people sinners, they seem to imply that it makes us guilty before God and needs to be forgiven or at least covered over by the merits of Christ. This was and is contrary to Catholic teaching. Catholics, by contrast, hold that concupiscence is not sin, and that justification removes all that can properly be called sin. The Council of Trent taught that justification effectively makes one righteous and condemned the view that justification is only an imputation of Christ's righteousness.[26] It also condemned under anathema the view that concupiscence is sin.[27]

Another formulation deriving from the Reformation is *Ecclesia semper reformanda* (the Church must be always reforming). This is a shortened form of a motto of the Protestant Reformation, *Ecclesia reformata semper reformanda est secundum Verbum Dei* ('the reformed Church must be always reforming according to the Word of God'), which refers to the Protestant position that the church must continually re-examine itself, reconsider its doctrines, and be prepared to accept change, in order to conform more closely to orthodox Christian belief as revealed in the Bible. The shortened form, *semper reformanda,* literally means 'always about to be reformed', but the usual translation is taken from the full sentence where it is used in a passive periphrastic construction to mean 'always reforming.' This expression is also inadequate to express the existence of sinful members of the Church, because it fails to consider the Church as essentially holy.

However, one can distinguish the *holiness of the Church* from *holiness in the Church*. The objective *holiness of the Church* founded on the missions of the Son and Spirit guarantees the continuity of the mission of the People of God until the end of time and stimulates and aids the believers in pursuing subjective personal holiness. Holiness *in the Church,* on the other hand, also depends on a human and fallible character. The baptized person is called to become in his entire existence that which has already taken place by virtue of his baptismal consecration. This only occurs with the consent of his freedom and the assistance of the grace that comes from God. Ideally, therefore, the holiness *in the Church,* must correspond to the holiness *of* the Church, but this does not always take place.[28]

Without obscuring the essential holiness of the Church, due to the presence of sin in her earthly members, there is a need for continual renewal and for constant conversion in the People of God. The holiness of the members of the Church needs to be perfected.[29] As Augustine observes: 'The Church as a whole says: Forgive us our trespasses! Therefore she has blemishes and wrinkles. However, by means of confession the wrinkles are smoothed away and the blemishes washed clean. The Church stands in prayer in order to be purified by confession and, as long as men live on earth it will be so.'[30] St Thomas Aquinas links that fullness of holiness with the eschatological dimension of the Church; in the meantime, the Church still on pilgrimage should not deceive herself by saying that she is without sin in her members: 'To be a glorious Church, with neither spot nor wrinkle, is the ultimate end to which we are brought by the Passion of Christ. Hence, this will be the case only in the heavenly homeland, not here on the way of pilgrimage, where "if we say we have no sin we deceive ourselves."'[31]

Thanks to the bond established by the Holy Spirit, the communion that exists among all the baptized in time and space is such that in this communion each person is himself, but at the same time is conditioned by others and exercises an influence on them in the living exchange of spiritual goods. In this way, the holiness of each one influences the growth in goodness of others; however, sin also does not have an exclusively individual relevance, because it burdens and clouds the way of salvation of all and, in this sense, unfortunately touches the Church in her entirety, across the various times and places. This distinction prompts the Fathers to make sharp statements, like that of St Ambrose: 'Let us beware then that our fall not become a wound of the Church.'[32] The Church therefore, although she is holy because of her incorporation into Christ, does not tire of doing penance. Before God and man, she always acknowledges as her own her sinful sons and daughters of both yesterday and today.[33]

In fact, through her sacramental system, the Church effectively produces in her members the holiness which she preaches. She cleanses them from original sin by Baptism, strengthens them by Confirmation, absolves them by Penance, and crowns these and other instruments of grace with the Holy Eucharist, the supreme sacrament and sacrifice of the Mystical Body, containing the living presence of Christ Himself. This is the method by which the Saviour who 'offered Himself for us' fulfils for each individual His plan in order 'to ransom us from all our faults and to purify a people to be His very own and eager to do good' (Tt 2:14). In this people, which is the Church, is found a delightful garden growing the fruits of the Holy Spirit, the source of sanctity: 'love, joy, peace, patience, kindness, goodness, trustfulness, gentleness and self-control' (Ga 5:22–23). In these many and varied ways, the Church reveals a marvellous holiness, and an inexhaustible fertility in every kind of goodness.[34] The universal nature of this holiness will be examined in the next chapter.

Notes

1. Pope John Paul II, *Discourse at General Audience*, (12 February 1992).
2. St Irenaeus, *Adversus haereses*, Book 3, chapter 24, 1 in *SC* 211, 474–475, and see p. 24 above.
3. St John Chrysostom, *Homilia de Capto Eutropio et de divitiarum vanitate*, 1 in *PG* 52, 397. See also the idea of the Church as the assembly of the persons sanctified by the sacraments on p. 37 above.
4. See Pope Benedict XVI, *Discourse to the Roman Curia* (22 December 2006): 'The solely pragmatic reasons, the reference to greater availability, is not enough: such a greater availability of time could easily become also a form of egoism that saves a person from the sacrifices and efforts demanded by the reciprocal acceptance and forbearance in matrimony; thus, it could lead to a spiritual impoverishment or to hardening of the heart. The true foundation of celibacy can be contained in the phrase: *Dominus pars*—You are my portion. It can only be theocentric. It cannot mean being deprived of love, but must mean letting oneself be consumed by passion for God and subsequently, thanks to a more intimate way of being with him, to serve men and women, too. Celibacy must be a witness to faith: faith in God materializes in that form of life which only has meaning if it is based on God.'
5. That priestly celibacy is not a medieval invention, but goes back to the earliest period of the Church, is shown clearly and convincingly by Cardinal A. M. Stickler, *The Case for Clerical Celibacy: Its Historical Development and Theological Foundations* (San Francisco: Ignatius Press, 1995). Cf. also S. L. Jaki, *Theology of Priestly Celibacy* (Front Royal, VA: Christendom Press, 1997); C. Cochini, *Origines apostoliques du célibat sacerdotal* (Paris-Namur: Culture et Vérité, 1981); S. Heid, *Zölibat in der frühen Kirche: die Anfänge einer Enthaltsamkeitspflicht für Kleriker in Ost und West* (Paderborn: Schöningh, 1997).
6. J. Ratzinger 'The Theological Locus of Ecclesial Movements' in *Communio* 25 (Fall 1998), p. 481.
7. Cf. *Letter to Diognetus*, 6 in *SC* 33, 64–67.

8. For the necessity of discerning religious movements from an historical perspective, see R. Knox, *Enthusiasm. A Chapter in the History of Religion* (Oxford: Clarendon Press, 1977).
9. St Francis de Sales, *Introduction to the Devout Life*, Part I, Chapter III.
10. St Augustine, *Enarratio in Ps. XXVI*, II, 2 in *CCL*, 38, 154ff.
11. Cf. Pope John Paul II, Apostolic Exhortation *Christifideles Laici*, 16. See also Vatican II, *Lumen Gentium*, 5, 39–42.
12. Pope John Paul II, *Christifideles Laici*, 17.
13. See Pope Pius XII, Encyclical Letter *Mystici Corporis*, 73.
14. See Pope Benedict XVI, *Deus caritas est*, 19.
15. See Pope Benedict XVI, *Deus caritas est*, 25. See also Congregation for Bishops, Directory for the Pastoral Ministry of Bishops *Apostolorum Successores* (22 February 2004), 194.
16. R. H. Benson, *Christ in the Church* (St Louis: Herder, 1913), Part III, III, 5.
17. St Ambrose, *Exposition of the Gospel according to Luke*, 8, 40 in *CCL* 14, 311: 'Novi enim tectum in quo Rahab, illa typo meretrix, mysterio ecclesia, sacramentorum consortio populis copulata gentilibus exploratores…'
18. Pope St Clement I, *First Letter to the Corinthians*, 12, 1 in *SC* 167, 118–119.
19. Origen, *Homily on the book of Joshua*, 3, 5 in *SC* 71, 142–143.
20. St Cyprian, *De Ecclesiae catholicae unitate*, 8 in *SC* 500, 194–197.
21. Cardinal G. Biffi, *Casta Meretrix: An Essay on the Ecclesiology of St Ambrose* (Tenby: St Austin Press, 2000).
22. *Ibid.*, p. 22.
23. *Ibid.*, p. 36.
24. See St Albert the Great, *De Sacrificio Missae*, II, 9, 9.
25. For the actual expression *simul justus et peccator* see M. Luther, *Lectures on Galatians* (1535) in *Luther's Works*, ed. J. Pelikan and H. T. Lehmann, 55 vols. (St Louis: Concordia; Philadelphia: Muhlenberg, 1955–1976), vol. 26, p. 232 (see footnote 49). A similar expression is found in vol. 26, p. 235 and in vol. 27, p. 231 (see note 39). The *Joint Declaration on the Doctrine of Justification by the Lutheran World Federation and the Catholic Church* (1999), 29, indicates that there is still

'difference in understanding sin in the justified' between Catholics and Lutherans.

26. See Council of Trent, *Decree on Justification* in DS 1560–1561.
27. See Council of Trent, *Canon on Justification* in DS 1515. See also A. Dulles, 'Two Languages of Salvation: The Lutheran-Catholic Joint Declaration' in *First Things* 98 (December 1999), pp. 25–30.
28. See International Theological Commission, *Memory and Reconciliation: the Church and the Faults of the Past* (1999), 3.2.
29. See Vatican II, *Lumen Gentium*, 50.
30. St Augustine, *Sermo* 181, 5,7 in *PL* 38, 982.
31. St Thomas Aquinas, *Summa Theologiae* III, q.8, a.3.
32. St Ambrose, *De virginitate* 8, 48 in *PL* 16, 278: 'Caveamus igitur, ne lapsus noster vulnus Ecclesiae fiat.' Vatican II, *Lumen Gentium*, 11 also speaks of the wound inflicted on the Church by the sins of her children.
33. See Pope John Paul II, Apostolic Letter *Tertio millennio adveniente*, 33. See also International Theological Commission, *Memory and Reconciliation*, 3.3.
34. See Vatican I, Chapter 3, on faith in DS 3013.

5

The Church is Catholic

For then, with the rending of the veil of the temple it happened that the dew of the Paraclete's gifts, which formerly had descended only on the fleece, that is on the people of Israel, fell copiously and abundantly on the whole earth, that is on the Catholic Church, which is confined by no boundaries of race or territory.

Pope Pius XII, *Mystici Corporis*, 31

The catholicity of the Church is foreshadowed in the Old Testament. While the old covenant was established with only one people chosen by God, the people of Israel, the Old Testament is not lacking in texts which foretell this future universality. This is indicated in the promise God made to Abraham: 'All the communities of the earth shall find blessing in you' (Gn 12:3), a promise renewed several times and extended to 'all the nations of the earth' (Gn 18:18). Other texts specify that this universal blessing would be communicated by the offspring of Abraham (cf. Gn 22:18), Isaac (cf. Gn 26:4) and Jacob (cf. Gn 28:14). The same concept is repeated in other expressions by the prophets, especially in the Book of Isaiah:

> It will happen in the final days that the mountain of the Lord's house will rise higher than the mountains and tower above the heights. Then all the nations will stream to it, many peoples will come to it and say, 'Come, let us go up to the mountain of the Lord, to the house of the God of Jacob that He may teach

> us His ways so that we may walk in His paths.' For the Law will issue from Zion and the word of the Lord from Jerusalem. Then He will judge between the nations and arbitrate between many peoples (Is 2:2–4).

The universality is also envisaged in the form of the Messianic banquet, which foreshadows at one and the same time the Holy Eucharist and the final eschatological Banquet: 'On this mountain the Lord of hosts will provide for all peoples a feast of rich food and choice wines... On this mountain He will destroy the veil that veils all peoples, the web that is woven over all nations' (Is 25:6–7). From Second Isaiah come the predictions concerning the 'servant of the Lord': 'I, the Lord... formed you and set you as a covenant of the people, a light for the nations' (Is 42:6). The Book of Jonah is also significant when it describes the prophet's mission to Nineveh, which was outside Israel's sphere (cf. Jon 4:10–11).[1]

The Chosen People of the Old Covenant constituted a prefiguration of and a preparation for the future People of God, which would be universal in breadth. Jesus Christ was the founder of this new People. When Jesus was a tiny Infant the aged Simeon saw in Him the 'light' coming 'for revelation to the Gentiles,' as Isaiah's prophecy had foretold (cf. Is 42:6). Christ opened the way for people to attain to the universality of the new People of God, as St Paul writes: 'For He is our peace, He who made both one and broke down the dividing wall of enmity' (Ep 2:14). The Apostle Paul was indeed the principal spokesman of the universal extension of the People of God. Especially from his teaching and action, derived from that of Jesus Himself, the Church reached the firm conviction that in Jesus Christ all are called, without distinction of nation, language or culture. As the Second Vatican Council proclaims, the messianic people which is born of the Gospel and Redemption through Christ's Cross, is a most firm seed (*firmissimum germen*) of unity, hope and salvation for the whole human race.[2]

Basis for catholicity

The catholicity of the Church is expressed in the New Testament in the mission of the Church to the whole world and to all peoples (Mt 28:18–20; Mk 16:15). The entire world has to hear the Gospel call before the end (Mt 24:15). Particularly significant is the miracle of the tongues on the day of Pentecost, when the Apostles were all filled with the Holy Spirit and began to speak different languages as the Spirit gave them power to express themselves, and the hearers each heard them speaking his own language (Ac 2:4,6). This is a clear sign that the Church reaches all peoples of every language and culture. The symbolism of the number of the twelve Apostles also expresses universality or catholicity. The number twelve in Hebrew thought represents completeness, as in the twelve tribes of Israel, and in the twelve Apostles where the whole is manifested. The multiplication of the loaves, where twelve baskets of scraps were collected, prefigures the generosity of God who gives His Son to the Church in the Holy Eucharist. The Apostles were prefigured in the twelve tribes of Israel, and the number twelve is obtained by the product of three by four, mystically signifying Christian faith in three divine Persons, extended to the four corners of the world.[3] St Peter's vision at Jaffa is an indication of the universality of God's call (Ac 10:10–16).

The phrase 'Catholic Church' first appears in St Ignatius of Antioch (who died in 117 AD), in his statement: 'wherever Christ Jesus is, there is the Catholic Church'.[4] Another very early testimony is found in letter of the Christian community in Smyrna concerning the martyrdom of St Polycarp, who had prayed for the 'whole Catholic Church'.[5] St Irenaeus affirms, against the Gnostics, that 'the Catholic Church possesses one and the same faith throughout the whole world'.[6] In St Cyprian, the concepts of the unity and catholicity of the Church are intertwined and mutually reinforce each other: 'The one Church is continually growing and increasing in number: just like the many rays of the sun which issue from only one luminous source… so also the Church, bathed in the light of her Lord, shines her rays upon all the world, while the light which penetrates everywhere remains undivided.'[7] St Vincent of Lerins further refined the concept of the catholicity of the Church:

> Now in the Catholic Church itself we take the greatest care to hold *that which has been believed everywhere, always and by all.* That is truly and properly 'Catholic', as is shown by the very force and meaning of the word, which comprehends everything almost universally. We shall hold to this rule if we follow universality, antiquity, and consent. We shall follow universality if we acknowledge that one Faith to be true which the whole Church throughout the world confesses; antiquity if we in no wise depart from those interpretations which it is clear that our ancestors and fathers proclaimed; consent, if in antiquity itself we keep following the definitions and opinions of all, or certainly nearly all, bishops and doctors alike.[8]

St Augustine reflected in more detail on the precise meaning of the expression *Catholic* in his dispute with the schismatic bishop Vincent:

> You think that you make a very acute remark when you affirm the name Catholic to mean universal, not in respect to the communion as embracing the whole world, but in respect to the observance of all Divine precepts and of all the sacraments, as if we (even accepting the position that the Church is called Catholic because it honestly holds the whole truth, of which fragments here and there are found in some heresies) rested upon the testimony of this word's signification, and not upon the promises of God, and so many indisputable testimonies of the truth itself, our demonstration of the existence of the Church of God in all nations.[9]

In the East, St Cyril of Jerusalem is a clear teacher of the doctrine of catholicity. For him, the Church is 'called Catholic or universal because it has spread throughout the entire world, from one end of the earth to the other'. This geographical catholicity is then extended to a metaphysical idea which denotes totality and perfection: 'Again, it is called Catholic because it teaches fully and unfailingly all the doctrines which ought to be brought to men's knowledge, whether concerned with visible or invisible things, with the realities of heaven or the things of earth.' Cyril also links the catholicity of the Church with the fact that she brings under religious obedience all classes of people, rulers and subjects, learned and unlettered. Finally, Cyril affirms that the Church 'deserves the title Catholic because it heals and cures unrestrictedly every type of sin that can be committed in soul or in body, and because it possesses within itself every kind of virtue that can be named, whether exercised in actions or in words or in some kind of spiritual charism.'[10] In the East, St John Chrysostom also proclaims the catholicity of the Church in these terms: 'He who dwells in Rome knows those in most distant parts to be his members.'[11]

The catholicity of the Church (derived from the Greek *kata* meaning through and *holos* signifying the whole), when the word is taken in its widest sense, means her existence in all places and all ages, and her preaching of Christ's doctrines in their entirety. Over the course of the centuries, Tradition maintained unaltered the Church's character of universality as she spread and came into contact with different languages, races, nationalities and cultures.[12] Thus it follows that the Church can be called 'Catholic' in a variety of senses: with reference to various qualities. First of all, the Church is Catholic with respect to *place,* inasmuch as she is diffused throughout the world. The First Vatican Council referred to the 'wonderful propagation' and to the 'Catholic unity' of the Church.[13] Not only is she one and undivided, but her unity is conspicuously diffused throughout all mankind. Hence she possesses a universality by which she appears as a constituted society in every part of the world. The Church grew to full statue, not suddenly but by a process of gradual development, as is clearly indicated by our Lord's parables of the mustard seed (Mt 13:31–32) and the yeast which leavens the dough (Mt 13:33). It is clear that this catholicity, far from arising by an accident of history, or by mere social and political development was part of the divine plan from the beginning. To this objective the Apostles had been directed from the outset of their ministry: 'Go out to the whole world; proclaim the Gospel to all creation' (Mk 16:15). The Apostles immediately set out to achieve this: 'they preached everywhere, the Lord working with them and confirming the word by the signs that accompanied it' (Mk 16:20).[14] The whole scheme of the redemption demands catholicity; all division of nation against nation, free man against slave, is to be transcended: 'There can be neither Jew nor Greek, there can be neither slave nor freeman, there can be neither male nor female: for you are all one in Christ Jesus' (Ga 3:28).

Second, the Church is Catholic with respect to *time,* because she will always exist. The third sense of catholicity refers to the *peoples within the Church,* members of every tribe, nation and tongue. Fourth, catholicity involves different *conditions and classes of people,* for neither masters nor slaves, neither wise nor foolish, are excluded from her fold. The Church is Catholic in a fifth sense, concerning *doctrine,* in that she possesses the entire teaching of Christ in its unimpaired truth. The Church is Catholic in a sixth way, as the *means of salvation,* because, as the whole of Christ's Paschal Mystery operates within her, she possesses a remedy against the spiritual ills of all people.[15] Seventh, catholicity also signifies the *obligation and necessity of embracing the Church* which bears upon all, as she is the divinely appointed means for their salvation.[16]

Universal and particular

Since Christ is One for the many, in the Church which is His body, the one and the many, the universal and the particular are necessarily simultaneous. Still more radically, because the one and only God is the communion of Three

Persons, the one and only Church is a communion of many communities and the local church a communion of persons. The one and unique Church finds her identity in the communion of the churches. Unity and multiplicity appear so linked that one could not exist without the other.

A *particular* Church, in Catholic theology and Canon law, is any of the individual constituent ecclesial communities in full communion with Rome that are part of the Catholic Church as a whole. The expression *particular Church* is preferable to *local Church*.[17] The term refers to aggregations that share a specific liturgical, theological and canonical tradition, namely, the western Latin Rite or Latin Church and the various Eastern Rites or Eastern Churches, called 'particular Churches or rites', and that are also referred to as autonomous (*sui iuris*) particular Churches.[18] In Catholic teaching, each diocese (Latin Rite term) or eparchy (Eastern Rite term) is also a local or particular Church, though it lacks the relative autonomy of the particular Churches described above:

> Particular Churches, in which and from which the one and only Catholic Church exists, are principally dioceses. Unless the contrary is clear, the following are equivalent to a diocese: a territorial prelature, a territorial abbacy, a vicariate apostolic, a prefecture apostolic and a permanently established apostolic administration.[19]

It lies within the competence of Papal authority alone to establish particular Churches; once they are lawfully established, the law itself gives them juridical personality.[20] Therefore, in no case can the parish be seen as the particular Church, since it is simply a part of a particular Church.[21]

Each particular Church is truly Catholic:

> The Church of Christ is really present in all legitimately organized local groups of the faithful, which, in so far as they are united to their pastors, are also quite appropriately called Churches in the New Testament… In them the faithful are gathered together through the preaching of the Gospel of

> Christ, and the mystery of the Lord's Supper is celebrated... In these communities, though they may often be small and poor, or existing in the diaspora, Christ is present, through whose power and influence the One, Holy, Catholic, and Apostolic Church is constituted.[22]

The idea of the communion of particular Churches must be clearly understood. A recent tendency to envisage a opposition between the universal Church and the particular must be avoided. Sometimes also it is wrongly asserted that every particular Church is a subject complete in itself, and that the universal Church is simply the result of a *reciprocal recognition* on the part of the particular Churches. This ecclesiological unilateralism impoverishes not only the concept of the universal Church but also that of the particular Church, and betrays an insufficient understanding of the concept of communion. As history shows, when a particular Church has sought to become self-sufficient, and has weakened its real communion with the universal Church and with its living and visible centre, its internal unity suffers too, and it finds itself in danger of losing its own freedom in the face of the various forces of slavery and exploitation.[23]

The relationship between the universal Church and the particular Churches is a mystery, and cannot be compared to that which exists between the whole and the parts in a purely human group or society. Each particular Church should not be conceived of as a part of a whole, but rather as the particular expression of the whole. They are not multiple diverse communities which flow into the unity and catholicity of the Church, but rather it is the Church who is always present herself in each of these communities.[24] For this reason, 'the universal Church cannot be conceived as the sum of the particular Churches, or as a federation of particular Churches'.[25] The universal Church is not the result of the communion of the Churches, but, in its essential mystery, it is a reality *ontologically and temporally* prior to every individual *particular* Church.[26] Indeed, according to the Fathers, *ontologically*, the one and unique Church, in her mystery, precedes creation, and gives birth to the particular Churches as her daughters.[27] She expresses herself in them; she is the mother and not the product of the particular Churches. Furthermore, the Church is manifested temporally, on the day of Pentecost, in the community of the one hundred and twenty gathered around Mary and the twelve Apostles, the representatives of the one unique Church and the founders-to-be of the particular Churches, who have a mission directed to the world: from the first the Church *speaks all languages*.[28]

From the Church, which in its origins and its first manifestation is universal, have arisen the various particular Churches, as expressions of the one unique Church of Jesus Christ. Arising *within* and *out of* the universal Church, they obtain their ecclesial nature in it and from it. Hence the formula of the Second Vatican Council: The Church in and formed out of the Churches (*Ecclesia in et ex Ecclesiis*),[29] is inseparable from this other formula: The Churches in and formed out of the Church (*Ecclesiae ex et in Ecclesia universali*).[30] The unity of the Church is strongly linked with the fact that it is universal. The fact that there is one Church implies it is unique, and this can be seen in its universality. The universal nature of the Church is also intrinsically linked with the nature of the Papacy which guarantees this universality. This note of the Church is very important especially today in a globalized era, when many other contrasting universal forces are at work, and humanity needs to see the truth in the midst of confusion.

Idea of sobornost

A particular development took place in Slavic Orthodoxy from the Greek word *katholikos* (catholic) to the Slav *sobornost*. This term that was developed by the Russian theologians expresses the ancient Orthodox ecclesiology as a community of catholicity while at the same time being in unity with the Holy Spirit. For the Orthodox, the theme of synodality or the conciliar nature of the Church, often described with the Slavic word *sobornost*, is of capital importance, intimately related to their understanding of the Trinity, the role of the Holy Spirit, and the very constitution of the Church. Its origins lie deep in Russian culture. Sobornost signifies the essentially extrapersonal (suprapersonal) and timeless nature of aesthetic consciousness. This is the consciousness of a community (*sobor*) of people, akin in spirit, who have reached, in the process of communal liturgical life, a spiritual unity both with each other and with the higher spiritual levels, ideally with God. For this reason, medieval Russian art and other products of the spirit are essentially anonymous. The medieval Russian learned writer, icon painter, or architect does not consider himself personally as the author or creator of his own work, but only as a voluntary executor of the supreme will which acts through him, a middle man in artistic activity, or an instrument which is guided by the communal (*sobornoe*) consciousness of the Orthodox Church. The communal (*sobornoe*) consciousness not only inspires creative activity in medieval artists, but also preserves carefully the forms, schemes and methods which have been worked out in the process of this activity, and which are considered to be the most capacious and adequate carriers and expressions of the Orthodox spirit.

The movement of 'slavophiles', and in particular the activities of Alexej S. Khomyakov (1804–1860) and Ivan V. Kireevsky (1806–1856), gave birth to a definition of *sobornost*. Their aesthetic vision is based on a peculiar mixture of ideas from German Romanticism and Orthodox aesthetics. It is Khomyakov who, for the first time in the Orthodox culture, finally furnished a definition of sobornost: according to him, it is a mystical 'unity of God and man,' or a certain ideal spirit of the people enlightened by the Christian faith. He understands art as an expression of this spirit on the basis of divine love, or as an artistic 'self-consciousness of life' through the mediation of the artist.[31] For him, the term contained an entire confession of faith, expressing the reality of the Church as a mystery of unity, as the gathering of believers in love and freedom in the image of the Trinity. Ivan Kireevsky also offered his definition of sobornost as: 'The sum total of all Christians of all ages, past and present, comprise one indivisible, eternal living assembly of the faithful, held together just as much by the unity of consciousness as through the communion of prayer.'[32]

In summary, the concept of sobornost involves applying the Trinitarian model to the life of the Church arriving at unity in multiplicity, oneness in diversity, togetherness in dispersal, a catholicity realized in quality not in quantity, in depth rather than in breadth, a characteristic communicated by the Holy Spirit which enables individual communities, and even persons, to give full and complete manifestation to the mark of catholicity. Unity, catholicity and conciliarity are the essence of the church's being; and *sobornost* is an overarching principle of their intertwinement.[33]

Catholic and Missionary

The Lord's missionary mandate is ultimately grounded in the eternal love of the Most Holy Trinity: 'The Church on earth is by her nature missionary since, according to the plan of the Father, she has as her origin the mission of the Son and the Holy Spirit.'[34] The ultimate purpose of mission is none other than to enable people to share in the communion between the Father and the Son in their Spirit of love.[35] The Trinity, as a 'community of divine sending,' has created a space for the Church to take part in God's mission, to be sent, empowered, and accompanied by grace unto the 'ends of the earth'. God shows the depth of his love by receiving the Church, with all its human frailty, into the divine missionary communion (1 Co 1:9). Jesus' command to His Apostles forms the basis of missionary catholicity: 'Go, therefore, make disciples of all nations; baptise them in the name of the Father and of the Son and of the Holy Spirit, and teach them to observe all the commands I gave you. And look, I am with you always; yes, to the end of time' (Mt 28:19–20). The catholicity of the Church, understood from the perspective of mission, refers generally to the geographic spread of the Christian faith throughout the world and the presence of the Church in every locality among countless cultures and subcultures. The Church's sacramental life, like leaven, not only permeates the whole dough, but also transforms it. With regard to individuals, groups, peoples and cultures it is often only gradually that the Church touches and penetrates them and so receives them into a fullness which is Catholic.[36]

Together the qualitative universality of faith and its incarnational implantation into every culture, and the quantitative spread of the Church are the result of the missionary effort of the Church. This universality encompasses believers of all times: God's people of past generations, of today, and of years to come. It is from God's love for all people that the Church in every age receives both the obligation and the vigour of her missionary dynamism, 'for the love of Christ urges us on' (2 Co 5:14).[37] Since God 'desires all men to be saved and to come to the knowledge of the truth' (1 Tm 2:4), He wills the salvation of everyone through the knowledge of the truth, for salvation is found in the Truth (Jn 14:6). Those who obey the prompting of the Spirit of truth are already on the way of salvation, and desire it. The Church, to whom this truth has been entrusted, must go out to meet their desire, so as to bring them the truth. Because she believes in God's universal plan of salvation, the Church must be missionary.

The Holy Spirit is the principal agent of the whole of the Church's mission.[38]

> This mission continues and, in the course of history, unfolds the mission of Christ, who was sent to evangelize the poor; so the Church, urged on by the Spirit of Christ, must walk the road Christ Himself walked, a way of poverty and obedience, of service and self-sacrifice even to death, a death from which He emerged victorious by His Resurrection.[39]

On this pilgrimage, the Church has also experienced the 'discrepancy existing between the message she proclaims and the human weakness of those to whom the Gospel has been entrusted.'[40] Only by taking the 'way of penance and renewal,' the 'narrow way of the Cross,' can the People of God extend Christ's Kingdom.[41] For 'just as Christ carried out the work of redemption in poverty and oppression, so the Church is called to follow the same path if she is to communicate the fruits of salvation to men'.[42]

Cosmic dimension of the Church

The Catholic nature of the Church can lead to a consideration also of its cosmic aspect, which is very popular also in Eastern Christendom. Cosmic Christology has theological roots in the Scriptures and the Fathers though its development has taken place during the past century.[43] Pope John Paul II has also articulated this dimension of the mystery of creation:

> The Incarnation, then, also has a cosmic significance, a cosmic dimension. The 'First-Born of all creation', becoming incarnate in the individual humanity of Christ, unites Himself in some way with the entire reality of man, which is also 'flesh'—and in this reality with all 'flesh', with the whole of creation.[44]

For the foundation of a sound cosmic Christology it is necessary to have a clear idea of the transcendence and immanence of Christ in relation to everything which was created through Him. In particular, the intimate bond between Christ and the cosmos should not be exaggerated at the expense of His sovereignty over all creation. Otherwise there is a danger of implying that Christ emerges or evolves from the cosmos. It would be equally false to regard Christ as part of the very fabric of nature itself, and that therefore He is a necessary part of the cosmos in the sense that God is somehow bound to send His Word cloaked in human flesh. This would destroy the gratuity of the Incarnation and the gratuity of grace. From this cosmic Christology also follows cosmic ecclesiology.

The Scriptural basis for the relation between the Church and the cosmos is outlined principally in the Letters to the Ephesians and to the Colossians. St Paul illustrates a double Lordship of Christ, that over the cosmos (Ep 1:10; 4:10; Ph 2:9–11) and that over the Church (Col 1:18). While the Church is presented as the Body of Christ (Col 1:18), the cosmos is never proposed as such and this contrasts sharply with the ancient Greek idea in which the universe is conceived as an enormous body. The glorified Christ acts in the cosmos through the mediation of the Church, the organ through which Christ gradually brings the universe into unity. Among the Greek Fathers it is especially Origen who highlights the idea that Church is 'the cosmos of the cosmos, because Christ has become its cosmos, He who is the primal Light of the cosmos'.[45] This is, in fact, a play on the Greek expression 'cosmos' which can mean either adornment, order or world, so that 'Christ is the initiator of order in the world and the Church its mediator.'[46] The Church is sent to the world 'to gather together all people and all things into Christ'.[47] Not simply 'all people' but also 'all things' which therefore implies a cosmic rôle for the Church.

The power of Christ through His Church does not bring human beings inexorably into an automatic unity with God: the free cooperation of rational creatures is required. This is at least implied by St Paul in his letter to the Romans: 'It was not for its own purposes that creation had frustration imposed on it, but for the purposes of him who imposed it—with the intention that the whole creation itself might be freed from its slavery to corruption and brought into the same glorious freedom as the children of God' (Rm 8:20–21). However, as regards the non-rational creation, Christ is dependent in a certain sense and up to a certain point on the cooperation of human beings for bringing about His plan, as expressed in the command to His apostles which seems to imply a cosmic dimension:

'Go out to the whole world; proclaim the Good News to all creation' (Mk 16:15).

St Maximus the Confessor developed a cosmic ecclesiology. He suggested that the Church may be seen as an image of the cosmos, regarded as made up of visible and invisible beings. He depicted the Church as a building, and more precisely as an edifice divided into two parts: the area for 'the priests and ministers alone', that is, the sanctuary (in Greek: *hierateion*), and the area for 'all the faithful people', which is called the nave (*naon*). He envisages this distinction echoed in the cosmos, in the separation between its invisible and visible parts.[48] These two sections are closely related; indeed, Maximus says, the Church is not properly speaking divided by the differences between the two parts, but rather the two portions subsist in a dynamic relationship, so that 'the nave is potentially the sanctuary since it is a holy place by reason of its relationship to the goal of sacred initiation, and the sanctuary is actually the nave, since it is there that the process of its own sacred initiation begins'. So, too, with the cosmos: 'for the whole intelligible cosmos is imprinted in a hidden way on the whole sensible cosmos through the symbolic forms, while the whole sensible cosmos can be understood to be present to the intelligible cosmos through its principles (*logoi*) that reveal its simplicity to the intellect.' The distinction found in cosmos and Church, that is the reason for one being an image of the other, is a matter of relationship rather than separation; it is a matter of connection, and not division, and it is an ordered connection, the visible pointing to the invisible realm, so that the visible finds its meaning in the invisible, and the invisible finds its expression in the visible, and in this way reflecting the close relationship between sanctuary and nave in a church.

The irruption of grace into the cosmos through the Church raises an important issue regarding the relationship between the sacred and the secular.[49] Some theologians would maintain that after the redemptive Incarnation, all creation has in a way become sacred, and that the old division between sacred and profane falls away. We would not go so far. First, the effects of Christ's Incarnation and Redemption are applied *through* the Church and her sacraments which implies a zone of greater efficacious sacredness. Also, the cosmos has not yet been completely set free in Christ, who is not yet 'all in all' (Col 3:11). Furthermore, there is a question of hierarchy, for some creatures are more sacred by reason of a higher position in the order of being (for instance, human life is more sacred than that of a dog) or of a greater participation in the life of grace. If it is true that the Church is the cosmos which redeems the universe, then men and women need the Church even to live as decent human beings. As a result of the Fall, the human intellect is darkened and the human will confused, though man is not totally wounded. Grace flows from the Church and heals the cosmos, just as the water issuing from Ezekiel's Temple brought health and life wherever it went (Ez 47:1–12). This healing power of the Church is imparted though the ministry of the Apostles and their successors, a theme which will be explored in the upcoming chapter.

Notes

1. See Pope John Paul II, *Discourse at General Audience* (13 November 1991).
2. Vatican II, *Lumen Gentium*, 9.
3. See St Augustine, *Enarratio in Psalmum* 86, 4 in *PL* 37, 1104; Pope St Gregory the Great, *Moralia*, I, 14, 19 in *PL* 75, 535.
4. St Ignatius of Antioch, *Epistle to the Smyrnaeans*, 8, 2 in *SC* 10, 126–127.
5. *Letter of the Church at Smyrna* in *PG* 5, 1036.
6. St Irenaeus, *Adversus Haereses*, Book 1, chapter 10, 3 in *SC* 264, 166–167: 'Ecclesia universa unam et eandem fidem habeat in universo mundo.'
7. St Cyprian, *De Ecclesiae catholicae unitate*, 5 in *SC* 500, 184–187.
8. St Vincent of Lerins, *Commonitorium adversus profanas omnium haereticorum novitates*, chapter 2, 6 in *PL* 50, 640.

9. St Augustine, *Letter to Vincent the Rogatist*, 93, 7, 23 in *PL* 33, 333.
10. St Cyril of Jerusalem, *Catecheses*, 18, 23–26 in *PG* 33, 1044–1047.
11. St John Chrysostom. *On St. John's Gospel* 65,1, in *PG* 59, 361, as quoted in Vatican II, *Lumen Gentium*, 13.
12. See Pope Benedict XVI, *Discourse to International Episcopal Conference of St. Cyril and St. Methodius* (4 May 2007). See also M. Briek, 'De vocis catholica origine et natura' in *Antonianum* 38 (1963), pp. 263–287.
13. Vatican I, Session 3, Chapter 3 *De Fide*.
14. See Vatican II, *Lumen Gentium*, 13.
15. See Vatican II, *Ad Gentes* 4, 6.
16. Cf. R.-M. Schultes, *De Ecclesia catholica praelectiones apologeticae* (Paris: P. Lethielleux, 1925), p. 179.
17. See P. Rodriguez, *Iglesias particulares y Prelaturas personales. Consideraciones teológicas a propósito de una nueva institución canónica* (Pamplona: Eunsa, 1985).
18. See Vatican II, *Orientalium Ecclesiarum* 2. See *CCEO* 27 which refers to 'a group of Christian faithful united by a hierarchy according to the norm of law which the supreme authority of the Church expressly or tacitly recognizes as *sui iuris*'.
19. *CIC* 386.
20. *CIC* 373.
21. See *CIC* 374 §1: 'Each diocese or other particular Church is to be divided into distinct parts or parishes.'
22. Vatican II, *Lumen Gentium*, 26. See *CCC* 832.
23. See Congregation for the Doctrine of the Faith, *Communionis Notio*, 8. Cf. Pope Paul VI, Apostolic Exhortation *Evangelii Nuntiandi*, 64.
24. See Pope Leo XIII, Encyclical *Satis Cognitum*, 4: 'Ecclesiam Jesus Christus non talem finxit formavitque, quae communitates plures genere similes complecteretur.'
25. Pope John Paul II, *Address to the Bishops of the United States of America* (16 September 1987), 3. See also Congregation for the Doctrine of the Faith, *Communionis Notio*, 9.

26. J. Card. Ratzinger, *Il cammino Pasquale* (Milano: Editrice Ancora, 1985), p. 131. See also G. Mansini, 'On the relation of particular to Universal Church' in *The Irish Theological Quarterly* 69/2 (2004), pp. 177–187.
27. See Hermas, *The Shepherd*, Vision 2, 4 in *PG* 2, 897–900; Pope St Clement I, *Second Letter to the Corinthians*, 14, 2 in F. Funk, *Patres Apostolici* I (Tübingen: 1901), p. 200.
28. See Ac 2:1ff. St Irenaeus, *Adversus Haereses*, Book 3, chapter 17, 2 in *SC* 211, 330–333: 'at Pentecost (...) all nations (...) had become a marvellous choir to intone a hymn of praise to God in perfect harmony, because the Holy Spirit had brought distances to nought, eliminated discordant notes and transformed the varieties of the peoples into the first-fruits to be offered to the Father.' Cf. also St Fulgentius of Ruspe, *Sermo 8 in Pentecoste*, 2–3, in *PL* 65, 743–744.
29. See Vatican II, *Lumen Gentium*, 23. This doctrine had been previously developed by Pope Pius XII in his Encyclical *Mystici Corporis*, 42: 'What we have thus far said of the Universal Church must be understood also of the individual Christian communities, whether Oriental or Latin, which go to make up the one Catholic Church.'
30. Pope John Paul II, *Address to the Roman Curia* (20 December 1990), 9.
31. Studies on Khomyakov and his ecclesiology include: N. S. Arseniev, 'Alexey Khomyakov' in *Saint Vladimir's Seminary Quarterly* 5 (1961) pp. 3–10; G. Cioffari, *La sobornost nella teologia russa: La visione della chiesa negli scrittori ecclesiastici della prima metà del XIX secolo* (Bari: 1978); P. P. O'Leary, *The Triune Church: A Study in the Ecclesiology of A. S. Xomjakov* (Fribourg: Universitätsverlag, 1982); M. G. Ritchey, 'Khomiakov and His Theology of Sobornost' in *Diakonia* 17 (1982) pp. 53–62; and J. Van Rossum, 'A. S. Khomiakov and Orthodox Ecclesiology' in *Saint Vladimir's Theological Quarterly* 35(1991) pp. 67–82.
32. From N. Smart, J. Clayton, P. Sherry, S. T. Katz, *Nineteenth-Century Religious Thought in the West* (Cambridge: Cambridge University Press, 1988), p. 183.
33. See T. Sabev, 'The nature and mission of councils in the light of the theology of sobernost' in *Ecumenical Review* 45 (1993), p. 261.
34. Vatican II, *Ad Gentes*, 2.

35. Cf. Pope John Paul II, *Redemptoris Missio*, 23.
36. See Vatican II, *Ad Gentes*, 6.2.
37. See Vatican II, *Apostolicam Actuositatem*, 6; Pope John Paul II, *Redemptoris Missio*, 11.
38. See Pope John Paul II, *Redemptoris Missio*, 21.
39. Vatican II, *Ad Gentes*, 5.
40. Vatican II, *Gaudium et Spes*, 43.6.
41. Vatican II, *Lumen Gentium*, 8.3; 15; *Ad Gentes* 1.3; cf. Pope John Paul II, *Redemptoris Missio*, 12–20.
42. Vatican II, *Lumen Gentium*, 8.3.
43. For a development of cosmic Christology terminology see J.A. Lyons, *The Cosmic Christ in Origen and Teilhard de Chardin* (New York: Oxford University Press, 1982), pp. 1–73.
44. Pope John Paul II, Encyclical Letter *Dominum et Vivificantem* §50.3.
45. See Origen, *Commentary on St. John's Gospel*, Book 6, n.38 in *PG* 14, 301–302: 'Mundus autem et ornamenti est Ecclesia, Christo exsistente mundo et ornamento Ecclesiae, quippe qui sit prima lux mundi.'
46. Lyons, *The Cosmic Christ in Origen and Teilhard de Chardin*, p. 142.
47. Congregation for the Doctrine of the Faith, *Communionis Notio*, 4.2.
48. See St Maximus the Confessor, *Mystagogia*, chapter 2, in *PG* 91, 667–670. Successive chapters suggest further images of the Church: in the visible world itself, consisting as it does of heaven and earth (chapter 3 in *PG* 91, 671–672), and then in the human person, consisting of body and soul (chapter 4 in *PG* 91, 671–672), and the soul, consisting of will and intellect (chapter 5 in *PG* 91, 671–684).
49. In chapter eight below we apply this principle to the relation between the Church and the world.

6

The Church is Apostolic

We shall confound all those who assemble other than where it is proper, by pointing out here the successions of the bishops of the greatest and most ancient Church known to all, founded and organized at Rome by the two most glorious apostles, Peter and Paul—that Church which has the tradition and the faith which comes down to us after having been announced to men by the apostles. For with this Church, because of its superior origin, all churches must agree, that is, all the faithful in the whole world. And it is in her that the faithful everywhere have maintained the apostolic tradition.

St Irenaeus, *Against the heresies*

The Church is called apostolic, because she is based upon the Apostles in four ways. First, in a foundational and historical sense, namely she was and remains built on the Apostles, the witnesses chosen and sent on mission by Christ Himself. The Apostles form the permanent and ontological foundation of the Church (see 1 Co 12:28; Ep 2:20; 4:11). Next, the Church is apostolic in a doctrinal sense since, with the help of the Spirit dwelling in her, she keeps and transmits the deposit of Revelation, which she has received from the Apostles. Third, the Church is apostolic in a sacramental way, as she continues to be taught, sanctified, and guided by the Apostles until Christ's return, through their successors in pastoral office: the college of bishops, assisted by priests, in union with the successor of Peter, the church's supreme Pontiff.[1] Finally, the Church is apostolic in an eschatological sense, since she will always be apostolic as part of her nature, and the Holy City is built 'on twelve foundation stones, each one of which bore the name of one of the twelve apostles of the Lamb' (Rev 21:14). The Final Judgment will be carried out in the context of the Church's apostolicity since when the Son of Man is seated on His throne of glory, the Apostles will sit on twelve thrones to judge the twelve tribes of Israel (Mt 19:28; cf. Lk 22:30). The Apostle thus appears as a uniquely authoritative figure not only at the foundation of the Church but also as a companion of the eschatological Christ at the judgment on the Last Day. This eschatological dimension does not only mean that the Church, founded on the Twelve, awaits its perfect form at the end of God's plan for history. It also means that the Church shares now in the finality, the irrevocable fullness, of God's action within the changes of history, precisely because the Twelve have passed on to the Church their witness to the presence of God's Kingdom in the risen Lord and their role as authoritative heralds of His coming in history.

The historical and eschatological dimensions of apostolicity are to be held together, since one of the characteristics of God's gift of apostolicity is that it manifests the events of the *end* to the present time. This is seen clearly in the mystery of the Eucharist, where the Holy Spirit brings the reality of the resurrected Christ to the Church. Therefore, apostolicity is not reduced simply to a reference in the past, nor is it related only to the reality of a future age. It means that, here and now, the life of the Church is being moulded, corrected, and governed by what has been received from the past *and* by what is awaited at the last day.

The Apostles in the New Testament

The Twelve are seen from the Gospels, for example that of St Matthew:

> These are the names of the twelve apostles: first, Simon who is known as Peter, and his brother

> Andrew; James the son of Zebedee, and his brother John; Philip and Bartholomew; Thomas, and Matthew the tax collector; James the son of Alphaeus, and Thaddaeus; Simon the Zealot and Judas Iscariot, who was also his betrayer. These twelve Jesus sent out, instructing them as follows: 'Do not make your way to gentile territory, and do not enter any Samaritan town' (Mt 10:2–5).

The title of Apostle was gradually extended beyond those who constituted the group of the Twelve. Matthias was elected to fill the place left by Judas, and so was listed as one of the twelve Apostles (Ac 1:15–26). James, mentioned in the Letter to the Galatians, is no longer considered to be James the son of Alphaeus, but rather one who had known Jesus and who held a certain prominence in the primitive Church. He is regarded as enjoying apostolic power (Gal 1:19; 2:9). The title of Apostle was also assigned to Paul and Barnabas (Ac 14:4, 14). The progression in the use of this title is seen in St Paul's description of the appearances of the risen Christ: 'First He appeared to Cephas and secondly to the Twelve. Next He appeared to more than five hundred of the brothers at the same time, most of whom are still alive, though some have died; then He appeared to James, and then to all the apostles; and last of all He appeared to me too' (1 Co 15:5–8). The office of being an Apostle involved an investiture which consisted of the laying-on of hands and a prayer, as can be seen in the case of Paul and Barnabas (Ac 13:3). Those who were Apostles, but not numbered among the Twelve, held in common with the Twelve an episcopal power and also the privilege of having seen the risen Christ, and shared the foundational quality of the experience of the early Church. However, being part of the Twelve involved more: it meant having been present the whole time the Lord Jesus was exercising His ministry, and having shared the experience of the Paschal Mystery (Ac 1:22). A disciple is a *follower* of Jesus; an Apostle is one who is *sent* by Jesus.

St Paul was conscious of the fact that he had received the priestly nature, which he was to transmit: 'He has appointed me as a priest of Jesus Christ, and I am to carry out my priestly duty by bringing the Good News from God to the pagans, and so make them acceptable as an offering, made holy by the Holy Spirit' (Rm 15:16). It is evident that the apostles shared with others the sacrament of Order which they possessed in its fullness. What remains less clear is the concrete way in which they handed on their power of orders in the primitive Church. Not all scholars agree that those who were designated with the title of overseer (*episcopos*) in the apostolic era were in fact endowed with the fullness of the priesthood.[2] Nevertheless, it is commonly held that at least Timothy and Titus, whom St Paul set over the churches of Ephesus and Crete, enjoyed episcopal orders. Titus was given the power of organizing the church in Crete and of appointing elders (*presbyteroi*) in the various towns (Tt 1:5). Timothy was reminded about the gift which he received in episcopal ordination: 'You have in you a spiritual gift which was given to you when the prophets spoke and when the body of elders laid their hands on you; do not let it lie unused' (1 Tm 4:14). This text can be taken to indicate the laying-on of hands as a central rite in ordination, its collegial quality and also the sacramental character imparted thereby.

As regards the delineation of a second rank of the sacrament of order, the issue remains that the Greek New Testament expressions elder (*presbyteros*) and overseer or presiding elder (*episcopos*), in the earliest times did not univocally correspond to the later terms priest and bishop.[3] Indeed in some passages, the overseers seem to be identified with the elders (Tt 1:5, 7; Ac 20:17, 28). What seems clear however, is that both in the Jewish-Christian communities and among the Gentiles, the primitive Christian communities were governed by a body of elders. It is probable that these elders were endowed with the fullness of the priesthood, so as to be able to confer the power of orders to other elders. In this primitive era, a high concentration of men of episcopal rank would have been necessary to ensure a rapid expansion of the Church. The spread of the Church would have required the convenient ordination of men to celebrate the Eucharist. This rapidity of expansion and corresponding ordination is borne out by St Paul's prudent injunction to Timothy: 'Do not be too quick to lay hands on any man' (1 Tm 5:22). The overseers and elders were appointed by the apostles (Ac 14:23) or their representatives (Tt 1:5) by the laying-on of hands (1 Tm 5:22), and their powers were of divine institution (Ac 20:28). The body of elders gradually developed into communities ruled by one bishop and a college of priests; a system involving a monarchical episcopate would have been in place by about 100 AD. There may have also been some intermediate development but this is subject to a certain amount of speculation. In other words, within a relatively short period, those with episcopal powers were regularly ordaining men of the second rank, who enjoyed sacramental orders corresponding to the priesthood which we know today.[4] In conclusion, it can be proposed that the Apostles had all the power of orders which they shared in different ways with those whom they subsequently ordained. It is also accepted that in the generation succeeding the apostles a hierarchy of bishops, priests and deacons was established everywhere in the early rapidly-growing Church of Christ.

The expression of apostolic power in the Church is shown in the triple *munera* or offices of Christ as priest, prophet and king.[5] The three-fold office (or *munera*) of the Apostles can be derived from the supreme command given by Christ to them before His Ascension into heaven: 'All authority in heaven and on earth has been given to me. Go, therefore, make disciples of all nations; baptise them in the name of the Father and of the Son and of the Holy Spirit, and teach them to observe all the commands I gave you. And look, I am with you always; yes, to the end of time' (Mt 28:18–20). The teaching or prophetic office corresponds to teaching all nations to observe Jesus' commandments. The sacerdotal office is expressed in the instruction to baptize, but this clearly would also involve the administration of the other sacraments as well. Finally, the regal or pastoral office is found in the words 'all authority is given to me', and this authority is shared by Christ with His Apostles, and given to them in order that they can 'make disciples of all nations'.

Over the past fifty years, much emphasis has been laid on the pastoral aspect of the apostolic and priestly action, often at the expense of the regal aspect, and also at the expense of the other roles of the priest, namely that of teaching and sanctifying. This has resulted on the one hand in an activist type of priesthood, incapable of contemplation, and reduced to the role of a psychologist, sociologist, capitalist manager, or Marxist political liberator. On the other hand, the full Catholic theological concept of priesthood has sometimes suffered a reduction to the Protestant notion of ministry.

The Petrine nature of the Church

After Jesus Christ, Peter is the figure best known and most frequently cited in the New Testament writings. Peter's name is mentioned more often than all the other disciples put together: 191 times (162 as Peter or Simon Peter, 23 as Simon, and 6 as Kephas). John is next in frequency with only 48 appearances, and Peter is present fifty per cent of the time that John appears in the Bible. In effect, Peter is named a remarkable sixty per cent of the time any disciple is referred to. He is mentioned 154 times with the special name of *Pétros*, 'rock', which is the Greek translation of the Aramaic name Jesus gave him directly: *Kephas*, attested to especially in St Paul's Letters. The frequently-occurring name Simon is a hellenization of his original Hebrew name *Symeon* (this occurs twice: in Ac 15: 14; and in 2 Pt 1: 1). He was the son of Jonah and was born in Bethsaida (Jn 1:42, 44), a little town to the east of the Sea of Galilee. The Apostle Andrew was his brother, and the Apostle Philip came from the same town. Simon pursued in Capernaum the profitable occupation of fisherman on Lake Gennesaret, possessing his own boat (Lk 5:3). Simon settled in Capernaum, where he was living with his mother-in-law in his own house (Mt 8:14; Lk 4:38) at the beginning of Christ's public ministry (around AD 26–28). Recent archaeological excavations have brought to light, beneath the octagonal mosaic paving of a small Byzantine church, the remains of a more ancient church built in that house, as the graffiti with invocations to Peter testify.[6] Simon was thus married, and, according to Clement of Alexandria, had children.[7] The same writer relates the tradition that Peter's wife also suffered martyrdom.[8]

Like so many of his Jewish contemporaries, Simon was attracted by John the Baptist's preaching of penance and was, with his brother Andrew, among John's associates in Bethania on the eastern bank of the Jordan. John the Baptist pointed to Jesus who was passing, saying, 'Behold, the Lamb of God' (Jn 1:36), and Andrew and another disciple followed the Saviour to His residence and remained with Him that day. Later, meeting his brother, Simon, Andrew said 'We have found the Messiah', and brought him to Jesus, who, looking upon him, said: 'You are Simon the son of John; you will be called Kephas' (Jn 1:42). Already, at this first meeting, the Saviour foretold the change of Simon's name to *Kephas*, the Aramaic for rock, which is translated *Pétros* in Greek (in Latin *Petrus*), a proof that Christ had already special plans with regard to Simon. Later, probably at the time of his definitive call to the Apostolate with the eleven other Apostles, Jesus actually gave Simon the name of *Kephas*, after which he was usually called Peter, especially on the solemn occasion of Peter's profession of faith (Mt 16:18).

After this first meeting, Peter with the other early disciples remained with Jesus for some time, accompanying Him to Galilee (for the Marriage at Cana), to Judaea, and to Jerusalem, and through Samaria back to Galilee (Jn 2–4). Here Peter resumed his occupation of fisherman for a short time, but soon received the definitive call of the Saviour to become one of His permanent disciples. Peter and Andrew were engaged at their work when Jesus met and addressed them: 'Come after me, and I will make you fishers of men' (Mt 4:19). On the same occasion, the sons of Zebedee were called (Mt 4:18–22; Mk 1:16–20; Lk 5:1–11; it is here assumed that Luke refers to the same occasion as the other Evangelists). Thereafter, Peter remained always in the immediate neighbourhood of Our Lord. After preaching the Sermon on the Mount and curing the son of the centurion in Capernaum, Jesus came to Peter's house and cured his wife's mother, who was sick with a fever (Mt 8:14–15; Mk 1:29–31). A little later, Christ chose His Twelve Apostles as His constant associates in preaching the kingdom of God.

The New Testament notes the growing prominence of Peter among the Twelve. Though of irresolute character, he clings with the greatest fidelity, firmness of faith, and inward love to the Saviour; rash alike in word and act, he is full of zeal and enthusiasm, though momentarily easily accessible to external influences and intimidated by difficulties. The more prominent the Apostles become in the Gospel narrative, the more conspicuous does Peter appear as the first among them. In the list of the Twelve on the occasion of their solemn call to the Apostolate, not only does Peter stand always at their head, but the name given him by Christ is especially emphasized. For example in the list of the Apostles we read: 'The names of the twelve apostles are these: first, Simon called Peter, and his brother Andrew; James, the son of Zebedee, and his brother John; Philip and Bartholomew, Thomas and Matthew the tax collector; James, the son of Alphaeus, and Thaddaeus; Simon the Cananean, and Judas Iscariot who betrayed Him' (Mt 10:2–4).[9] On various occasions Peter speaks in the name of the other Apostles (Mt 15:15; 19:27; Lk 12:41). When Christ's words are addressed to all the Apostles, Peter answers in their name (see, for example Mt 16:16). Frequently the Saviour turns specially to Peter (Mt 26:40; Lk 22:31).

Peter's name occurs first in all lists of apostles (Mt 10:2; Mk 3:16; Lk 6:14; Ac 1:13). Matthew even calls him the 'first' (πρῷτος in Greek, see Mt 10:2). The name of Judas Iscariot, however, is invariably mentioned last. Peter is almost without exception named first whenever he appears with anyone else. Peter's name is always the first listed of the 'inner circle' of the disciples (Peter, James and John—Mt 17:1; 26:37,40; Mk 5:37; 14:37). In one example to the contrary, Galatians 2:9, where he ('Cephas') is listed after James and before John, he is clearly pre-eminent in the entire context (e.g., 1:18–19; 2:7–8). Peter is often the central figure relating to Jesus in dramatic gospel scenes, such as walking on the water (Mt 14:28–32; Lk 5:1 ff., Mk 10:28; Mt 17:24 ff.). Peter first professes Christ's divinity (Mt 16:16). Peter alone among the apostles receives a new name, *Rock*, solemnly conferred by Jesus Christ (Jn 1:42; Mt 16:18). Likewise, Peter is regarded by Jesus as the Chief Shepherd after Himself (Jn 21:15–17), singularly by name, and over the universal Church, even though others have a similar but subordinate role (Ac 20:28; 1 Pt 5:2). Peter alone among the apostles is mentioned by name as having been prayed for by Jesus Christ in order that his 'faith may not fail' (Lk 22:32). Peter alone among the apostles is exhorted by Jesus to 'strengthen your brethren' (Lk 22:32). Peter alone is told that he has received divine knowledge by a special revelation (Mt 16:17).

Peter is regarded by the Jews (Ac 4:1–13) as the leader and spokesman of Christianity, and is regarded by the common people in the same way (Ac 2:37–41; 5:15). Jesus Christ uniquely associates Himself and Peter in the miracle of the tribute-money (Mt 17:24–27). Christ teaches from Peter's boat, and the miraculous catch of fish follows (Lk 5:1–11): perhaps a metaphor for the Pope as a 'fisher of men' (cf. Mt 4:19). Peter was the first apostle to set out for, and enter the empty tomb (Lk 24:12; Jn 20:6). Peter is specified by an angel as the leader and representative of the apostles (Mk 16:7). Peter leads the apostles in fishing (Jn 21:2–3,11). The barque of Peter is regarded as a figure of the Church, with Peter at the helm. Peter alone casts himself into the sea to come to Jesus (Jn 21:7). Peter's words are the first recorded and most important in the upper room before Pentecost (Ac 1:15–22).

Very characteristic is the expression of true fidelity to Jesus, which Peter addressed to Him in the name of the other Apostles. Christ, after He had spoken of the mystery of the reception of His Body and Blood (Jn 6:22 ff.) and many of His disciples had left Him, asked the Twelve if they too would leave Him. Peter's answer comes immediately: 'Master, to whom shall we go? You have the words of eternal life. We have come to believe and are convinced that you are the Holy One of God' (Jn 6:68–69). Christ Himself unmistakably accords Peter a special precedence and the first place among the Apostles, and designates him as such on various occasions. Peter was one of the three Apostles (with James and John) who were with Christ on certain special occasions like the raising from the dead of the daughter of Jairus (Mk 5:37; Lk 8:51); the Transfiguration of the Lord (Mt 17:1; Mk 9:1; Lk 9:28), the Agony in the Garden of Gethsemane (Mt 26:37; Mk 14:33). On several occasions, also Christ favoured him above all the others. For example, Jesus enters Peter's boat on Lake Gennesaret to preach to the multitude on the shore (Lk 5:3). When He was miraculously walking upon the waters, He called Peter to come to Him across the lake (Mt 14:27–32). In this episode, Peter's apparent lack of trust is often pointed out. Yet his faith is strong, for even in his weakness he cries out 'Lord save me!' (Mt 14:30). This expression indicates that he did not rely on his own strength, but on the help which comes from Christ. Therefore, despite the fact that Jesus refers to Peter in that moment as having so little faith (Mt 14:31), that faith is nevertheless growing. This miracle is a prelude to Peter's profession of faith in Matthew 16:13–19, and is a rich illustration of the Church as the barque of Peter.

St Peter's profession of faith took place at Caesarea Philippi. This place was so named because it had been rebuilt by the tetrarch Philip in honour of Caesar Augustus. It was the summer before the Crucifixion, with Jesus filled with presentiments of His Death. Perhaps Jesus withdrew here because it is a pleasant place to escape in summertime the torrid heat of the Lake of Galilee. However, the area has other associations which make it a suitable site for this scene. Hermon is traditionally a holy mountain, a meeting place of God and man, a suitable background to this episode of revelation and solemn mission. They walked a while up the mountain road to Mount Hermon. The Jordan had its source in these mysterious ravines; the spring of the Jordan is, in Jewish legend, the opening to hell.[10] The precipitous southern end of one of the foothills of Mount Hermon forms a wall of bare rock about 200 feet high and 500 feet wide, which formed the backdrop for Peter's profession of faith.[11] Here, Jesus asked His disciples: 'Who do people say that the Son of Man is?' (Mt 16:13). Some of them had heard that people took Him for the risen John the Baptist, others for Elijah or one of the prophets. 'But who do you say that I am?', continued Jesus. Quicker than any of the others, came Peter's profession of faith: 'You are the Christ, the Son of the living God' (Mt 16:16). Jesus responded with the words: 'Blessed are you, Simon son of Jonah. For flesh and blood has not revealed this to you, but my heavenly Father.' Then Jesus added 'And so I say to you, you are Peter, and upon this rock I will build my Church, and the gates of hell shall not prevail against it. I will give you the keys to the kingdom of heaven. Whatever you bind on earth shall be bound in heaven; and whatever you loose on earth shall be loosed in heaven' (Mt 16:18–19). These words of the Lord, written down in the latter half of the first century are inscribed in Latin, in golden letters, within the dome of St Peter's Basilica in Rome.

In Hebrew thought, a person's name expresses the reality concerning that person. St Peter's new name encapsulates his mission as bedrock of the Church and foundation of its unity in Christ. In the Sermon on the Mount Jesus gave the example of the 'wise man who built his house on rock' (Mt 7:24). Addressing Simon, Jesus declared to him that because of his faith, a gift from God, he had the solidity of rock upon which an unshakable edifice could be built. Jesus then stated His own decision to build on this rock just such a building, namely His Church.[12] By the word 'rock' the Saviour cannot have meant Himself, but only Peter, as is so much more apparent in Aramaic in which the same word (*Kipha*) is used for 'Peter' and 'rock'. His statement means that He wished to make Peter the head of the whole community of those who believed in Him as the true Messiah; that through this foundation (Peter) the Kingdom of Christ would be unconquerable; that the guidance of the faithful was placed in the hands of Peter, as the special representative, or Vicar, of Christ. Moreover, *Rock* also embodies a metaphor applied to him by Christ in a sense analogous to the suffering and despised Messiah (1 Pt 2:4–8; cf. Mt 21:42).

Without a solid foundation a house falls. St Peter is the foundation, but not founder of the Church; the administrator, but not the Lord of the Church. The Good Shepherd (Jn 10:11) gives us other shepherds as well (Eph 4:11). Christ says to St Peter 'I will give you the keys of the kingdom of heaven' (Mt 16:19). This 'power of the keys' concerns ecclesiastical discipline and administrative authority with regard to the requirements of the faith, as prefigured in Isaiah 22:22 (cf. Is 9:6; Jb 12:14; Rev 3:7). From this power flows the use of censures, excommunication, absolution, baptismal discipline, the imposition of penances, and legislative powers. In the Old Testament a steward, or prime minister, is a man who is set 'over a house' (Gn 41:40; 43:19; 44:4; 1 Ki 4:6; 16:9; 18:3; 2 Ki 10:5; 15:5; 18:18; Is 22:15,20–21). Jesus adds 'whatever you bind on earth shall be bound in heaven, and whatever you loose on earth shall be loosed in heaven' (Mt 16:19). The words 'bind' and 'loose' are not merely metaphorical, but are concrete Jewish juridical rabbinical terms, which meant to 'forbid' and 'permit' with reference to the interpretation of the law, and secondarily to 'condemn' or 'place under the ban' or 'acquit'. Thus, St Peter and the Popes are given the authority to determine the rules for doctrine and life, by virtue of revelation and the Spirit's leading (Jn 16:13), and to demand obedience from the Church. 'Binding and loosing' represent the legislative and judicial powers of the Papacy and the bishops

(Mt 18:17–18; Jn 20:23). St Peter, however, is the only apostle who receives these powers by name and in the singular, making him pre-eminent. The close link between Christ and St Peter after his profession of faith is illustrated by the episode in which Jesus sent him to the lake to catch the fish in whose mouth Peter found the coin to pay as tax for both of them (Mt 17:24 ff.).

The position of Peter among the other Apostles and in the Christian community formed the basis for the Kingdom of God on earth, that is, the Church of Christ. Peter was personally installed as Head of the Apostles by Christ Himself. This foundation created for the Church by its Founder could not disappear with the person of Peter, but was intended to continue and did in fact continue (as actual history shows) in the primacy of the Roman Church and its Popes.

In spite of his firm faith in Jesus, Peter had thus far no clear knowledge of the mission and work of the Saviour. The sufferings of Christ especially, transcended his worldly conception of the Messiah, and were inconceivable to him. Peter's incomplete conception occasionally elicited a sharp reproof from Jesus (Mt 16:21–23; Mk 8:31–33). During the Passion, Peter's weakness was manifested. The Saviour had already told him that Satan had desired to sift him as wheat. However, Christ had prayed for Peter that his faith may not fail, and, after being converted, he would confirm his brothers (Lk 22:31–32). Peter's assurance that he was ready to accompany his Master to prison and to death, elicited Christ's prediction that Peter would deny Him (Mt 26:30–35; Mk 14:26–31; Lk 22:31–34; Jn 13:33–38). When Christ proceeded to wash the feet of His disciples before the Last Supper, and came first to Peter, the latter at first protested, but, on Christ's declaring that otherwise he should have no part with Him, immediately said: 'Lord, not only my feet, but also my hands and my head' (Jn 13:1–10). In the Garden of Gethsemane, Peter had to submit to the Saviour's reproach that he had slept like the others, while his Master suffered deadly anguish (Mk 14:37). At the seizing of Jesus, Peter in an outburst of anger wished to defend his Master by force, but was forbidden to do so. At first he fled with the other Apostles (Jn 18:10–11; Mt 26:56); then turning he followed his captured Lord to the courtyard of the High Priest, and there denied Christ, asserting explicitly and swearing that he did not know Him (Mt 26:58–75; Mk 14:54–72; Lk 22:54–62; Jn 18:15–27). This denial did not constitute a lapse of interior faith in Christ, but was an expression of exterior fear and cowardice. His sorrow was thus so much the greater, when, after his Master had turned His gaze towards him, he clearly recognized what he had done.

In spite of this weakness, Peter's position as head of the Apostles was later confirmed by Jesus, and his precedence was at least as clear after the Resurrection as before. The women, who were the first to find Christ's tomb empty, received from the angel a special message for Peter (Mk 16:7). To him alone of the Apostles did Christ appear on the first day after the Resurrection (Lk 24:34; 1 Co 15:5). Moreover, most important of all, when He appeared at the Lake of Gennesaret, Christ renewed to Peter His special commission to feed and defend His flock, after Peter had thrice affirmed his special love for his Master (Jn 21:15–17). The encounter involves a very significant play on words. In Greek, the term '*fileo*' means the love of friendship, which is limited and not all-encompassing; instead, the word '*agapao*' signifies a total and unconditional love without reserve. Jesus asks Peter the first time: 'Simon... do you love me *(agapas-me)*' with this total and unconditional love (Jn 21:15)? Prior to the experience of betrayal, the Apostle Peter certainly would have said: 'I love you *(agapo-se)* unconditionally.' Now that he has known the bitter sadness of infidelity, the drama of his own weakness, he says with humility: 'Lord; you know that I love you *(filo-se)*', that is, 'I love you with my poor human love.' Christ insists: 'Simon, do you love me with this total love that I want?' And Peter repeats the response of his humble human love: '*Kyrie, filo-se*', 'Lord, I love you as I am able to love you.'

The third time Jesus only says to Simon: *'Fileis-me?'*, 'Do you love me?' Simon Peter understands that his poor love is enough for Jesus, it is the only one of which he is capable, nonetheless he is grieved that the Lord spoke to him in this way. He thus replies: 'Lord, you know everything; you know that I love you *(filo-se).'*[13] In conclusion, Christ foretold the violent death Peter would have to suffer, and thus invited him to follow Him in a special manner (Jn 21:20–23). In this manner, Peter was called and prepared to exercise the primacy of the Apostles, which he carried out with courage after Christ's Ascension into Heaven.

Among the crowd of Apostles and disciples who, after Christ's Ascension into Heaven from the Mount of Olives, returned to Jerusalem to await the fulfilment of His promise to send the Holy Spirit, Peter clearly stands out as the leader of all, and is henceforth constantly recognized as the head of the original Christian community in Jerusalem. He takes the initiative in the appointment to the Apostolic College of another witness of the life, Death and Resurrection of Christ to replace Judas (Ac 1:15–26). After the descent of the Holy Spirit on the first feast of Pentecost, Peter standing at the head of the Apostles delivers the first public sermon to proclaim the life, Death, and Resurrection of Jesus, and wins a large number of Jews as converts to the Christian community (Ac 2:14–41). As the first among the Apostles he worked a public miracle, when with John he went up into the temple and cured the lame man at the Beautiful Gate. To the people crowding in amazement about the two Apostles, he preaches a long sermon in the Porch of Solomon, and brings new members to the flock of believers (Ac 3:1–4:4).

In the subsequent examinations of the two Apostles before the Jewish High Council, Peter defends in a courageous fashion the cause of Jesus and the obligation and liberty of the Apostles to preach the Gospel (Ac 4:5–21). When Ananias and Sapphira attempt to deceive the Apostles and the people, Peter appears as judge of their action, and God executes the sentence of punishment passed by the Apostle by causing the sudden death of the two guilty parties (Ac 5:1–11). By numerous miracles, God confirms the apostolic activity of Christ's witnesses, and here also special mention is made of Peter, since it is recorded that the inhabitants of Jerusalem and neighbouring towns carried their sick in their beds into the streets so that the shadow of Peter might fall on them and they might thereby be healed (Ac 5:12–16). The ever-increasing number of the faithful caused the Sanhedrin to adopt new measures against the Apostles, but 'Peter and the Apostles' answer that they 'ought to obey God rather than men' (Ac 5:29 ff.). Not only in Jerusalem itself did Peter labour in fulfilling the mission entrusted to him by his Master. He also retained connection with the other Christian communities in Palestine, and preached the Gospel both there and in the lands situated farther north. When Philip the Deacon had won a large number of believers in Samaria, Peter and John were deputed to travel there from Jerusalem to organize the community and to invoke the Holy Spirit to descend upon the faithful. Peter appears a second time as judge, in the case of the magician Simon, who had wished to purchase from the Apostles the power that he also could invoke the Holy Spirit (Ac 8: 14–25). On their way back to Jerusalem, the two Apostles preached the joyous tidings of the Kingdom of God. Subsequently, after Paul's departure from Jerusalem and conversion on the road to Damascus, the Christian communities in Palestine were left in peace by the Jewish council.

Peter now undertook an extensive missionary tour, which brought him to the maritime cities, Lydda, Joppe, and Caesarea. In Lydda he cured the paralyzed Aeneas, in Joppe he raised Tabitha (Dorcas) from the dead; and at Caesarea, instructed by a vision which he had in Joppe, he baptized and received into the Church the first non-Jewish Christians, the centurion Cornelius and his kinsmen (Ac 9:32–10:48). On Peter's return to Jerusalem a little later, the strict Jewish Christians, who regarded the complete observance of the Jewish law as binding on all, asked him why he had entered and eaten in the house of the uncircumcised. Peter tells of his vision and defends his action, which was ratified by the Apostles and the faithful in Jerusalem (Ac 11:1–18).

A confirmation of the position accorded to Peter by Luke, in the Acts, is afforded by the testimony of St Paul (Gal 1:18–20). After his conversion and three years' residence in Arabia, Paul came to Jerusalem 'to see Peter'. Here the Apostle of the Gentiles clearly designates Peter as the authorized head of the Apostles and of the early Christian Church. Peter's long residence in Jerusalem and Palestine soon came to an end. Herod Agrippa I began (AD 42–44) a new persecution of the Church in Jerusalem; after the execution of James, the son of Zebedee, this ruler had Peter cast into prison, intending to have him also executed after the Jewish Passover was ended. Peter, however, was freed in a miraculous manner, and, proceeding to the house of the mother of John Mark, where many of the faithful were assembled for prayer, informed them of his liberation from the hands of Herod, commissioned them to communicate the fact to James and the brethren, and then left Jerusalem to go to 'another place' (Ac 12:1–18). Concerning St Peter's subsequent activity we receive no further connected information from the Scriptural sources, although we possess short notices of certain individual episodes of his later life.

It is certain that St Peter remained for a time at Antioch; he may even have returned there several times. The Christian community of Antioch was founded by Christianized Jews who had been driven from Jerusalem by the persecution (Ac 11:19ff.). Peter's residence among them is proved by the episode concerning the observance of the Jewish ceremonial law even by Christianized pagans, related by St Paul (Gal 2:11–21). The chief Apostles in Jerusalem, the 'pillars', Peter, James, and John, had unreservedly approved St Paul's Apostolate to the Gentiles, while they themselves intended to labour principally among the Jews. While Paul was dwelling in Antioch (the date cannot be accurately determined), St Peter came there and mingled freely with the non-Jewish Christians of the community, frequenting their houses and sharing their meals. However, when the Christianized Jews arrived from Jerusalem, Peter, fearing lest these rigid observers of the Jewish ceremonial law should be scandalized, and his influence with the Jewish Christians be endangered, afterwards avoided eating with the uncircumcised. His conduct made a great impression on the other Jewish Christians at Antioch, so that even Barnabas, St Paul's companion, now avoided eating with the Christianized pagans. As this action was entirely opposed to the principles and practice of Paul, and might lead to confusion among the converted pagans, this Apostle addressed a public reproach to St Peter, because his conduct seemed to indicate a wish to compel the pagan converts to become Jews and accept circumcision and the Jewish law. The whole incident is another proof of the authoritative position of St Peter in the early Church, since his example and conduct was regarded as decisive. Tradition makes Peter the first bishop of Antioch, and thus its first Patriarch. Some scholars interpret Paul's mention of Peter in 1 Corinthians 1:12 as evidence that Peter had also visited Corinth.

Peter returned occasionally to the original Christian Church of Jerusalem, the guidance of which was entrusted to St James, the relative of Jesus, after the departure of the Prince of the Apostles (AD 42–44). The last mention of St Peter in the Acts (15:1–29; see Gal 2:1–10) occurs in the report of the Council of the Apostles on the occasion of such a passing visit. Between Peter and Paul there was no dogmatic difference in their conception of salvation for Jewish and Gentile Christians. The recognition of Paul as the Apostle of the Gentiles (Gal 2:1–9) was entirely sincere, and excludes all question of a fundamental divergence of views. St Peter and the other Apostles recognized the converts from paganism as Christian brothers on an equal footing.

It is an established historical fact that St Peter laboured in Rome during the last portion of his life, and there ended his earthly course by martyrdom. As to the duration of his Apostolic activity in the Roman capital, the continuity or otherwise of his residence there, the details and success of his labours, and the chronology of his arrival and death, all these questions are uncertain, and can be solved only on more or less well-founded hypotheses. The essential fact is that Peter died at Rome, which is linked to the historical foundation of the claim of the Bishops of Rome to the Apostolic Primacy of Peter. The manner, and therefore the place of his death, must have been known in widely extended Christian circles at the end of the first century. This is clear from the remark, in the Gospel of St John, concerning Christ's prophecy that Peter would be led where he did not want to go, signifying by this the type of death with which he would glorify God (Jn 21:18–19).

St Peter's First Letter was written almost undoubtedly from Rome, since the salutation at the end reads: 'The chosen one at Babylon sends you greeting, as does Mark, my son.' (1 Pt 5:13). Babylon must here be identified with the Roman capital; since Babylon on the Euphrates, which lay in ruins, or New Babylon (Seleucia) on the Tigris, or the Egyptian Babylon near Memphis, or Jerusalem cannot be meant, the reference must be to Rome, the only city which is called Babylon elsewhere in ancient Christian literature (Rev 17:5; 18:10). From Bishop Papias of Hierapolis and Clement of Alexandria, who both appeal to the testimony of the old disciples of the Apostles, we learn that Mark wrote his Gospel in Rome at the request of the Roman Christians, who desired a written memorial of the doctrine preached to them by St Peter and his disciples, and this is confirmed by St Irenaeus.[14]

A testimony concerning the martyrdom of Peter and Paul is supplied by Pope Clement of Rome, around AD 95–97: 'Through jealousy and envy the greatest and most righteous supports of the Church have suffered persecution and been put to death. Let us place before our eyes the good Apostles, like St Peter, who in consequence of unjust jealousy, suffered not one or two, but numerous miseries, and, having thus given testimony, has entered the merited place of glory.'[15] He then mentions Paul and a number of elect, who were assembled with the others and suffered martyrdom 'among us' (namely among the Romans). He is speaking undoubtedly of the persecution under Nero, and thus refers the martyrdom of Peter and Paul to that epoch.

St Irenaeus of Lyons, a native of Asia Minor and a disciple of Polycarp of Smyrna (himself a disciple of St John the Apostle), passed a considerable time in Rome shortly after the middle of the second century, and then proceeded to Lyons, where he became bishop in AD 177. Irenaeus described the Roman Church as the most prominent and chief preserver of the Apostolic tradition:

> However, since it would be too long to enumerate in such a volume as this the succession of all the churches, we shall confound all those who, in whatever manner, whether through self-satisfaction or vainglory, or through blindness and wicked opinion, assemble other than where it is proper, by pointing out here the successions of the bishops of the greatest and most ancient church known to all, founded and organized at Rome by the two most glorious apostles, Peter and Paul, that church which has the tradition and the faith which comes down to us after having been announced to men by the apostles. With that church, because of its superior origin, all the churches must agree, that is, all the faithful in the whole world, and it is in her that the faithful everywhere have maintained the apostolic tradition.[16]

Eusebius records that Paul was beheaded in Rome itself, and Peter, likewise, was crucified, during the reign of the Emperor Nero:

> The account is confirmed by the names of Peter and Paul over the cemeteries there, which remain to the present time. And it is confirmed also by a stalwart man of the Church, Caius by name, who lived in the time of Zephyrinus, Bishop of Rome (198–217 AD).

> This Caius speaks of the places in which the remains of the aforementioned apostles were deposited: 'I can point out the trophies of the apostles. For if you are willing to go to the Vatican or to the Ostian Way, you will find the trophies of those who founded this Church.'[17]

Around 210 AD, Tertullian provides a further testimony to the martyrdom of St Peter and St Paul and its importance for Rome: 'But if you are near Italy, you have Rome, where authority is at hand for us too. What a happy church that is, on which the apostles poured out their whole doctrine with their blood; where Peter had a passion like that of the Lord, where Paul was crowned with the death of John the Baptist, by being beheaded.'[18]

Tradition has it that St Peter suffered martyrdom under Nero in the year 67, having arrived in Rome under the Emperor Claudius (according to Jerome, in 42 AD). He would thus have completed in Rome twenty-five years of Papacy. Eusebius also records the manner of St Peter's crucifixion, from a theologian named Origen (who wrote about 230 AD): 'Peter appears to have preached through Pontus, Galatia, Bithynia, Cappadocia, and Asia, to the Jews that were scattered abroad; who also, finally coming to Rome, was crucified with his head downward, having himself requested to suffer in this way.'[19] These facts are also borne out by St Jerome:

> Simon Peter, the son of Jonah, from the village of Bethsaida in the province of Galilee, brother of Andrew the apostle, and himself chief of the apostles, after having been bishop of the church of Antioch and having preached to the Dispersion … pushed on to Rome in the second year of Claudius to over-throw Simon Magus, and held the sacerdotal chair there for twenty-five years until the last, that is the fourteenth, year of Nero. At his hands, he received the crown of martyrdom being nailed to the cross with his head towards the ground and his feet raised on high, asserting that he was unworthy to be crucified in the same manner as his Lord.[20]

In art, St Peter is featured with the keys, based on Christ giving to him the keys of the kingdom of heaven (Mt 16:19); these keys are of silver and gold, referring to the miracle in Acts 3:6.

The Papacy in the Church

Jesus' intention to make Simon Peter the foundation 'rock' of His Church (cf. Mt 16:18) has a value that outlasts Peter's earthly life. Jesus actually conceived His Church and desired her presence and activity in all nations until the ultimate fulfilment of history (cf. Mt 26:14; 28:19; Mk 16:15; Lk 24:47; Ac 1:8). Therefore, He foresaw and desired successors for Peter and He also willed successors for the other Apostles in order to continue His work in the various parts of the world. The Papal office was not to terminate with the death of Peter, and so the Kingdom of God was to endure for all ages (Mt 28:18–20; cf. 13:38–50). Accordingly, unless the gates of hell were to prevail, there could never come a time when Christ's sheepfold would be deprived of its shepherd, never a time when His Church would be without its rock foundation. The successors of St Peter would be charged with the same pastoral mission and equipped with the same power, beginning with the mission and power of being Rock, the visible principle of unity in faith, love and the ministry of evangelization, sanctification and leadership entrusted to the Church.[21]

The most ancient tradition of the Church clearly indicates the consciousness that the office and ministry of St Peter is handed on within the Church in the Papacy. Around the year 107 AD, St Ignatius of Antioch wrote a letter to the Church of Rome which he addressed as that 'which presides in the land of the Romans, worthy of God, worthy of honour, deservedly blessed, worthy of happy success, worthily chaste, which presides over charity, observing the law of Christ, and bearing the Father's name.'[22] Charity (*agápe*) in St Ignatius' language refers to ecclesial communion. Presiding over charity expresses the primacy in that communion of charity which is the Church, and necessarily includes the service of authority, the *ministerium Petrinum*. In no other letter to the other churches, did St Ignatius address any such terms expressing such high respect, honour, veneration, and deference.

St Irenaeus, bishop of Lyons, around 202 AD actually lists the succession of the bishops of Rome.

> The blessed Apostles [Peter and Paul], having founded and built up the Church [of Rome], handed over the office of the episcopate to Linus. Paul makes mention of this Linus in the Epistle to Timothy. To him succeeded Anacletus; and after him in the third place from the Apostles, Clement was chosen for the episcopate. He had seen the blessed Apostles and was acquainted with them. It might be said that He still heard the echoes of the preaching of the Apostles, and had their traditions before his eyes. And not only he, for there were many still remaining who had been instructed by the Apostles... To this Clement, Evaristus succeeded; and Alexander succeeded Evaristus. Then, sixth after the Apostles, Sixtus was appointed; after him, Telesphorus, who also was gloriously martyred. Then Hyginus; after him, Pius; and after him, Anicetus. Soter succeeded Anicetus, and now, in the twelfth place after the Apostles, the lot of the episcopate has fallen to Eleutherius. In this order, and by the teaching of the Apostles handed down in the Church, the preaching of the truth has come down to us.[23]

St Jerome, around 376 AD, in the context of Christological heresies circulating in the East affirmed:

> Since the East... is tearing piecemeal the undivided tunic of Christ, woven from the top throughout, and foxes are destroying the vine of Christ, so that among the broken cisterns which have no water it is hard to know where is the sealed fountain and the garden enclosed, I have considered that I ought to consult the Chair of Peter and the faith praised by the mouth of the Apostle, asking now the food of my soul where of old I received the garment of

> Christ. Neither the vast expense of ocean nor all the breadth of land which separate us could preclude me from seeking the precious pearl... From the priest I ask the salvation of the victim; from the shepherd the safety of his sheep... Following none in the first place but Christ, I am in communion with your beatitude, that is, with the Chair of Peter. On that rock I know the Church is built. Whosoever shall eat the Lamb outside that house is profane. If any be not with Noah in the Ark, he shall perish beneath the sway of the deluge.[24]

St Ambrose of Milan proposed in a concise way the inseparability of the Papacy and the Church in his epithet: 'Where Peter is, there is the Church; where the Church is, eternal life is to be found.'[25]

Around the year 400 AD, St Augustine detailed a complete list of the Papal succession, thus indicating the unbroken unity of the Petrine office:

> For if the lineal succession of bishops is to be taken into account, with how much more certainty and benefit to the Church do we reckon back till we reach Peter himself, to whom, as bearing in a figure the whole Church, the Lord said: 'Upon this rock will I build my Church, and the gates of hell shall not prevail against it!' The successor of Peter was Linus, and his successors in unbroken continuity were these: Clement, Anacletus, Evaristus, Alexander, Sixtus, Telesphorus, Iginus, Anicetus, Pius, Soter, Eleutherius, Victor, Zephyrinus, Calixtus, Urban, Pontianus, Antherus, Fabian, Cornelius, Lucius, Stephen, Xystus, Dionysius, Felix, Eutychianus, Gaius, Marcellinus, Marcellus, Eusebius, Miltiades, Sylvester, Marcus, Julius, Liberius, Damasus, and Siricius, whose successor is the present Bishop Anastasius.[26]

St Augustine also encapsulated his understanding of the Petrine succession in the pithy saying: 'Peter is the Rock, and the Rock is the Church.'[27] Pope St Leo the Great affirmed, before the year 461:

> For the solidity of that faith which was praised in the chief of the Apostles is perpetual: and as that which Peter believed in Christ remains, so that remains which Christ instituted in Peter... The dispensation of Truth therefore abides, and the blessed Peter persevering in the strength of the Rock, which he has received, has not abandoned the helm of the Church, which he undertook. For he was ordained before the rest in such a way that from his being called the Rock, from his being pronounced the Foundation, from his being constituted the Doorkeeper of the kingdom of heaven, from his being set as the Judge to bind and to loose, whose judgments shall retain their validity in heaven, from all these mystical titles we might know the nature of his association with Christ. And still to-day he more fully and effectually performs what is entrusted to him, and carries out every part of his duty and charge in Him and with Him, through Whom he has been glorified.[28]

The continuity of the Papal succession was solemnly defined by the First Vatican Council: 'What Christ the Lord, prince of pastors and great shepherd of the sheep, established in the blessed Apostle Peter for eternal salvation and for the everlasting welfare of the Church, must always perdure, by the will of the same Christ, in the Church which, founded on rock, will remain indestructible until the end of time.'[29] The same Council defined as a truth of the faith: 'It is by the institution of Christ the Lord, that is, by divine right, that blessed Peter has endless successors in his primacy over the whole Church.'[30] This is an essential element of the Church's organic and hierarchical structure, which no one has the power to change. For the Church's entire duration, there will be successors of Peter in virtue of Christ's will.

The First Vatican Council solemnly defined that the Roman Pontiff is the successor of blessed Peter in the same primacy.[31] This excludes the idea that Peter and Paul were joint heads of the Church. The Jansenist Martin de Barcos, inspired by Antoine Arnauld, had proposed this theory.[32] This notion of dual church authority, implying an equality of the two Apostles, had been condemned under Pope Innocent X, in 1647.[33]

The definition binds the primacy of Peter and his successors to the See of Rome, which cannot be replaced by any other see. However, it can happen that, due to circumstances of the times or for particular reasons, the bishops of Rome take up residence temporarily in places other than the Eternal City. Certainly, a city's political condition can change extensively and profoundly over centuries. Nevertheless Rome remains a determinate space to which the concrete institution of the See of Peter is always referred.[34] The decisive historical event is that the fisherman of Bethsaida came to Rome and suffered martyrdom in this city. This fact is rich in theological significance, because it shows the mystery of the divine plan which arranges the course of human events to serve the Church's beginnings and development.

The Papacy is attached to the See of Rome for ever. Peter was prompted by the Spirit to come to Rome, the same Holy Spirit who assisted the Apostles in founding the Church. Peter was expressly led by the divine will to unite the Papacy to the See of Rome for all future time. The Church of Christ, the Church of Peter, the Church of the successors of Peter, is Roman for ever. The title 'Roman' is more than a merely historical one reminding us that after twenty centuries the primacy of jurisdiction remains attached to the Roman See; it is a prophetic title signifying that for all ages to come the primacy of jurisdiction will be linked with the See of Rome. The See of Rome is to be distinguished from residence in Rome. The Pope can leave Italy, and go to Avignon. In ecclesiastical law, which is always revocable, he could even annex the episcopate of Avignon to the universal episcopate. He remains however, by divine right, the Roman Pontiff; and there can be no other legitimate Bishop of Rome. If Rome one day should be utterly destroyed, we should then have to say that the exclusive authority of the Pope over it would have become in fact without object, though continuing to exist in right. The See associated with the Petrine authority cannot be detached or changed by any human authority. No matter where he lives, the true successor of St Peter will necessarily remain the Bishop of Rome.[35]

The office entrusted by Christ to St Peter and his successors cannot simply be reduced to a special 'charism', a gift belonging to the category of prophecy. Rather his power derives from the natural jurisdiction of his office, whether he exercises this in an ordinary or in an extraordinary manner. This power and this authority does not come to him from the consent of the people of God, nor does it emerge from the community, it does not come from 'flesh and blood'; it is given from above. It is the apex of the priestly office at its point of first adhesion into the personal Priesthood of Jesus Christ, before the descent of power through Order in the whole Church.[36] The founding foundation (*fundamentum fundans*) of the Church is Christ, and her founded foundation (*fundamentum fundatum*) is St Peter.

The Papal election

In the early centuries of Christianity the bishop of Rome (like other bishops) was chosen by the consensus of the clergy and people of Rome.[37] For example, St Cyprian described the manner in which Pope Cornelius was elected:

> He was made bishop by very many of our colleagues who were then present in the city of Rome, who sent to us letters concerning his ordination, honourable and laudatory, and remarkable for their testimony in announcement of him. Moreover, Cornelius was made bishop by the judgment of God and of His Christ, by the testimony of almost all the clergy, by the suffrage of the people who were then present, and by the assembly of ancient priests and good men, ... when the place of Fabian, that is, when the place of Peter and the degree of the sacerdotal throne was vacant.[38]

As regards the question whether the Pope can select his own successor, it is possible that Peter, the first Pope chose his own immediate successor, St Linus. History records the case of Felix IV who in 530, on his deathbed, chose his successor, Boniface II. Felix even handed him his pallium. However the question then arises whether the latter become Pope in virtue of this election or in virtue of the later ratification by the Roman clergy. Nevertheless, the fact that the Senate published an edict forbidding discussion of Papal succession during a reigning Pontiff's lifetime, indicates that this was indeed an example of a Pope naming his successor. Boniface II, in his turn, made the Roman clergy promise to maintain after his death the choice he had made of Vigilius as his successor: but fearing, later on, for the consequences of such an act, he publicly retracted it.[39] For certain theologians, like Cajetan, the direct election of a successor by the reigning Pope would be invalid. According to Cajetan, the power to elect a successor resides in the Pope not in a formal manner, apt to pass into act (as the mason's art is in the mason), but in an eminent manner, inapt for immediate exercise (as the mason's art is in the architect).[40] This is an extreme position, and other theologians would simply point out that it is not fitting, since the act of electing a Pope precedes, strictly speaking, any exercise of the papal power; and so it is fittingly assigned to the Church and not to the Pope.[41] For many other theologians, however, it would be simply contra-indicated in the present state of things. It could well be proposed that as the Pope can appoint a coadjutor bishop to any other see, he could do the same to his own See of Rome.

At the Lateran Synod of 13 April 1059, Pope Nicholas II decreed (*In nomine Domini*) that the pope is to be elected by the six cardinal bishops.[42] The Second Council of the Lateran in 1139 removed the requirement that the assent of the lower clergy and the laity be obtained. In 1179 the Third Lateran Council (Eleventh General Council) decreed that papal elections require a two-thirds majority. During this Council, Pope Alexander III (*Licet de vitanda*) restricted papal elections solely to the three orders of Cardinals. A history of political interference in these elections and consequently long vacancies between popes, and especially the interregnum of 1268–1271, prompted the Second Council of Lyons to decree in 1274 that the electors should be locked in seclusion *cum clave* (Latin for 'with a key'), and not permitted to leave until a new Bishop of Rome is elected. Conclaves are now held in the Sistine Chapel in the Palace of the Vatican. Since then other details of the process have developed. In 1970 Pope Paul VI limited the electors to those cardinals under 80 years of age. Electors formerly made choices by three methods: by acclamation, by compromise and by scrutiny. When voting by acclamation, the cardinals would unanimously declare the new Pope *quasi afflati Spiritu Sancto* (as if inspired by the Holy Spirit). When voting by compromise, the deadlocked College of Cardinals would select a committee of cardinals to conduct an election. When voting by scrutiny, the electors cast secret ballots.[43] The last election by compromise was that of John XXII (1316), and the last election by acclamation was that of Gregory XV (1621). New rules introduced by Pope John Paul II have formally abolished these long-unused systems; now, election is always by ballot.[44]

Teaching, Governing, Sanctifying

In the threefold charge entrusted to the Church of preaching the Good News of salvation, of gathering together the dispersed children of God, and of sanctifying the believers, we find a special and supreme responsibility of the Pope in the Church's threefold mission of teaching, governing and sanctifying, as Prophet, Priest and Shepherd.

The Church's doctrinal authority is vested in the Roman Pontiff. The teaching office of Peter's successor has been affirmed in East and West, for example by St John Chrysostom: 'Peter the leader (*coryphaeus*) of the choir of apostles, the mouth of the disciples, the foundation of the faith, the base of the confession, the fisherman of the world, who brought back our race from the depth of error to heaven, he who is everywhere fervent and full of boldness, or rather of love than of boldness.'[45] The mission of the Magisterium is linked to the definitive nature of the covenant established by God with his people in Christ. It is the task of the Magisterium to preserve God's people from deviations and defections and to guarantee them the objective possibility of professing the true faith without error. Thus, the task of the Magisterium is aimed at ensuring that the People of God abides in the truth that liberates. To fulfil this service, Christ endowed the Church's shepherds with the charism of infallibility in matters of faith and morals.

In this regard, the Pope enjoys the charism of infallibility in his office as teacher. As the First Vatican Council defined:

> We teach and define it to be a dogma divinely revealed that the Roman Pontiff, when he speaks *ex cathedra*, that is, when acting in his office of pastor and teacher of all Christians, by his supreme Apostolic authority, he defines a doctrine concerning faith or morals to be held by the whole Church, through the divine assistance promised him in Blessed Peter, he enjoys that infallibility with which the divine Redeemer willed his Church to be endowed in defining doctrine concerning faith and morals; and therefore such definitions of the said Roman Pontiff are irreformable of themselves, and not from the consent of the Church.[46]

An *ex cathedra* definition is one in which the Pope employs the fullness of his apostolic authority to make a final and irrevocable decision (*definit*) on a question of faith or morals, with the clear intention of binding all the faithful to its acceptance, as involving, directly or indirectly, the deposit of faith.

The Ordinary Magisterium of the Pope can also be infallible under certain circumstances as Vatican I defined: 'Wherefore, by divine and Catholic faith all those things are to be believed which are contained in the word of God as found in Scripture and Tradition, and which are proposed by the Church as matters to be believed as divinely revealed, whether by her solemn judgment or in her ordinary and universal Magisterium.'[47] When the Church through its supreme Magisterium proposes a doctrine for belief as being divinely revealed, and as the teaching of Christ, the definitions 'must be adhered to with the obedience of faith'.[48] This infallibility extends as far as the deposit of divine Revelation itself.[49]

Clearly, infallibility does not necessarily include the normal teaching authority by which the Pope frequently addresses the faithful, either directly or through the medium of the Roman Congregations. Teaching of the latter kind, though it is to be received with all reverence, does not enjoy the charism of infallibility. The Holy Father may speak, for example, merely as Bishop of Rome; or, as Pope, he may give instruction to only a section of the universal Church; or again, he may address the whole Church, but without the intention of defining anything as of faith. In none of these activities does he enjoy, within the terms of the definition, immunity from error. The same may be said of the occasions when the Pope expresses his mind *motu proprio*, namely by initiating a question himself, or else in response to queries submitted to him by others. Teaching which is technically non-infallible may be imparted in Pontifical Decrees and Instructions and in Encyclical Letters, for all of which the Pope is the responsible author. His authorization of the decisions of the Roman Congregations is not generally to be regarded in the light of a solemn definition. Divine assistance is, however, given in a particular way to the bishop of Rome, Pastor of the whole Church, when, without arriving at an infallible definition and without pronouncing in a 'definitive manner', he proposes in the exercise of the ordinary Magisterium a teaching that leads to better understanding of Revelation in matters of faith and morals. To this ordinary teaching the faithful 'are to adhere with religious assent' which, though distinct from the assent of faith, is nonetheless an extension of it.[50]

The successor of Peter is the pastor of all the faithful, with a mission to promote the common good and unity of the universal Church and the particular good of all the churches. Early on, around the year 250 AD, this truth was well expressed by St Cyprian:

> On him [Peter] He builds the Church, and to him He gives the command to feed the sheep; and although He assigned a like power to all the Apostles, yet he founded a single Chair, and He established by His own authority a source and an intrinsic reason for that unity. Indeed, the others were that also which Peter was; but a primacy is given to Peter, whereby it is made clear that there is but one Church and one Chair… If someone does not hold fast to this unity of Peter, can he imagine that he still holds the faith? If he desert the chair of Peter upon whom the Church was built, can he still be confident that he is in the Church?[51]

Later, in the East, St John Chrysostom expressed this universal role of Peter and his successors as shepherd of Christ's whole flock: 'Peter, the foundation of the Church, the vehement lover of Christ, at once unlearned in speech, and the vanquisher of orators, the man without education who closed the mouth of philosophers, who destroyed the philosophy of the Greeks as though it were a spider's web, he who ran throughout the world, he who cast his net into the sea, and fished the whole world…'[52] The Pope is therefore endowed with the primacy of ordinary power over all the churches. 'The Roman Pontiff, as the successor of Peter, is the perpetual and visible source and foundation of the unity both of the bishops and of the whole company of the faithful.'[53] The college of bishops exercises power over the universal Church in a solemn manner in an ecumenical council; however, there never is an ecumenical council which is not confirmed or at least recognized as such by Peter's successor.[54]

The sanctifying office of the Pope means that the sacraments and the liturgy are referred to the successor of Peter for their ecclesial celebration. St Cyprian expressed the fact that historically the sacramental ministry was given to Peter before the other Apostles: 'But it is plain where and by whom remission of sins can be given, that is to say, the remission that is given in baptism. First, the Lord gave that power to Peter, on whom He built the Church and whom He appointed and declared the origin of unity, that what he loosed should be loosed. And, after the Resurrection, He speaks to the apostles also…'[55] Sacramental ministry in the Church is a service exercised in the name of Christ. It has a personal character and a collegial form. This is evidenced by the bonds between the episcopal college and its head, the successor of St Peter, and in the relationship between the bishop's pastoral responsibility for his particular church and the common solicitude of the episcopal college for the universal Church. It belongs to the sacramental nature of ecclesial ministry that it have a personal character. Although Christ's ministers act in communion with one another, they also always act in a personal way. For this reason every bishop exercises his ministry from within the episcopal college, in communion with the bishop of Rome, the successor of St Peter and head of the college. So also priests exercise their ministry from within the *presbyterium* of the diocese, under the direction of their bishop.[56] The Pope offers the people of God the liturgy of the Church to which they have a right. This sanctifying office is oriented toward that day when every eye will see Christ, in the Church and in His risen body, even of those who pierced Him. The Pope sanctifies so that the people of God become holy in truth and in love.

The bishops

The Apostles collectively received from Christ a commission no less explicit than that given to their head, Peter: 'Go therefore and make disciples of all the nations, baptizing them in the name of the Father and the Son and the Holy Spirit, teaching them to observe all that I commanded you; and lo, I am with you always, even to the end of the age' (Mt 28:19–20; cf. Ac 10:40–42). Nevertheless this commission was given to them after the supreme office was conferred on Peter. The divine mission, entrusted by Christ to the apostles, will last until the end of the world, since the Gospel they are to teach is for all time the source of all life for the Church. For this reason the Apostles, appointed to guide the Church, took care to appoint successors. Therefore, the bishops by divine institution have succeeded to the place of the apostles, as shepherds of the Church, and he who hears them, hears Christ, and he who rejects them, rejects Christ and Him who sent Christ (Cf. Lk 10:16).[57]

Bishops, with priests as co-workers, have as their first task to preach the Gospel of God to all men, in keeping with the Lord's command. They are heralds of faith, who draw new disciples to Christ; they are authentic teachers of the apostolic faith endowed with the authority of Christ.[58] The bishop is the steward of the grace of the supreme priesthood, especially in the Eucharist which he offers personally or whose offering he assures through the priests, his co-workers. Bishops are authentic masters and judges in matters of faith, and their teaching is to be presumed sound until the contrary is proved. Should doubt arise as to a Bishop's orthodoxy, the question is to be settled, not by his subjects, but by an appeal to the Roman Pontiff. However, whatever be the possibility of individual Bishops falling into error, the Bishops collectively, namely the body of the episcopate, whether dispersed throughout the world in union with the Pope, or assembled under the presidency of the Pope in General Council, are infallible teachers of Christ's doctrine. The Eucharist is the centre of the life of the particular Church. The bishop and priests sanctify the Church by their prayer and work, by their ministry of the word and of the sacraments.[59] The bishops, as vicars and legates of Christ, govern the particular Churches assigned to them by their counsels, exhortations, and example, but moreover by the authority and sacred power which they exercise so as to edify, in the spirit of service which is that of their Master.[60] The power which the bishops exercise personally in the name of Christ, is 'proper, ordinary, and immediate, although its exercise is ultimately controlled by the supreme authority of the Church.'[61] It should be noted that the bishops are not merely the Pope's delegates, as, for example, are Apostolic Vicars in missionary countries; their jurisdiction is *proper* (belonging to them *ex officio*) and *ordinary* (not delegated). The ordinary and immediate authority of the Sovereign Pontiff over the whole Church does not annul, but on the contrary confirms and defends that of the bishops. Their authority must be exercised in communion with the whole Church under the guidance of the Pope.[62] The Roman Pontiff's supremacy implies that the exercise of the Bishops' powers may be controlled by him, either by limitation, or extension, or, in a particular case, by their total removal.

Certain bishops enjoy, under the Pope, a jurisdiction over other bishops. In the West, patriarchates are now little more than honorific titles, and archbishoprics have their origin in ecclesiastical law; their authority descends to them from that of Peter and his successors. It was found to facilitate the government of the Church to raise certain Bishops to a higher rank and give them, within prescribed limits, powers of delegating faculties to others; but they exercise these powers, not in virtue of their own episcopacy, but as sharing in the governing authority of the Apostolic See. However, in the East, the authentic Eastern form of Church governance is synodal, not monarchical, so the Patriarch actually governs the Church of which he is the head, together with the Synod of Bishops. The Patriarch exercises executive power and the Synod of Bishops exercises legislative power. Present Eastern Canon Law distinguishes between the powers of the Patriarch and Synod of Bishops inside the 'Patriarchal Territory' and outside of it; and it expressly states that their powers are exercised validly only inside the Patriarchal Territory, with certain limited exceptions.[63] The reason for this distinction is that, from the very earliest times, Patriarchal power or jurisdiction has been subject to a geographical limitation. This restriction, known as the Patriarchal Territory, refers to those regions in which the proper rite of the Church is observed and in which the Patriarch has the right to establish ecclesiastical provinces, eparchies and exarchies.[64] Only the Pope can change the Patriarchal Territory.[65] Even the Cardinals, as such, have no powers distinct from those proper to the Holy See, governed by the Pope. They are his counsellors and assistants in the government of the Universal Church; to them also pertains the negotiation of such business as must be done while the Roman See is vacant, notably the supervision of arrangements for the election of the succeeding Pontiff; but the cardinalate, unlike the episcopate, is not of divine institution.

Collegial aspect

The College of Bishops can be traced back to the Apostolic College. The Apostles were chosen and sent out by Christ the Lord not 'independently of one another, but rather as part of the group of the twelve'.[66] This collegial aspect among the Apostles is expressed by the use of the Scriptural term 'one of the Twelve',[67] by the sending out of the Apostles two by two and by Christ's prayer for the unity of the Apostles.[68] In the early Church, the Apostolic College was a body united in heart and soul under the guidance of the Holy Spirit. The origins of the College of Bishops lie in the affirmation that just as St Peter and the Apostles formed one Apostolic College, so also 'the Roman Pontiff, Peter's Successor, and the Bishops, the successors of the Apostles are joined to one another'.[69] This collegial aspect does not undermine the power which each Bishop enjoys by divine institution in his own diocese.

The unity of the College of Bishops is based upon the union of the Bishops with their head, the Roman Pontiff, who enjoys full, free, supreme and universal power within the Church.[70] The supreme power which the College of Bishops enjoys can only be exercised together with the head. Supreme collegial actions 'cannot be carried out at the level of particular Churches or of gatherings of such

Churches called together by their respective Bishops'.[71] The universal Church 'is not the result of the communion of the Churches, but, in its essential mystery, it is a reality ontologically and temporally prior to every individual particular Church'.[72] Thus the power of the College of Bishops is not the summation of the powers of the individual Bishops, nor a federation of the individual Bishops, but rather a 'pre-existing reality in which individual Bishops participate'.[73] Hence individual Bishops are related in one way with the Episcopal College on the one hand and in an essentially different way with such bodies as Episcopal Conferences on the other.

A Church Council may be defined as a legitimate assembly of the Pastors of the Church for judging and legislating in matters of doctrine and ecclesiastical discipline. Such a council is described as *provincial* when there are present at it the bishops of a single province, under the presidency of its Archbishop or Metropolitan; these were held from the second century onwards, but became less frequent after the Council of Trent. *Plenary councils* (at one time called *national*) are those composed of the bishops of one kingdom or nation. *General* or *ecumenical* councils represent the Universal Church, with the Roman Pontiff presiding, either personally or through his representative. The decrees of provincial and plenary councils are not, of themselves, infallible; they may, however become embodied in the rule of faith, if they are so regarded by the Bishops throughout the world, or are ratified by the Pope with his full teaching authority; as happened, for example, with the decrees of the plenary council of Carthage (418) and the second council of Orange (529).

The Episcopal Conference is 'a form of assembly in which the bishops of a certain country or region exercise their pastoral office jointly in order to enhance the Church's beneficial influence on all men, especially by devising forms of the apostolate and apostolic methods suitably adapted to the circumstances of the times'.[74] The primary purpose of Episcopal Conferences is 'to foster unity, collaboration and communion among the bishops within a nation or a determined territory and to promote common pastoral action.'[75]

Episcopal Conferences are to be situated within the context of the College of Bishops. The collegial aspect has been expressed in various ways during the course of history. Historically, 'the origin of the bishops' conference can be traced back to the spontaneous assembly of bishops in Belgium (1830) and in Germany (1848) in the first half of the nineteenth century'.[76] The Second Vatican Council desired that Particular Councils be revitalized, but also treated the question of Episcopal Conferences, and laid down norms concerning the latter. Pope Paul VI in his Motu Proprio *Ecclesiae Sanctae* of 1966 requested that Episcopal Conferences be erected wherever they did not already exist. The Code of Canon Law of 1983 laid down precise norms regulating the purposes and powers of these structures.[77]

The College of Bishops is part of the very nature of the Church, while Bishops' Conferences are groupings based on human language, culture and history. Moreover, these Conferences derive any binding power that they have from the fact that the Apostolic See has erected them and allocated to them specific areas of competence. There exists also a fundamental difference between Episcopal Conferences and the Synods of the Eastern Churches.[78] In the Oriental Churches the heads are the Patriarchs and the Major Archbishops, and government is carried out by the Synods of Bishops, which possess legislative, judicial and, in certain cases, administrative power.[79] Hence no analogy may be drawn between such Synods and Episcopal Conferences.

Episcopal Conferences are usually national in that 'the links of culture, tradition and common history, as well as the interconnection of social relations among citizens of the same nation require more constant collaboration among the members of the episcopate of that territory than the ecclesial circumstances of another territorial entity might require'.[80] However, Canon Law makes allowances for Episcopal Conferences to be set up with a size smaller than the national unit, or with a super-national extension.[81] A collaboration between Episcopal Conferences is also encouraged, and this has sometimes taken institutional form in the shape of International Meetings of Episcopal Conferences, which are not themselves properly to be regarded as Episcopal Conferences.[82]

The Episcopal Conference and its sphere of competence 'are in strict relation to the authority and action of the diocesan Bishop'.[83] It must support the 'inalienable responsibility of each Bishop'.[84] The Code of Canon Law specifies that the diocesan Bishop possesses all the ordinary and immediate power needed for the exercise of his pastoral office, save for those cases 'which the law or a decree of the Supreme Pontiff reserves to the supreme authority of the Church or to some other ecclesial authority'.[85] Hence, in order that the joint exercise of episcopal ministry in the Episcopal Conference be legitimate and binding on the individual Bishops, the intervention of the supreme authority of the Church is required which entrusts certain questions to the Conference.[86] Episcopal Conferences enable the Bishops of a given territory to collaborate on certain specific issues. These include the promotion and safeguarding of faith and morals, the translation of liturgical books, the promotion and formation of priestly vocations, the preparation of catechetical aids, the promotion and safeguarding of Catholic universities and other educational centres, ecumenical concerns, relations with civil authorities, the defence of human life, of peace, and of human rights, also in order to ensure their protection in civil legislation, the promotion of social justice, and the use of the means of social communication.

There are several instances in the common law in which the Bishops' Conference legislates. According to a letter issued by the Cardinal Secretary of State on 8th November 1983, there are 21 cases in which the Conference *must* legislate and in 22 cases it *can* promulgate particular norms.[87] An example of where the Bishops' Conference must legislate concerns the final determination of common law as regards what is the most appropriate form of clerical dress in the territory concerned.[88] An example of where the Conference can issue a norm is the determination of the age which is deemed suitable for the administration of the sacrament of Confirmation.[89] As regards the specific question of the teaching office of the Bishops gathered in Episcopal Conferences, their pronouncements 'do not have the characteristics of the universal Magisterium'.[90] However, when they jointly teach Catholic faith and morals, 'the faithful must adhere to the authentic teaching of their own Bishops with a sense of religious respect'.[91] Nevertheless, an Episcopal Conference can only issue a joint doctrinal declaration if this be approved unanimously by the Conference. In certain cases when the approval is not unanimous, a *recognitio* (validating recognition) can be obtained from the Holy See, but this is only conceded if a substantial majority of the Bishops composing the Conference have voted favourably. No organism of the Episcopal Conference, outside of its plenary assembly, has the authority to teach as the authentic Magisterium.[92]

Our Lady, Queen of Apostles

To complete the apostolic picture of the Church, the Marian dimension always complements the Petrine dimension.[93] In the hierarchy of our heavenly homeland, Our Lady, whom the Church greets as Queen of Angels, Patriarchs, Apostles, Martyrs and all the Saints, will have, under Christ, the supreme role as indeed she has now. However, here in the hierarchy of exile she also plays an invisible part. Although the Blessed Virgin Mary was more worthy, higher, and more holy than all the Apostles, it was yet not to her but to them that the Lord gave the keys of the Kingdom of Heaven. She sustained the newborn Church by the power of her contemplation and of her love. She was of even greater aid to the Church than were the Apostles who acted outwardly. She was the hidden root in which was secreted the sap that was to burst into flower and fruit. She did not bear the keys of the Kingdom, but by her prayer she guided and sustained those who bore them, and those also who came and knocked at their door. This role she still fulfils today.[94] She guides the Church in the way of salvation, as will now be examined in the upcoming chapter.

Notes

1. See *CCC* 857.
2. See A. Piolanti, *I sacramenti* (Città del Vaticano: Libreria Editrice Vaticana, 1990), pp. 480–481.
3. See M. Schmaus, *I sacramenti* (Casale: Marietti, 1966), p. 665.
4. A further question regards the diaconate. The ordination of the Seven described in the Acts of the Apostles (Ac 6:1–6), the earliest existing account of an ordination, is accepted by many theologians, right from the time of St Irenaeus, to refer to that of deacons. (See St Irenaeus, *Adversus Haereses*, Book 3, chapter 12, 10; Book 4, chapter 15, 1 in *SC* 211, 224–225; *SC* 100, 550–551.) Nevertheless, there is another school of thought, dating back to St John Chrysostom, which does not make this rapid identification. (See St John Chrysostom, *Homilia 14 in Acta Apostolorum*, 3 in *PG* 60, 116.) More recently some scholars consider that the Seven were ordained presbyters. On this point see, for example, J. Galot, *Theology of the Priesthood* (San Francisco: Ignatius Press, 1985), pp. 160–164. However, the presence of a diaconal office elsewhere in the New Testament (1 Tm 3:8–13) indicates that a lower rank of orders existed which was associated with service (they should 'carry out their duties well') and preaching ('conscientious believers in the mystery of faith'). It is possible that the *diaconos* mentioned in the New Testament is also not yet the deacon known by the later Church, but a figure endowed with a higher power of orders; however he was entrusted with a specific role of service.
5. The term *munera* seems to have its origins in the gladiatorial combats in which men and women fought to the death to entertain crowds of spectators. The Romans are said to have adopted these combats, called munera (singular, munus), from the Etruscans. The Etruscan city–states exerted a strong cultural influence over the early Romans, who freely borrowed numerous artistic and social concepts from their more refined neighbours. The Romans were

particularly impressed by Etruscan funeral rites, which operated under the belief that, when an important man died, his spirit required a blood sacrifice to survive in the afterlife. Supposedly, the spirits of the dead would not be satisfied until they received an infusion of fresh blood from someone still living. (In fact, the literal translation of *munera* is 'duties' or 'offerings' to the dead.) It was the duty of the dead person's relatives to carry out this sacrifice. The word developed in Christian usage, but is difficult to render into English, and is variously translated as task or office.

6. See P. Haffner, *New Testament Theology. An Introduction* (Rome: 2006), pp. 76–77.
7. Clement of Alexandria, *Stromata*, 3, 6 in *PG* 8, 1157–1158.
8. *Ibid*., 7, 11 in *SC* 428, 202–203.
9. See also the parallels in Mark 3:14–19, and Luke 6:13–16.
10. See *Revue Biblique* 62 (1955), p. 405. See also Mt 16:18.
11. See S. L. Jaki, *And on this Rock. The Witness of One Land and Two Covenants* (Manassas, Va.: Trinity Communications, 1987[2]), p. 16.
12. See Pope John Paul II, *Discourse at General Audience* (25 November 1992).
13. See Pope Benedict XVI, *Discourse at General Audience* (24 May 2006).
14. See Eusebius, *Ecclesiastical History*, 2, 15; 3, 39; 6, 14 in *PG* 20, 171–174; 295–302; 549–554. See also St Irenaeus, *Adversus Haereses*, Book 3, chapter 1, 1 in *SC* 211, 22–25. Clement of Alexandria stated: 'After Peter had announced the Word of God in Rome and preached the Gospel in the Spirit of God, the multitude of hearers requested Mark, who had long accompanied Peter on all his journeys, to write down what the Apostles had preached to them.' From Eusebius, *Ecclesiastical History*, 6, 14 in *PG* 20, 551–552.
15. Pope Clement I, *Letter to the Corinthians*, 5, 1–4 in SC 167, 106–109.
16. See St Irenaeus, *Adversus Haereses*, Book 3, chapter 3, 2 in *SC* 211, 32–33.
17. Eusebius, *Ecclesiastical History*, 2, 25 in *PG* 20, 209–210. He quotes Caius, *Disputation with Proclus*.

18. Tertullian, *On the prescription of heretics*, 36, 3 in *CCL* 1, 216. Tertullian also cites the tradition that St John the Apostle was immersed in boiling oil, but emerged unscathed.
19. Eusebius, *Ecclesiastical History*, 3,1 in *PG* 20, 215–216.
20. St Jerome, *Lives of Illustrious Men*, 1 in *PL* 23, 607.
21. See Pope John Paul II, *Discourse at General Audience* (27 January 1993).
22. St Ignatius of Antioch, *Letter to the Romans*, Introduction, in *SC* 10, 94–95.
23. St Irenaeus, *Adversus Haereses*, Book 3, chapter 3, 3 in *SC* 211, 32–39.
24. St Jerome, *Epistle to Pope St. Damasus* 15 in *CSEL* 54, 62–64.
25. St Ambrose, *Enarrationes in XII Psalmos davidicos* in *PL* 14, 1082: 'Ipse est Petrus cui dixit: "Tu es Petrus et super hanc petram aedificabo Ecclesiam meam". Ubi ergo Petrus, ibi Ecclesia; ubi Ecclesia, ibi nulla mors, sed vita aeterna.'
26. St Augustine, *Epistle 53 to Generosus*, 2 in *PL* 33, 196.
27. St Augustine, *Homily on Psalm 103*, 3, 3 in *PL* 37, 1359: 'Petrus Petra, Petra Ecclesia.'
28. Pope St Leo the Great, *Sermon 3*, chapters 2–3, in *PL* 54, 145–146.
29. Vatican I in DS 3056.
30. Vatican I in DS 3058.
31. *Ibid.*
32. See M. de Barcos, *De l'autorité de St. Pierre et de St. Paul* (Paris: 1645), Idem, *Grandeur de l'Eglise de Rome qui repose sur l'autorité de St. Pierre et de St. Paul* (Paris: 1645) ; Idem, *Eclaircissements sur quelques objections que l'on a formées contre la grandeur de l'Eglise de Rome* (Paris: 1646).
33. See *Decree of the Holy Office* (24 January 1647) in DS 1999: 'Sanctissimus Dn. … propositionem hanc: "S. Petrus et S. Paulus sunt duo Ecclesiae principes, qui unicum efficiunt", vel: "sunt duo Ecclesiae catholicae coryphaei ac supremi duces summa inter se unitate coniuncti", vel: "sunt geminus universalis Ecclesiae vertex, qui in unum divinissime coaluerunt", vel: "sunt duo Ecclesiae summi pastores ac praesides, qui unicum caput constituunt", ita explicatam, ut ponat omnimodam aequalitatem inter S. Petrum et S. Paulum sine

subordinatione et subiectione S. Pauli ad S. Petrum in potestate suprema et regimine universalis Ecclesiae, haereticam censuit et declaravit.'

34. See Pope John Paul II, *Discourse at General Audience* (27 January 1993).
35. See C. Journet, *The Church of the Word Incarnate* (London: Sheed and Ward, 1955), Chapter 8, 5, B, 3.
36. E. Holloway, *Catholicism: a new synthesis* (Wallington: Faith Keyway, 1976), p. 301.
37. Cf. F. J. Baumgartner, *Behind Locked Doors: A History of the Papal Elections* (New York: Palgrave MacMillan, 2003), p. 4.
38. St Cyprian, *Epistula 10 ad Antonianum*, 8 in *PL* 3, 770–773.
39. See J. N. D. Kelly, *The Oxford Dictionary of Popes* (Oxford: University Press, 1987), pp. 56–57.
40. Cajetan, *Apologia de Comparata Auctoritate Papae et Concilii,* cap. xiii, no. 736.
41. See C. Journet, *The Church of the Word Incarnate* (London: Sheed and Ward, 1955), Chapter 8, excursus 8, 2.
42. See H. Kühner, *Das Imperium der Päpste* (Frankfurt am Main: Fischer Taschenbuch Verlag, 1980), p. 128: 'Eine Synode im Lateran brachte ein Papstwahldekret heraus, nach welchem Klerus und Volk der Kardinäle nur noch zustimmen konnten.'
43. Each ballot paper was divided into three parts; in the first was written the cardinal's name, in the second the name of the individual voted for, and in the third a motto of the cardinal's choice and the number of votes taken so far. (The motto and number were to be used to verify the authenticity of each ballot.) The first and third divisions were folded down and sealed, with the middle exposed; the back was heavily decorated so that the writing would not be visible. Thus, when the Scrutineers (the vote counters) removed a ballot paper from the ballot box, they could see only the name of the candidate voted for. If the winning candidate received exactly two-thirds of the votes, the ballot papers were unsealed to ensure that the winning cardinal did not vote for himself. Modern ballots differ from the complicated older ballots in that the cardinals do not write anything other than the name of the individual for whom they are

voting; furthermore, they are only folded once and need not be specially sealed.

44. Pope John Paul II, Apostolic Constitution *Universi Dominici Gregis*. See also Benedict XVI, *Litterae Apostolicae Motu Proprio Datae de aliquibus mutationibus in normis de electione Romani Pontificis* (11 June 2007), which restored the necessity of a two-thirds majority in the Papal election. Pope John Paul II had altered the voting process in 1996, allowing the Pope to be elected by an absolute majority if the cardinals were unable to agree after several days of balloting in which a two-thirds majority was needed.
45. St John Chrysostom, *De decem millium talentorum debitore homilia*, 3 in *PG* 51, 20.
46. Vatican I in ND 831–839. See also Vatican II, *Lumen Gentium,* 12, 25; Congregation for the Doctrine of the Faith, *Mysterium ecclesiae,* 5.
47. Vatican I, *Dei Filius* 8.
48. Vatican II, *Lumen Gentium,* 25.2; see Vatican II, *Dei Verbum* 10.2.
49. Cf. Vatican II, *Lumen Gentium,* 25.
50. Vatican II, *Lumen Gentium,* 25.
51. St Cyprian, *De Ecclesiae catholicae unitate,* 4 in *SC* 500, 176–183.
52. St John Chrysostom, *In illud, Vidi dominum,* 4, 3 in *PG* 56, 123.
53. Vatican II, *Lumen Gentium,* 23.
54. See Vatican II, *Lumen Gentium,* 22; cf. *CIC*, can 336, 337 # 1.
55. St Cyprian, *Epistle 73,* 7 in *PL* 3, 1114: 'Nam Petro primum Dominus, super quem aedificavit Ecclesiam, et unde unitatis originem instituit et ostendit, potestatem istam dedit ut id solveretur in coelis quod ille solvisset in terris. Et post resurrectionem quoque ad Apostolos loquitur …'
56. See *CCC* 877–879.
57. See Vatican II, *Lumen Gentium,* 20.
58. Cf. *CCC* 888. See also Vatican II, *Presbyterorum Ordinis,* 4; Idem, *Lumen Gentium,* 25; cf. Mk 16:15.
59. Cf. *CCC* 893. See Vatican II, *Lumen Gentium,* 26.
60. Cf. *CCC* 894. See Vatican II, *Lumen Gentium,* 27; cf. also Lk 22:26–27.

61. Vatican II, *Lumen Gentium*, 27.
62. Cf. *CCC* 894.
63. See *CCEO* 78, § 2 and 150, §§2 and 3.
64. See *CCEO* 146, § 1.
65. See *CCEO* Canon 146, § 2.
66. Pope John Paul II, Motu Proprio *Apostolos Suos* on the theological and juridical nature of Episcopal Conferences, 1.1. For a brief explanation of the history of the document see A. Antón Gómez, 'La Lettera Apostolica *Apostolos suos* di Giovanni Paolo II' in *La Civiltà Cattolica* 150/I (1999), pp. 119–121.
67. Cf. Mt 26:14; Mk 14:10,20,43; Lk 22:3,47; Jn 6:72; 20:24.
68. Cf. Jn 17:11, 18, 20–21.
69. Vatican II, *Lumen Gentium*, 22.
70. See Vatican II, *Lumen Gentium*, 22.
71. Pope John Paul II, *Apostolos Suos*, 10.1.
72. Congregation for the Doctrine of the Faith, Letter *Communionis Notio* (1992), 9.
73. Pope John Paul II, *Apostolos Suos*, 12.2.
74. Vatican II, *Christus Dominus*, 38.1.
75. P. Pallath, *Local Episcopal Bodies in East and West* (Kottayam, Kerala: Oriental Institute of Religious Studies India: 1997), p. 357.
76. Pallath, *Local Episcopal Bodies in East and West*, p. 344.
77. See *CIC* 447–459.
78. See Pope John Paul II, *Apostolos Suos*, note 1.
79. See *CCEO*, Canons 110 and 152.
80. Pope John Paul II, *Apostolos Suos*, 16.
81. See *CIC* 449 §1.
82. See Vatican II, *Christus Dominus*, 38.5; *CIC* 459 #1. This type of cooperation has in fact been fostered by such International Meetings of Episcopal Conferences as the Consejo Episcopal Latinoamericano(C.E.L.A.M.), the Consilium Conferentiarum Episcopalium Europae (C.C.E.E.), the Secretariado Episcopal de América Central y Panama (S.E.D.A.C.), the Commissio Episcopatuum Communitatis Europaeae (COM.E.C.E.), the Association des Conférences Episcopales

de l'Afrique Centrale (A.C.E.A.C.), the Association des Conférences Episcopales de la Région de l'Afrique Centrale (A.C.E.R.A.C.), the Symposium des Conférences Episcopales d'Afrique et de Madagascar (S.C.E.A.M.), the Inter-Regional Meeting of Bishops of Southern Africa (I.M.B.S.A.), the Southern African Catholic Bishops' Conference (S.A.C.B.C.), the Conférences Episcopales de l'Afrique de l'Ouest Francophone (C.E.R.A.O.), the Association of the Episcopal Conferences of Anglophone West Africa (A.E.C.A.W.A.), the Association of Member Episcopal Conferences in Eastern Africa (A.M.E.C.E.A.), the Federation of Asian Bishops' Conferences (F.A.B.C.), and the Federation of Catholic Bishops' Conferences of Oceania (F.C.B.C.O.).

83. Pope John Paul II, *Apostolos Suos*, 19.
84. Synod of Bishops 1985, *Final Report*, II, C.
85. *CIC* 381 #1.
86. See Pope John Paul II, *Apostolos Suos*, 20.
87. See Pallath, *Local Episcopal Bodies in East and West*, p. 383.
88. See CIC 284.
89. See *CIC* 891.
90. See Pope John Paul II, *Apostolos Suos*, 22.
91. *CIC* 753.
92. See Pope John Paul II, *Apostolos Suos*, 23 and Norms, Article 2.
93. See Pope John Paul II, Apostolic Letter *Mulieris Dignitatem* note 55 to §27.
94. See C. Journet, *The Church of the Word Incarnate* (London: Sheed and Ward, 1955), Chapter 9, 8.

7

The Church and Salvation

The Church in the world is a great harbour, full of peace; whoever toils, let him come in and rest at her table. Her doors are open, and her eye is good, and her heart is wide. Her table is full, and sweet is her mingled cup to those who are worthy. All you lovers of the world, come in from wandering in the evil world, and rest at the Inn that is full of comfort to him that enters it.

Jacob of Sarug, *On the Reception of the Holy Mysteries*

Sacrament of salvation

The Church renders Christ present to the world, and continues His action in the world. This theme of the Church as sacrament has already been outlined.[1] First of all, she is the sacrament of the inner union of people with God. Because human communion is rooted in union with God, the Church is also the sacrament of the unity of the human race. In her, this unity is already begun, since she gathers men 'from every nation, from all tribes and peoples and tongues' (Rv 7:9).[2] As the primordial sacrament, the Church is Christ's sign and instrument of the full realization of the unity yet to come. In this sense she is also the instrument for the salvation of all or 'the universal sacrament of salvation,' by which Christ is 'at once manifesting and actualizing the mystery of God's love for men'.[3] The Church is the visible plan of God's love for humanity, because God desires 'that the whole human race may become one People of God, form one Body of Christ, and be built up into one temple of the Holy Spirit'.[4] Thus the Church is the visible sacrament of saving unity:

> For it is through Christ's Catholic Church alone, which is the universal help toward salvation, that the fullness of the means of salvation can be obtained. It was to the apostolic college alone, of which Peter is the head, that we believe that our Lord entrusted all the blessings of the New Covenant, in order to establish on earth the one Body of Christ into which all those should be fully incorporated who belong in any way to the People of God.[5]

Since salvation only comes to us through Christ, and because Christ and His Church are inseparable, then salvation only comes through the Church. The classic expression of this truth is that outside the Church there is no salvation or, in Latin: *extra Ecclesiam nulla salus*.

Necessary for salvation

The absolute necessity for salvation of the Catholic Church may already be found in the Gospels. 'Unless a man be born again of water and the Holy Spirit,' Christ told Nicodemus, 'he cannot enter the kingdom of God' (Jn 3:5). The kingdom to which the Lord refers is two-fold; on earth it is the visible Church of which Christ is the invisible Head, and in heaven, it is the consummation of human destiny in the beatific vision. Consequently, the Church is indispensable for salvation as is baptism, whereby souls are cleansed of original sin and are made partakers in the divine life.

When schisms and heresies arose in the early centuries, ecclesiastical writers stressed the need to belong to the true Church by remaining faithful to her teaching and to her legitimate pastors. St Ignatius of Antioch, writing to the Philadelphians about the year 100 AD, is the most ancient witness to this truth after the New Testament. The problem in Philadelphia was a certain rejection of episcopal authority and flirting with false doctrine. 'All who belong to God and Jesus Christ,' they were reminded, 'are with the bishop. Those, too, will belong to God who have returned, repentant, to the unity of the Church so as to live in accordance with Jesus Christ. Make no mistake, brothers. No one who follows another into schism inherits the kingdom of God. No one who follows heretical doctrine is on the side of the Passion.'[6] A century later, this time in Alexandria, Origen developed a concept of the Church as the body of Christ's disciples scattered over the face of the earth, yet never to be confused with the rest of the human race. It is the home of the elect: 'If someone from this people wants to be saved, let him come into this habitation so that he may be able to attain his salvation... Let no one deceive himself. Outside of this habitation, that is, outside the Church, no one is saved. He who leaves it is responsible for his own death.'[7] About the same time, in nearby Carthage, St Cyprian penned his famous treatise *On the unity of the Catholic Church*, to combat the schismatic proclivities of a rival bishop in his own diocese and, many think, to meet the challenge of a concurrent rivalry in the See of Rome: 'Who does not have the Church for mother cannot have God for his Father. If anyone outside the ark of Noah could escape, then he who is outside the Church may also be saved.'[8] Around the year 307, Lactantius proclaimed this same doctrine: 'It is, therefore, the Catholic Church alone which retains true worship. This is the fountain of truth; this, the domicile of faith; this, the temple of God. Whoever does not enter there or whoever does not go out from there, is a stranger to the hope of life and salvation.'[9]

In a beautiful image illustrating her salvific value, St Augustine pictures the Church as a nest hewn from the wood of Christ's Cross, a nest which offers tender shelter to all the peoples of the world.[10] An important development comes again from St Augustine regarding his classic description of those who may have all the external or formal clothing of Catholicism but, unless they belong to the true Church, they cannot be saved. Augustine formulated this concept in the context of the Donatist crisis. 'No one can be saved,' he declared, 'except in the Catholic Church.

He can have everything but salvation outside the Catholic Church. He can have honours, he can have the sacraments, he can sing "Alleluia," he can answer "Amen," he can hold the Gospels, he can have faith and preach in the name of the Father and of the Son and of the Holy Spirit. But nowhere except in the Catholic Church will he find salvation.'[11] Augustine stressed that a Christian must fear nothing so much as separation from the Body of Christ. Once he is separated he is no longer a member of Christ; and if he is not a member of Christ, he is no longer animated by the Holy Spirit of Christ, without Whom there is no salvation.[12]

Following the tradition of the Fathers, the doctrine of no salvation outside the Church was first repeated in papal documentation and, as occasion arose, was solemnly defined by the Church's Magisterium. Already in the fifth century, the Athanasian Creed or *Quicumque*, as it is commonly known, was authorized for the sacred liturgy as a preparation for baptism. 'Whoever wishes to be saved,' the Creed begins, 'must, above all, keep the Catholic faith. For unless a person keeps this faith whole and entire he will undoubtedly be lost forever.'[13]

The doctrine of the necessity of the Church for salvation was further refined during the Middle Ages, in a series of three definitions. The first of these took place at the Fourth Lateran Council in the year 1215. While directly concerned with the Albigensian heresy, the Council also formulated a profession of faith which began with the declaration, 'There is but one universal Church of the faithful, outside which no one at all is saved and in which the priest Himself, Jesus Christ, is the Victim, whose Body and Blood are truly contained in the Sacrament of the altar under the appearances of bread and wine.'[14] Early in the following century, Pope Boniface VIII published the Bull *Unam Sanctam*. This document met the challenge of Philip IV, King of France, and here Pope Boniface adopted the fullness of apostolic power: 'We declare, say, define and pronounce that it is absolutely necessary for the salvation of every human creature to be subject to the Roman Pontiff.'[15] Taken in conjunction with an opening sentence of the Bull, 'Outside this Church there is no salvation and no remission of sins,' the meaning of the definition cannot be misunderstood.[16] The last of this triad of definitions was made at the Council of Florence in 1442, where, after a breach of four centuries, the Eastern and Western Churches were temporarily reunited. On 4 February of that year, Pope Eugenius IV published a profession of Catholic belief to which the oriental dissidents (specifically the Jacobites) were required to subscribe:

> The holy Roman Church believes, professes and preaches that no one remaining outside the Catholic Church, not just pagans, but also Jews or heretics or schismatics, can become partakers of eternal life; but they will go to the everlasting fire which was prepared for the devil and his angels, unless before the end of life they are joined to the Church. For union with the body of the Church is of such importance that the sacraments of the Church are helpful to salvation only for those remaining in it; and fasts, almsgiving, other works of piety, and the exercise of Christian warfare bear eternal rewards for them alone. And no one can be saved, no matter how much alms he has given, even if he sheds his blood for the name of Christ, unless he remains in the bosom and unity of the Catholic Church.[17]

This profession of faith is a most unequivocal statement of the Church's indispensability.

If one considered solely the doctrine of the Church's absolute necessity, one might be tempted to opt for a type of Calvinist predestination that God has predestined some for heaven and others for hell, irrespective of their virtues or vices. What else could one say faced with millions of people in non-Christian countries who never had the Gospel preached to them and therefore never enjoyed the opportunity of entering the Church of Christ; also what can be said about many other millions who are living where the Church is established but psychologically have no chance of learning the true faith or embracing its sacred invitation?

Universal Divine salvific will

Another dogma must be considered alongside that of the necessity of the Church. As it is true that no salvation is possible outside the Church, it is equally true that God wants all people to be saved and that Christ died for the universal salvation of mankind. This doctrine is clear from the New Testament in St Paul's first letter to Timothy: 'God our Saviour wants everyone to be saved and reach full knowledge of the truth. For there is only one God, and there is only one mediator between God and humanity, Himself a human being, Christ Jesus, who offered Himself as a ransom for all' (1 Tm 2:3–6). The Apostle also taught in his letter to the Romans that God did not spare His own Son, but gave Him up for the sake of all of us (Cf. Rm 8:32). Back in the ninth century, the provincial Council of Quiercy, in France, approved by Pope St Leo IV, decreed that 'Almighty God wishes all men without exception to be saved, though all may not attain salvation. For those who are saved it is a gift of the Saviour, for those who are lost it is the guilt of the fallen.'[18] In the sixteenth century, the Council of Trent defined the universal salvific will of God.[19] More recently, when the Jansenists began to teach, 'It is Semi-Pelagian to say that Christ died or shed His blood for all men without exception,' that proposition was condemned.[20] The Second Vatican Council clearly taught that Christ died for all people.[21]

The issue is then how to reconcile the apparent limitation of God's salvific will to those who belong to the Catholic Church, with the non-limitation of this will as declared in the texts quoted above. As a premise to this, one question must be definitely answered: is it possible for a person to be saved without actual membership in the Catholic Church? The answer is in the affirmative and traceable to the earliest Christian tradition: it has also been confirmed by the authority of the Holy See. Parallel with the emphasis on the Church as the ark of salvation, professed by all the

Fathers, is an equally distinct though less frequent admission that under certain conditions a person can be saved even if he dies without having been an explicit member of the Mystical Body of Christ.[22]

The tradition on this point is very clear and ancient, because until recent times the Church's concern with the problem was quite minimal and overshadowed by the larger and more important question of safeguarding and propagating the true faith. For a variety of reasons the custom in the early Church was to defer the baptism of prospective converts for a much longer time than is the current practice.[23] Several years was not too long, and some even waited until shortly before death. The Roman Emperor Valentinian II had been taking instruction in the Catholic faith and was planning to be baptized when death suddenly overtook him before he actually entered the Church. St Ambrose preached his funeral homily in 492 AD, in which he raised the issue of Valentinian's salvation. He told his listeners:

> I hear you are grieving, because he did not receive the sacrament of baptism. But tell me what else is in our power except our will and desire? For a long time and even before he came to Italy, he wanted to be received into the Church and said he wished to be baptized by me in the near future… Did he, then, not have the grace he desired? Did he not receive what he sought? Surely he obtained what he asked for, as we read, 'The just man, though he die early, shall be in rest.' Why should not he who had your spirit, receive your grace? If it is objected that the sacrament of baptism was not solemnly administered, then even the martyrs do not attain glory if they die as mere catechumens, on the assumption there is no heaven for the unbaptized. On the other hand, if they are cleansed of their sins by the shedding of blood, then also his piety and good will saved Valentinian.[24]

In this earliest patristic evidence for the salvation of non-Catholics, the concession is severely limited. Valentinian was under instruction and professed belief in the Catholic Church. Consequently though dying before actual reception, he was saved by a baptism of desire which was regarded as salvific, like martyrdom for the faith.

St Augustine followed his teacher St Ambrose with the same indulgence towards catechumens, and extended the concept of baptism by desire, even preferring, on occasion, a virtuous candidate for the sacrament to an unfaithful Catholic.

> I have no doubt that a Catholic catechumen, possessed of divine charity, is better than a heretic who received baptism. Even in the Catholic Church we prefer a good catechumen, possessed of divine charity to a wicked person who is baptized... For the centurion Cornelius, not yet baptized, was better than Simon Magus, already baptized; since the former was filled with the Holy Spirit before baptism, while the latter, even after baptism, was inflated with the spirit of the devil... The more I think about it, the more I believe that not only suffering for the name of Christ, but also faith and conversion of heart can supply what is wanting on the part of baptism if perchance, for lack of time, the mystery of baptism cannot be approached.[25]

Augustine, therefore, goes beyond Ambrose; where the latter spoke of an isolated case, Augustine generalizes. He sees no difficulty in sanctifying grace being infused prior to baptism, and identifies faith (along with conversion of spirit) with actual martyrdom as an instrument of justification. However, like Ambrose, he postulates an explicit desire for baptism and entrance into the Church before divine charity is received.

The saving power of Christ through His Church also extends back before the time of her visible foundation, as St Irenaeus testified: 'Christ came not only for those who believed from the time of Tiberius Caesar, nor did the

Father provide only for those who are living now, but for absolutely all men from the beginning, who according to their ability, feared and loved God and lived justly… and desired to see Christ and to hear His voice.'[26] Eusebius even assigns the idea that the just who lived before Christ's coming are implicit (but not anonymous) Christians:

> However, even if we (Christians) are certainly new, and this really new name of Christians is just recently known among the nations, yet our life and mode of conduct, in accord with the precepts of religion, has not been recently invented by us; but from the first creation of man, so to speak, it is upheld by natural inborn concepts of the ancient men who loved God, as we will here show… But if someone would describe as Christians those who are testified to as having been righteous (going back) from Abraham to the first man, he would not be far from the truth.[27]

Within Eastern Christendom, there were also those who saw the Church as instrumental in the salvation of those outside her visible structure. In the early fifth century, St Nilus of Sinai remarked:

> In every nation, the one who fears God and does justice is acceptable to Him. For it is clear that such a one is acceptable to God and is not to be cast aside, who at his own right time flees to the worship of the blessed knowledge of God. God will not allow him to die in ignorance, but will lead him to the truth, and will enlighten him with the light of knowledge, like Cornelius.[28]

St John Damascene, often considered the last of the Fathers, stresses that the salvation which the Church brings is catholic or universal: 'The Creed teaches us to believe also in one holy Catholic and Apostolic church of God. The Catholic Church cannot be only apostolic, for the all-powerful might of her Head, which is Christ, is able through the Apostles to save the whole world. So there is a Holy Catholic Church of God, the assembly of the Holy Fathers who are from the ages, of the patriarchs, of prophets, apostles, evangelists, martyrs, to which are added all the gentiles who believe the same way.'[29]

Until the Middle Ages there seems to have been no further development on this doctrine. However, in the twelfth century, St Bernard of Clairvaux was asked by Hugh, the abbot of St Victor in Marseilles, to settle a theological problem created by the so-called *Ecclesiastical Dogmas*, falsely attributed to St Augustine. Among other strange doctrines, it was said that 'no catechumen has life everlasting, although he has died in good works'. Bernard refuted this rigorism by invoking the authority of Ambrose and Augustine. He remarked:

> With these I am willing to err or to be right, believing that a man with the desire of receiving the sacrament (of baptism) can be saved by faith alone, if death should prevent him from fulfilling his desire or any other invincible force stands in the way. Was not this perhaps why the Saviour, after He had said, 'He that believes and is baptized shall be saved', carefully and prudently did not add, 'but he that is not baptized', but only, 'he that does not believe, shall be condemned.'? This suggests that at times faith alone is sufficient for salvation, and that without it nothing avails.[30]

This idea is an advance on the formulations of Ambrose and Augustine. Besides unexpected death which prevents a catechumen from being baptized, Bernard allows 'any other invincible force (*vis invincibilis*) that stands in the way'. The implication is that the implicit (and not only the explicit) desire to become a Catholic, may be enough to merit salvation.

Actual and intentional Church membership

By the end of the thirteenth century, the concept of justification without baptism by water was firmly established in Catholic theology. In his *Summa Theologiae* (written between 1271 and 1274), Thomas Aquinas crystallized all the preceding tradition when treating of the effects of baptism. He asks himself 'whether grace and virtue are bestowed through baptism' and answers with St Augustine that since 'the effect of baptism is to incorporate the baptized into Christ as His members', and all grace and virtues flow from Christ, it logically follows that we receive grace and virtue in the sacrament. However, if this is true, he objects, how could the centurion Cornelius be called religious and a God-fearing man according to the Acts of the Apostles? He answers that 'a man receives the forgiveness of sins before baptism in so far as he has baptism of desire, explicitly or implicitly; and yet when he actually received baptism, he receives a fuller remission, as to the remission of the entire punishment.'[31]

Parallel passages in the *Summa Theologiae* are amplified in *De Veritate*, where St Thomas is treating of faith and handling the problem of a pagan living out of contact with Christianity. If explicit faith in certain truths revealed by God is absolutely necessary, how can the pagan be saved? Thomas answers that 'divine providence will provide whatever such a person needs for salvation, as long as he places no obstacles in the way. If a man of that kind followed the dictates of natural reason in doing good and avoiding evil, it is certain that God would either reveal by internal inspiration what he has to believe, or send someone to preach the faith to him.'[32] St Thomas brought about a further clarification of the traditional belief that non-Catholics can be saved, with an accent on two elements that are intrinsic to the whole problem: baptism of water can be substituted by baptism of desire, and this latter, whether explicit or implicit, confers sanctifying grace. Faith, which must be explicit, is provided (if need be) by a miraculous revelation from God.

St Thomas' doctrine was effectively adopted by the Council of Trent, which defined justification as 'a passing from the state in which a man is born a son of the first Adam, to the state of grace and adoption as sons of God through the second Adam, Jesus Christ our Saviour. Since the gospel was promulgated, this passing cannot take place without the water of regeneration, or the desire for it.'[33] Although the Council did not qualify whether the desire needed to be explicit or implicit, theologians commonly agree that both kinds are covered by the Tridentine decree.

Within the life span of the original Reformers, one theory was proposed by the Spaniard, Melchior Cano (1509–1560), a conspicuous figure at the Council of Trent. Cano's solution distinguished the concept 'Church' in the doctrine 'no salvation outside the Church'. He explained that the Church can be understood in two senses:

> First there is the Church which is composed of the assembly of all the faithful from the beginning of the world to its end. In this sense, catechumens (or non-Catholics in good faith) are most truly in the Church. However, that which is entered through baptism in the name of Christ is also called the Church, and of this Church, catechumens (or non-Catholics generally) are not a part.[34]

His contemporary rival, St Robert Bellarmine (1542–1621), the father of modern ecclesiology, criticized the solution as unsatisfactory because 'since the coming of Christ there is no true Church except that which is properly called Christian'. Thus, if non-Catholics do not belong to this Church, they belong to none. Cano properly distinguished between his hypothetical Church of the faithful and the Church of Christ on the point of baptism. Real baptism of water, he admitted, is essential to become a member of the Church of Christ. However, he dismissed the problem instead of solving it by proposing another Church besides the one founded by the Saviour, misunderstanding certain statements in the Fathers about a 'Church' that began with Abel in the Old Testament and includes all the predestined till the end of time.

Somewhat later than Cano, two other theories were proposed by Bellarmine. His first theory follows St Augustine, who described the Church as a living Body, in which there is a body and soul. The soul is constituted by the internal gifts of the Holy Spirit: faith, hope and charity. The body is connected with the external profession of faith and communication of the sacraments:

> Some people belong to both the body and soul of the Church, and are therefore united to Christ, the Head, both interiorly and exteriorly. These are most perfectly in the Church. They are like living members in the body, although among them, too, some participate more and some less (in the life of the body), and some have only the beginnings of life, having, as it were, sensation without movement, like those who have faith with charity. Others, however, are of the soul but not of the body (of the Church), as catechumens and those who have been excommunicated, who may have faith and charity, which is possible. Finally, some belong to the body and not to the soul (of the Church), like those who have no internal virtue, but yet out of hope or moved by some temporal fear, they profess the faith and share in the sacraments, under the rule of legitimate pastors.[35]

According to this hypothesis, the soul of the Church means the Holy Spirit with His gifts of grace and internal virtue; the body is the eternal profession of the Catholic faith. Non-Catholics, whether actual catechumens or not, will belong to the soul if they have the gifts of the Holy Spirit. Professed Catholics, if they have any internal virtue at all, belong to the Church's body and also to the soul, depending on the strength of their interior life.

Bellarmine's second explanation has become standard in Catholic theology, though much amplified and clarified. He began by admitting Cano's presupposition, that baptism is the only way to become a member of the Church of Christ, as distinct from the Church of the faithful. This paved the way for his own thesis, that non-Catholics (for him, catechumens) can be saved, even without baptism of water or martyrdom, provided they die with a baptism of desire. His argument runs as follows. First, baptism is the only entrance into the Church. However, baptism can be actual (*in re*) or intentional (*in voto*). Therefore entrance into the Church can be actual or intentional. Second, the kind of association with the Church is determined by the kind of entrance a person makes. However, there are two kinds of entrance into the Church, actual or intentional. Therefore, if a person enters the Church through actual baptism he becomes an actual member. On the other hand, if he enters baptism by intention (*in voto*), he belongs intentionally to the Church. In Bellarmine's own words: 'When it is said that outside the Church no one is saved, this is to be understood of those who do not belong to the Church either in reality or in desire, as theologians commonly speak of baptism. However, since catechumens are in the Church, if not in reality, at least in desire, therefore they can be saved.'[36]

Less than a century after the Council of Trent, when a new generation of born-Protestants was established in the Western world, the problem of the salvation of non-Catholics entered theological circles and opinions were expressed that ranged from rigid formalism to the most extreme laxism. The dilemma was between rigidly interpreting the necessity of the Church that no one but a professed Catholic can be saved, or so freely allowing salvation to anyone on any terms that the Church's necessity is compromised. The rigorist school found support in certain statements of the Fathers and in the relative silence of the Church. They held that since the promulgation of the Gospel became world-wide soon after the Ascension of Christ, explicit faith in Christ and actual baptism, or at least the explicit desire to be baptized, was necessary for all to be saved. The laxist school maintained that even a natural act of faith in the existence of God, implicitly containing everything else, including the desire for baptism and entrance into the Church, was enough for salvation.[37]

St Robert Bellarmine, who coined the now familiar actual and intentional adherence to the Church, was not concerned with defending the condition of those who had broken with Catholic unity, except to expose their errors and appeal to their better judgment to return to the one true Church, outside of which no one can see God. By the middle of the nineteenth century, however, it was seen that, while traditional principles on Church membership were immutable, they needed to be re-examined. New conclusions had to be drawn from the ancient truths to meet the current problem, notably the delicate question of how millions of apparently sincere non-Catholics could be saved. Fundamentally it was a problem of how to relate these people to the Catholic Church. They were born and educated outside the true faith and, although living among Catholics, never entered the Church, and, perhaps, were never baptized.

Pope Blessed Pius IX appears to have made the first *ex officio* pronouncement of the Holy See on the condition of non-Catholics in good faith, who are living not only among pagans but also in countries where the Church is established. Blessed Pius IX has been called the greatest defender of the Church since Gregory the Great.[38] At least nine of his official documents repeat and defend the necessity of belonging to the Catholic Church. However, in two of these, and both before the First Vatican Council, the Pope deals with the complementary problem of how it is possible for a person to be saved without actually professing the true religion. The day after his solemn definition of the Immaculate Conception, he gave an allocution to the several hundred bishops who had assembled in Rome for the occasion. First, he exhorted them to oppose the error which claims that we can hope for the salvation of those who 'in no way' belong to the true Church of Christ. Then he explained how 'time and again' he was asked to declare 'what is going to be the fate and condition after death of those who have never yielded themselves to the Catholic faith'. Without presuming 'to establish limits to the divine mercy, which is infinite', we must hold it as certain that 'those who labour in ignorance of the true religion, if that ignorance is invincible, will never be charged with any guilt on this account before the eyes of the Lord. Who is there that would arrogate to himself the power to point out the extent of such ignorance according to the nature and variety of peoples, regions, talents, and so many other things?'[39]

Nine years later, during the wars of unification, Blessed Pius IX issued a strong appeal to the bishops of Italy for a more concerted effort to stem the tide of immorality and indifference that was sweeping over the peninsula. 'It is again necessary to mention and censure a very grave error entrapping some Catholics,' he warned. 'They imagine that men living in errors and apart from the true faith and from Catholic unity, can attain to eternal life.' They cannot.

> It is known to us and to you that those who labour in invincible ignorance of our most holy religion, and who, carefully observing the natural law and its precepts, which God has inscribed in the hearts of all, and being ready to obey God, live an honest and upright life can, through the workings of divine light and grace, attain eternal life. The reason is because God, who clearly sees, searches and knows the mind, intentions, thoughts and habits of all, will, by His supreme goodness and kindness, never allow anyone who is not guilty of deliberate sin to suffer eternal punishments.[40]

On the other hand, 'Eternal salvation cannot be obtained by those who oppose the authority and statements of the same Church and are stubbornly separated from the unity of the Church and also from the successor of Peter, the Roman Pontiff, to whom the custody of the vineyard has been committed by the Saviour.'[41]

Papal teaching has always followed the line proposed by Pope Blessed Pius IX, whereby he extended the possibility of salvation not only to catechumens, as in Ambrose and Augustine, or to pagans out of touch with Christianity, as in Thomas Aquinas, but to all men of good will throughout the world, not excluding those living among Christians and in some contact with the Catholic faith. The subject of the salvation of sincere non-Catholics was on the agenda of the

First Vatican Council. For this purpose, the two documents of Blessed Pius IX on invincible ignorance were quoted extensively and the essential terms were fully explained. 'By the words, "those who labour in invincible ignorance" is indicated the possibility that a person may not belong to the visible and external communion of the Church, and yet may attain to justification and eternal life.'[42] Moreover the saving clause on invincibility was incorporated into a proposed definition, namely:

> It is a dogma of faith that no one can be saved outside the Church. However, those who labour in invincible ignorance of Christ and His Church are not to be punished for this ignorance with eternal pains, since they are not burdened with guilt on this account in the eyes of God, who wishes all men to be saved and to come to the knowledge of the truth, and who does not deny His grace to the person who does what he can, to enable him to attain to justification and eternal life. But this salvation no one attains, who leaves this life culpably separated from the unity of faith and communion of the Church.[43]

The doctrine of Blessed Pius IX remained part of the unfinished business of the Vatican Council and was not formally defined.

However, the Council did express itself more directly on the subject in another context. The final draft of the Constitution on the Faith (infallibly defined) includes two successive statements. The first is an exposition of the object of faith, that 'by divine and Catholic faith all those things must be believed which are contained in the word of God.' Then follows a declaration on the necessity of faith: 'Since without faith it is impossible to please God and attain to the fellowship of His children, therefore, without faith no one has ever attained justification, nor will anyone obtain eternal life unless he shall have persevered in faith unto the end.'[44] The essential word in the second statement is evidently 'faith.' In the original draft of the dogmatic constitution, the pertinent passage, describing the necessity of faith, was logically connected with the preceding paragraph on the scope of Catholic belief. However, before the final and definite form was drawn up and presented to the Council for acceptance, an important amendment was made and the reason for the change explained to the assembly by the delegate for the Commission *De Fide*. He stated:

> We have made a substitution in the paragraph which begins, 'This is that faith…' The emendation of the beginning of this paragraph is the following, namely, that instead of the words, 'This is that faith…' there be substituted the following words, 'Since, without faith, it is impossible to please God…Unless he shall have persevered in faith unto the end.' I explained to you yesterday, Most Reverend Fathers, our reason for this change. The reason, to repeat in brief, is this: to remove the close connection between this and the preceding paragraph, lest it appear that an act of the Catholic faith is necessary for salvation, for all people. For this is false. I ask you, therefore, to accept the formula modified by us.[45]

They accepted the revised formula, *verbatim*, and the reason for the change, we may infer, was also accepted by the Vatican Council to be solemnly confirmed by Pius IX, that a person can reach heaven by professing that faith without which no one can please God, but not necessarily the explicit faith of the Roman Catholic Church.

The relation of non-Catholics to the Church and the prospect of their salvation reached a high degree of development under Pope Pius XII. In the Encyclical on the Mystical Body, he invited 'those who do not belong to the visible Body of the Catholic Church, … to correspond to the interior movements of grace, and to seek to withdraw from that state in which they cannot be sure of their salvation. For even though by an unconscious desire and longing (*desiderio ac voto*), they have a certain relationship with the Mystical Body of the Redeemer, they still remain deprived of those many heavenly gifts and helps which can only be enjoyed in the Catholic Church.'[46] The Pope is here contrasting the intentional (*in voto*) relation of non-Catholics with the actual (*in re*) members of the Church, 'who have been baptized and profess the true faith'.

Around this time, Father Leonard Feeney, SJ (1897–1978) followed a rigorist interpretation of the doctrine that there is no salvation outside the Church. He denounced the baptism of blood and baptism of desire as 'heretical innovations' and believed that all unbaptized persons were condemned to hell. Feeney insisted that all who did not formally enter the Church would go to hell. Hence he even affirmed that unbaptized babies would be damned. Further, all adults who did not formally enter the Church, would also go to hell, even if they never had a chance to hear there was a Church. Apart from the documents of the Church as interpreted by the Church which should have kept him from this error, merely common sense, and the realization that God is infinitely good, should have checked him. In 1949, the Holy Office, under Pius XII, sent a letter to the Archbishop of Boston, condemning Feeney's error. After three letters were sent inviting Feeney to appear before the Holy Office, to which he refused, in 1953 he was officially excommunicated, in a decree confirmed by Pope Pius XII, for failing to submit to ecclesiastical authority.[47] Subsequently, in 1972, Fr Leonard Feeney was reconciled and absolved from the excommunication by Pope Paul VI and Vatican delegates. Many of his followers were afterwards reconciled to the local diocese. Feeney was not required to retract his position on the doctrine in question, which is inscribed on his tombstone.

The letter of the Holy Office to the Archbishop of Boston firmly reiterated the infallible statement by which we are taught that there is no salvation outside the Church. Yet people can be saved, even if they die before actual incorporation into the Mystical Body of Christ. The reason is that belonging to the Church can be considered in two ways, as a precept and as a means, for entering eternal glory. Under both aspects, it is possible to attain heaven without actual membership in the Roman Catholic Church. The Church teaches, first of all, that she is the object of 'a very strict command of Jesus Christ. In unmistakable terms He gave His disciples the command to teach all nations to keep whatever He had commanded.' Among these commands, 'not the least is the one which orders us to be united to Christ and His Vicar, through whom He Himself governs the Church on earth in a visible way'. This precept is so binding that 'no one who knows that the Church has been divinely established by Christ and, nevertheless, refuses to be a subject of the Church, or refuses to obey the Roman Pontiff, the vicar of Christ on earth, will be saved'.[48] On this level of necessity, therefore, actual profession of the Catholic faith, visible and participation in the sacraments and submission to the Roman Pontiff are required for salvation provided that a person has reached the age of discretion which enables him to recognize the law, that the divine mandate is clearly made known to him, and that he is not otherwise excused from obedience to a positive command of God, through circumstances that would make adherence to Catholicism a moral impossibility.

There is another and deeper sense, however, in which the Church is necessary for salvation. 'The Saviour did not make it necessary merely by precept for all nations to enter the Church. He also established the Church as a means of salvation without which no one can enter the kingdom of heavenly glory.'[49] If we compare that two necessities, of precept and of means, the former is external and imposed from without (like the divine choice of the Sabbath as a day of rest, or the Church's precept of Friday abstinence), the latter is intrinsic and part of the structure of a given function. Unless the given means are used, the end is simply not attained. Incapacity because of age, or ignorance or grave obstacles that stand in the say (all of which excuse from sin where only precepts are involved) do not apply where it is a question of means. In the supernatural order, the end in view is always salvation or the beatific vision, and the means required are of two kinds. Some are necessary by strict internal necessity. Thus sanctifying grace, the infused virtues of faith, hope and charity, are so indispensable that nothing can supply for them. Without them salvation is impossible for anyone, before the time of Christ and ever since. Unless a person is raised to the family of God and his soul infused with supernatural life, he will never reach the beatific nature which is utterly beyond his native capacity as a creature. However, these are not the only means of salvation. There are others, established by God as vehicles or instruments by which the indispensable supernatural grace is obtained or retained, and may therefore be called instrumental means of salvation. Such are the sacraments of Baptism, the Holy Eucharist and Penance, as well as membership of the Catholic Church.

While absolutely speaking, God might have required that these instrumental means be used actually and physically as a condition for salvation, He did not do so: 'Of those helps to salvation that are ordered to the last end only by divine institution, not by intrinsic necessity, God, in His infinite mercy, willed that such effects of those helps as are necessary to salvation can, in certain circumstances, be obtained when the helps are used only in desire and intention. We see this clearly stated in the Council of Trent about the sacraments of regeneration and penance.'[50] The effects of these sacraments, which is remission of sin, may be obtained by the desire (expressed or implied) to receive Baptism or Penance, provided there is perfect contrition.

> The same, in due proportion, should be said of the Church insofar as it is a general help of salvation. To gain eternal salvation it is not always required that a person be incorporated in fact as a member of the Church, but it is required that he belong to it at least in desire and intention. It is not even necessary that this desire be explicit as it is with catechumens. When a man is invincibly ignorant, God also accepts an implicit desire, so-called because contained in the good disposition of soul by which

> a person wants his will to be conformed to the will of God.[51]

Examined psychologically, the desire to enter the Church, although implicit, requires a considerable degree of generosity of will. It means that a person has that disposition which God sees would make him ready to embrace Catholicism if he recognized this as the divine will. Only because he fails to realize the obligation does he not become a Catholic. However, there is more to this situation. On the side of his supernatural condition, 'it is necessary that the desire by which a man is related to the Church be informed with perfect charity. An implicit desire cannot have its effect unless a man has supernatural faith.'[52] Consequently, knowledge of the natural law is not enough. There must be a divinely-inspired obedience to the voice of conscience. Correspondence with actual grace is also required, to the point where perfect contrition is aroused for past sins and an act of perfect love for God is formulated.

It should be clarified that this relationship to the Church by desire does not constitute membership. While theological writers on occasion speak of actual (*in re*) and intentional (*in voto*) members of the Mystical Body, ecclesiastical documents carefully distinguish between the two. Only professed Catholics are credited with membership. Non-Catholics in good faith (and in the state of grace) are variously described as related (*ordinare*) or adhering (*adhaerere*) to the Church. The terms are significant. *Ordinare* in classic theology means the movement of an object towards a preconceived end, implying that the end is not yet achieved. So when Pius XII says that non-Catholics may be related (*ordinentur*) to the Mystical Body, he implies two things: that they are not yet members of the visible communion of the true Church; but they are moving towards membership if they sincerely wish to accomplish the entire will of God. In many cases, the incorporation will not be attained until the Mystical Body in heaven; but whether on earth or in heaven, their relationship is a dynamic progress towards a divinely recognized end.

Adherence to the Church also implies the absence of real membership, which technically would be inherence, because when an object adheres to something the supposition is that the two are really distinct. More than relationship (*ordinare*) or active movement towards the Church, adherence (*adhaerere*) suggest an active influence from the Church, even upon those who are not incorporated in the Mystical Body. As might be expected, the extent of this influence will be greater or less depending on the degree of personal response to the invitation of Jesus Christ. Now the body of the Church can be considered in terms of the contribution of the human beings who compose the visible society founded by Christ; and the soul of the Church is the Holy Spirit, animating this contribution by His grace. By analogy, we may speak of sincere non-Catholics as adhering to the Church and deriving grace from the Holy Spirit, who is the soul of the Mystical Body, according to the measure of their generosity in cooperating with the will of God, fully manifested in the doctrinal and sacramental nature of the Roman Catholic faith. Thus we may legitimately conclude that the Eastern Churches in partial communion, who have a valid priesthood, the seven sacraments and most of the doctrines of the true Church, adhere more closely (and hence efficaciously) to the Mystical Body than others who profess only a skeleton of Christian teaching and perhaps are not even baptized.

One may ask how the readiness to do God's will can include the desire to enter the Church, even where a person is quite oblivious of Christ's mandate to that effect. The fact is that God's will, objectively, includes this commandment and therefore a disposition to obey God in all things implicitly means a willingness to obey Him also in the injunction regarding the Church. Upon closer analysis, the discussion concerning intentional adherence to the Church still leaves the fundamental problem unsolved. The fact that non-Catholics can be saved without actual membership may be taken as established. Under given circumstances, as described, God may accept their fidelity to His will as an implicit desire to become Catholics, and they are saved accordingly. However, the critical issue is how the Church is responsible for their salvation, as it must be, if the dogma *Extra Ecclesiam nulla salus* is to be adequately explained. Granted it does not mean that only professed members can be saved; but how do others reach the beatific vision? What influence must the Church exert on anyone who attains eternal glory? This is not an academic question, as indicated by the warning of Pope Pius XII against the tendency in some circles to 'reduce to an empty formula the necessity of belonging to the true Church in order to gain salvation'.[53]

It has already been seen that Christ established the Church as 'a means of salvation', which is another way of saying that she is an instrument or vehicle of divine grace and, without grace, glory is unattainable. For, although by His absolute power God can infuse supernatural life into souls without human cooperation, in the existing order of providence He does not do so. He has, so to speak, united the bestowal of grace with some very definite instrumentalities. This means effectively that the Church is the sacrament of salvation. If these means are operative, grace is obtained; otherwise it is not received. Some of the means are visible or at least sensibly communicated, and need to be used; others are perfectly invisible and may be identified with the person of Christ, Head of the Mystical Body and universal source of supernatural life for the human race.

At the bedrock of the supernatural order is the invitation which mankind has received, to recognize and accept God's intervention in the world, when He communicated to man certain truths to be believed, precepts to observe and rites to practice as instruments of His salvation. It may be assumed that some form of knowledge of God is necessary for all who have reached the age of reason, if they are freely to work out their eternal destiny. However, merely rational knowledge, derived from reflection on created things, is not sufficient. Such knowledge would indeed suffice as the foundation for natural religion and natural beatitude after death; that is, if we had not been elevated to a supernatural order whose end is the beatific vision. However, since we have been so elevated, God requires that besides knowing Him from pure reason, we also believe in Him and accept the truth which He communicated to us by Revelation. The Council of Trent laid down as the first necessity for justification, a true faith in the promises revealed. The First Vatican Council repeated this necessity against the errors of rationalism, declaring that 'we are obliged to render by faith a full submission of intellect and will to God when He makes a revelation,' and 'this faith is the beginning (or basis) of human salvation.'[54]

The absolute minimum belief requirement for salvation is described in the Letter to the Hebrews: 'it is impossible to please God without faith, since anyone who comes to Him must believe that He exists and rewards those who seek Him' (Heb 11:6). Consequently unless the existence of God as a remunerator of those who serve Him is believed on the word of God, there is no salvation. As commonly explained, this means that a necessary and objective link is established between a true historical revelation (primitive to our first parents, or Judaic in the Old Law, or Christian till the death of the last Apostle) and the mind and heart of the believer. How the revelation comes to him or how clear the subjective motives for accepting it, are matters of legitimate speculation. However, in the framework of ordinary providence, there must be an objective communication, through human instruments, from God the Revealer to man the receptive believer. Since all who have reached the age of reason are bound by this injunction, one may ask whether, historically, all those who are not Catholic have access to divine revelation without the assistance of the Catholic Church.

Non-Catholics who believe in a historical revelation are beneficiaries in large measure, if not exclusively, of the Catholic and apostolic Church. Those who once had but lost their supernatural belief in God depend, again in large measure, on the Catholic Church to bring them at least the minimum essentials of faith, without which it is impossible to please God. We may admit the Church's necessity to bring and preserve the basic deposit of faith among all peoples, is not absolutely universal because we allow for the perdurance of primitive and Mosaic revelation. However, this necessity becomes more and more imperative when we realize that, since the time of Christ, only the Catholic Church is divinely assisted not merely to proclaim the word of God but to confirm this preaching (as did Christ) with signs and wonders that make the belief in revealed doctrine rationally acceptable.

It is commonplace in theology to say that all the grace of salvation that anyone receives is the grace of Christ. As God, He is the creator of His gifts, as Man He merited them on the Cross, and as Head of the Mystical Body, He distributes them to all of mankind. There is no difficulty accepting on faith the mystery of sanctification, wherein the members of the Mystical Body are animated by the Spirit of Christ and from Him receive all the blessings of the supernatural life. For He said: 'Remain in Me, as I in you. As a branch cannot bear fruit all by itself, unless it remains part of the vine, neither can you unless you remain in Me. I am the vine, you are the branches. Whoever remains in Me, with Me in him, bears fruit in plenty; for cut off from Me you can do nothing' (Jn 15:4–5). Can this concept be extended to include also those who are not actually in the Body of Christ? There is a legitimate sense in which non-Catholics derive supernatural grace from Christ precisely as Head of the Mystical Body. When we speak of Christ as Head of the Church we mean the Saviour in His capacity of governing the society of human beings of which His own Holy Spirit is the animating principle. He governs this society in two ways: the first by imparting sanctity to individual persons and the second by uniting these individuals into a living organism that is destined to last for all eternity. These two aspects are distinct but related. A person can be in the Mystical Body and not be in sanctifying grace, as he can be in the state of grace without being an actual member of the Church. However, in the latter case, he obtains justification only because he is somehow in relation with the Church. For an infant this means baptism by water, for an adult it implies that degree of response to the divine will which God recognizes as implying the desire to be incorporated in His Body. It matters little that psychologically a non-Catholic is not aware of the full implications of his generosity; ontologically God sees the implications and credits the soul accordingly. Proceeding on the axiom that God will not deny grace to the one who does what he is able to (*Facienti quod in se est Deus non denegat gratiam*), the medieval theologians believed that a person could prepare himself or herself and thereby 'merit' (*meritum de congruo*) the created grace of initial justification by performing works of righteousness in response to the external, and in cooperation with the internal, prevenient graces.[55] Origen had already proposed this as regards the knowledge of God: 'For ourselves, we maintain that human nature is in no way able to seek after God, or to attain a clear knowledge of Him without the help of Him whom it seeks. He makes Himself known to those who, after doing all that their powers will allow, confess that they need help from Him, who reveals Himself to those whom He approves, in so far as it is possible for man and the soul still dwelling in the body to know God.'[56]

Equally important and more subtle is the second way that Christ operates as Head of the Mystical Body. In the plan of God, we are not only to be personally sanctified but also united with Christ and each other in a communion whose intimacy is incomprehensible to the purely natural man. If a person is in the state of grace but not actually in the Church, Christ's function will be to draw him ever closer to actual membership, until (at least after death) he is fully incorporated into the Body of Christ. The very analogy with a human organism permits us to see how the Body of Christ can be active beyond its own physical self, by radiating power that affects others besides its own members and by assimilating elements from the outside for its growth and amplification. However, we are not to suppose that Christ acts independently of the Church in His action of sanctifying and incorporating non-Catholics to Himself. He uses the Church on every level of her ministration, especially in the Sacrifice of the Mass and the prayers and sacrifices of the faithful. The most important medium in the Church for the salvation of those outside the visible Church is the Sacrifice of the Mass. On the altar is renewed the oblation of Calvary because it is the same Priest and Victim who offered Himself on the Cross. Moreover, the appointed ends are the same, notably the expiation of sin and impetration of grace from Almighty God.

The Church's tradition has always recognized the Mass as a universal instrument for the salvation of those who were still outside the City of God. One of the most eloquent comes to us from the fifth century under the authority of the then reigning pontiff, St Celestine I:

> When priests fulfil the sacerdotal office entrusted to them, they are pleading the cause of the human race before the divine clemency, and while the whole Church mingles its sighs with theirs, they beg and pray that faith may be given to the infidels, that idolaters may be freed from the errors of their impiety, that the light of truth may appear to the Jews, that heretics may return to wisdom with the true comprehension of the Catholic faith, that schismatics may receive the spirit of charity once more revived in them and that those who have relapsed may be given the remedy of repentance.[57]

This doctrine, wrote Pope Celestine, was handed down from the Apostles, and therefore represents the mind of Christ, whose prayer for unity at the Last Supper is perpetuated in every Sacrifice of the Mass. Pope Pius XII wrote: 'Certainly, no one was better fitted to make satisfaction to Almighty God for all the sins of men than was Christ. Therefore, He desired to be immolated upon the Cross as a propitiation for our sins, "not for ours only but also for those of the whole world" and likewise He daily offers Himself upon our altars for our redemption...'[58]

Correlative with the Mass are the prayers and sacrifices of the faithful, imploring from Christ the graces which He dispenses outside the Mystical Body. As with the Mass, this tradition dates back to the early Church and is based on the dogmatic principle that the fruits of the Redemption are applicable to all the members of the human family. Following the example of his Master, Stephen prayed for his persecutors and Paul for the Jews, even to becoming anathema if this were necessary to win their salvation. However, besides the salvific will of God another principle is also operative in this tradition of apostolic prayer and sacrifice in favour of the non-Catholic world. While believing that conversion to Catholicism and especially final perseverance is a gift of divine liberality, we recognize the corresponding need of human activity antecedent to the reception of grace, notably the necessity of prayer. It may be the prayer that a person says for himself, asking for divine guidance and strength to follow the will of God; it may also be the prayer that others say in addition to his own or in his stead. For Catholics as well as non-Catholics, the latter prayer for others is indispensable. We need the prayers of the living members of the Mystical Body of Christ to reach our heavenly destiny.

In a famous letter that St Augustine wrote against the Pelagians we find all the essentials of this doctrine with reference to those who are eventually converted to God. Augustine pleads with his correspondent to recognize the Church's duty of praying for those outside of her fold. 'Surely you will not forbid the Church to pray for unbelievers that they may be believers, for those who refuse to believe that they may be willing to believe, for those who are at variance with God's law and doctrine, that God may give them what He promised by the prophet, "A heart for understanding Him and ears for hearing."'[59] As a general principle, therefore, 'these and other divine testimonies prove that God by His grace takes away the stony heart from unbelievers and forestalls merit in men of good will... This is shown both by thanksgiving and by prayer: prayer for unbelievers; thanksgiving for believers. Prayer is to be made to Him that He might do what we ask; thanksgiving is to be offered when He has done it.'[60] Pope Pius XII confirmed the same tradition when he declared that he had committed to the protection and guidance of heaven those who do not belong to the visible body of the Catholic Church, and united with the prayers of the whole Church, he desired most ardently that they may have life and have it more abundantly.[61] An example of the praying Church for those who are not yet united with her is the presence of contemplative communities, whose mission is directed precisely towards those who are still searching for salvation.

The Church is necessary for the salvation of all mankind. By divine ordinance she is the great sacrament through whom graces are dispensed to the entire human family. Within her Body, members receive these gifts as by a special privilege to which, by God's mercy, they have a supernatural title. However, even outside her Body, whoever is eventually saved, must credit his salvation to the instrumentality of the Catholic Church, whose invisible Head is the fountain of all life and holiness, and of whose fullness anyone who is sanctified must have received.

Anonymous Christians

Karl Rahner's definition of the concept of the anonymous Christian runs like this: 'the "anonymous Christian" in our sense of the term is the pagan after the beginning of the Christian mission, who lives in the state of Christ's grace through faith, hope and love, yet who has no explicit knowledge of the fact that his life is orientated in grace-given salvation to Jesus Christ.'[62] Rahner pointed out that his theory arose from two facts: first, the possibility of supernatural salvation and of a corresponding faith which must be granted to non-Christians, even if they never become Christian; and second, that salvation cannot be gained without reference to God and Christ, since it must in its origin, history and fulfilment be a theistic and Christian salvation.[63] Rahner then made clear that he adopted this expression to bypass the 'pessimistic outlook common in the past' whereby the possibility of supernatural salvation for such people was denied, thereby 'consigning them to hell or limbo'.[64] Also, Jesus Christ is man's only way of salvation. This must mean that the non-Christians who end up in heaven must have received the grace of Christ without their realising it.

This theory proposes that since all men are by nature ordered toward God and capable of sensing His sanctifying grace operative in themselves, those who existentially accept that grace manifest an implicit desire for incorporation into Christ and His Church. Insofar as they live justly and according to their consciences, they are in fact Christians and therefore redeemed men. Although Rahner was careful to indicate that not all non-Christians were anonymous Christians and that any and all who were saved were saved through the Paschal Mystery of Christ, the concept has developed in many minds that anyone who is basically of good will is oriented to Christ and saved: everyone is really a Christian in his heart of hearts.

One main danger of Rahner's theory is that it is a very short leap from implicit Christianity as a path toward salvation, to non-Christian religions being considered as paths to salvation in their own right. In the end it jeopardizes the belief that Jesus Christ is the only Saviour and Mediator. Steps in the direction of reducing Christianity simply to a type of first among equal religions have been taken, for example, in the thought of Jacques Dupuis.[65] Moreover, many members of non-Christian religious would themselves be very uneasy, to say the least, being considered anonymous Christians. In point of fact, not all people are Christians—explicitly or implicitly. Moreover Christianity, incorporation into Christ and His Church through the sacrament of baptism, does matter and is salvific. The term 'anonymous Christian' could well be a disincentive for evangelization, even if Rahner may not have intended it so.

Related to the Church

We would propose instead that those who have not yet received the Gospel are related in various ways to the visible Church.[66] There are various degrees of intimacy in this relationship. The closest are the Jewish people 'to whom the Testament and the promises were given and from whom Christ was born according to the flesh'.[67] On account of their fathers this people remains most dear to God, for God does not repent of the gifts He makes nor of the calls He issues (cf. Rm 11:28–29). Next in this plan of the plan of salvation are those who acknowledge the Creator. In the first place amongst these, there are the Muslims, 'who, professing to hold the faith of Abraham, along with us adore the one and merciful God, who on the last day will judge mankind'.[68] In a yet more distant relationship are those who are seekers: 'Nor is God far distant from those who in shadows and images seek the unknown God, for it is He who gives to all men life and breath and all things, and as Saviour wills that all men be saved.'[69] The Second Vatican Council made it clear that those who through no fault of their own do not know the Gospel of Christ or His Church, can also attain to salvation. The condition is that they sincerely seek God, and moved by His grace strive by their deeds to do His will as it is known to them through the dictates of conscience. Divine Providence does not deny the help necessary for salvation to those who, without blame on their part, have not yet arrived at an explicit knowledge of God and with His grace strive to live a good life.[70] The elements of goodness and truth found amongst these people is looked upon by the Church as a preparation for the Gospel.[71]

The difficulty is that this goodness and truth is also mixed with much error, since often men, deceived by the Evil One, have become vain in their reasoning and have exchanged the truth of God for a lie, serving the creature rather than the Creator.[72] These negative aspects, present in non-Christian religions, depend not so much and not only on the way in which these religions are professed or incarnated by different persons or by different peoples, in varied times and cultures. Rather, these shadowy elements are due in great measure also to the very nature of the non-Christian religions. In fact, these religions (except for the Jewish religion) are mainly the fruit and effect of man's efforts and attempts to reach God and enter in contact with Him, although one does not exclude that, in some cases, the founders of these natural religions might have received some special gifts from above. Thus, precisely due to their human origin, these religions easily contain deformed, erroneous and incomplete elements; often due to the fact that the divinities reflect man, they are in the image and likeness of the same limits and defects of man. The history of religions attests to the fact that in many cases men have made, imagined and constructed divinities in their own image and likeness. The unfortunate presence of these negative aspects is still greater if one considers that man is a sinner, and lives under the influence of personal sin, of the world, and of 'the prince of evil' or the devil. On the contrary, the Bible, in the first pages, attests that God created the human person in His own image and likeness, and calls man and woman to share in His life, giving them also the capacity and strength to realise this objective.

The fact that God can save those outside the visible confines of His Church does not diminish the importance of the Church. There is a difference between receiving what is a merciful gift from the Lord, and receiving the fullness of His treasury. Thus, the certainty of the universal salvific will of God does not diminish, but rather increases the duty and urgency of the proclamation of salvation and of conversion to the Lord Jesus Christ. Although in ways known to Himself God can lead those who, through no fault of their own, are ignorant of the Gospel, to that faith without which it is impossible to please Him, the Church still has the obligation and also the sacred right to evangelize all peoples.[73] The mentality of indifferentism must thus be avoided; it is characterized by a religious relativism which leads to the false notion that 'one religion is as good as another'.[74] While it is true that the followers of other religions can receive divine grace, it is also certain that objectively speaking they are in a gravely deficient situation in comparison with those who, in the Church, have the fullness of the means of salvation.[75] The Church is related to the world to which she is sent in mission, and this relationship will be explored in detail in the next chapter.

Notes

1. See chapter two, pp. 36–39 above.
2. Cf. *CCC* 775.
3. Vatican II, *Lumen Gentium*, 9.2, 48.2, 59; Idem, *Gaudium et Spes*, 45.1.
4. See Pope Paul VI, *Discourse to the Sacred College* (22 June 1973); Vatican II, *Ad Gentes*, 7.2; cf. Idem, *Lumen Gentium*, 17.
5. Vatican II, *Unitatis Redintegratio*, 3.5. See Vatican II, *Lumen Gentium*, 9; Idem, *Lumen Gentium*, 42; Idem, *Sacrosanctum Concilium*, 26.
6. St Ignatius of Antioch, *Letter to the Philadelphians*, 3, 2–3 in *SC* 10, 110–111. See also J. Hardon, manuscript *Christ to Catholicism*, chapter X 'No Salvation outside the Church' which provided material for some of the following points.
7. Origen, *Homilies on Joshua*, 3, 5, in *PG* 12, 841.
8. St Cyprian, *De Ecclesiae catholicae unitate*, 6 in *SC* 500, 188–189 To this day, Cyprian's formula, '*Habere iam non potest Deum patrem qui Ecclesiam non habet matrem*,' is a most concise expression of the doctrine under consideration.
9. Lactantius, *Divine Institutes*, 4, 30, 11–13, in *PL* 6, 542.
10. See St Augustine, *Enarratio in Psalmum 101*, 8 in *PL* 37, 1300: 'Ecclesia Dei nidum de lignis crucis ipsius.'
11. St Augustine, *Sermo ad Caesariensis Ecclesiae plebem* in *PL* 43, 695.
12. See St Augustine, *In Joannis EvangeliumTractatus*, XXVII, 6, in *PL* 35, 1618.

13. See DS 75. Curiously, the Church of England has retained the *Quicumque* in the Book of Common Prayer and one of the thirty-nine Articles of the Anglican communion prescribes its recitation. In America, the more liberal Episcopalian Church has dropped the Athanasian Creed.
14. Lateran IV, Chapter 1, *On the Catholic Faith* in DS 802.
15. Pope Boniface VIII, Bull *Unam Sanctam* in DS 870.
16. *Ibid.*, in DS 875.
17. Council of Florence, *Decree for the Jacobites*, in DS 1351.
18. Council of Quiercy, *De libero arbitrio hominis et de praedestinatione*, cap. 3, in DS 623.
19. Cf. Council of Trent, Decree *De iustificatione*, cap. 7 in DS 1529, 1530.
20. Pope Innocent X, Constitution *Cum Occasione* (31 May 1653) in DS 2005.
21. Vatican II, *Gaudium et Spes*, 22; Idem, *Sacrosanctum Concilium*, 5.
22. For the idea of the Church as an ark see chapter two, pp. 47–48 above.
23. For more information on this point see my work, *The Sacramental Mystery*.
24. St Ambrose, *De Obitu Valentiniani Consolatio*, in *PL* 16, 402–403.
25. St Augustine, *De Baptismo*, in *PL* 43, 172–173.
26. St Irenaeus, *Contra Haereses*, Book 4, chapter 22, 2 in SC 100, 688–689.
27. Eusebius of Caesaria, *Church History*, 1, 1, 4, in *PG* 20, 77.
28. St Nilus of Sinai, *Letter to Maximian*, 1, 154, in *PG* 79, 145. For information about Cornelius see Ac 10:1–42.
29. St John Damascene, *Against the Iconoclasts*, 11 in *PG* 96, 1357.
30. St Bernard, *Epistola seu Tractatus de Baptismo*, in *PL* 182, 1036.
31. St Thomas Aquinas, *Summa Theologiae*, III, q. 69, a. 4.
32. St Thomas Aquinas, *De Veritate*, q. 14, a. 11.
33. Council of Trent, Session 6, *Decree on Justification*, cap. 4 in DS 1524: '…quae quidem translatio post Evangelium promulgatum sine lavacro regenerationis aut eius voto fieri non potest…'
34. M. Canus, *De Locis Theologicis* (Paris: 1678), vol. I, p. 187.

35. St Robert Bellarmine, *De Ecclesia Militante*, cap.2. To safeguard the Church's visibility, Bellarmine here seems to defend actual membership in the Church for occult heretics, namely those who externally profess to be Catholic but internally reject the Church's teaching. Other passages in Bellarmine make it doubtful whether he really held this theory.
36. *Ibid.*, cap.3.
37. Among others, the French Jesuit Père Berruyer (1681–1758) was condemned by ecclesiastical authorities because his *L'Histoire du Peuple de Dieu* (Paris: 1728) suggested that faith based on revelation was not absolutely necessary for salvation.
38. Cf. G. S. Pelczar, *Pio IX e il suo pontificato sullo sfondo delle vicende della Chiesa nel secolo XIX*, vol. I, (Torino: Berruti, 1909), p. 5.
39. Pope Bl Pius IX, Allocution *Singulari Quidam* (9 December 1854), c.8, in *Codicis Iuris Canonici Fontes*, vol. II, (Roma: 1924), p. 894: 'Poiché si deve tener per fede che nessuno può salvarsi fuori della Chiesa Apostolica Romana, questa è l'unica arca di salvezza; chiunque non sia entrato in essa perirà nel diluvio. Ma nel tempo stesso si deve pure tenere per certo che coloro che ignorano la vera religione, quando la loro ignoranza sia invincibile, non sono di ciò colpevoli dinanzi agli occhi del Signore. Ora, chi si arrogherà tanto da poter determinare i limiti di codesta ignoranza secondo l'indole e la varietà dei popoli, delle regioni, degl'ingegni e di tante altre cose?'
40. Pope Bl Pius IX, Encyclical *Quanto Conficiamur Moerore* (10 August 1863), 7.
41. *Ibid.*, 8.
42. Acta Concilii Vaticani, *Collectio Lacensis*, vol. VII, col. 591.
43. *Ibid.*, col. 569.
44. Vatican I, Session 3, Cap. 3 *On Faith*, in DS 3011–3012.
45. Acta Concilii Vaticani, *Collectio Lacensis*, vol. VII, coll. 177–178.
46. Pope Pius XII, Encyclical Letter *Mystici Corporis*, 103.
47. Holy Office, *Decree of Excommunication* (13 February 1953) in *AAS* 45(1953), p. 100.

48. Holy Office, *Letter to the Archbishop of Boston* (8 August 1949) in DS 3867. English version from *American Ecclesiastical Review* 127, 4 (October 1952), p. 308.
49. *Ibid.*, in DS 3868. English version from *American Ecclesiastical Review* (October 1952), p. 308.
50. *Ibid.*, in DS 3869. English version from *American Ecclesiastical Review* (October 1952), pp. 308–309.
51. *Ibid.*, in DS 3870. English version from *American Ecclesiastical Review* (October 1952), pp. 308–309.
52. *Ibid.*, in DS 3872. English version from *American Ecclesiastical Review* (October 1952), p. 309.
53. Pope Pius XII, Encyclical Letter *Humani Generis,* 27.
54. Vatican I, Session 3, Chapter 3 *On Faith,* in DS 3008.
55. For the axiom *Facienti quod in se est Deus non denegat gratiam,* see St Thomas Aquinas, *Summa Theologiae,* I–IIae, q. 112, a. 3.
56. Origen, *Contra Celsum* VII, 42 in SC 150, 114–115.
57. Pope St Celestine I, *Epistola ad Episcopos Galliarum,* in *PL* 50, 535.
58. Pope Pius XII, Encyclical Letter *Mediator Dei,* 73. Cf. 1 Jn 2:2.
59. St Augustine, *Epistola ad Vitalem* in *PL* 33, 988.
60. *Ibid.*
61. See Pope Pius XII, Encyclical Letter *Mystici Corporis,* 103.
62. K. Rahner, *Theological Investigations* Vol 14 (London: Darton, Longman & Todd, 1976), p 283. Rahner's ideas on this matter are spread over a number of his writings. For a succinct understanding of his thought, see K. Riesenhuber, 'Der Anonyme Christ nach Karl Rahner' in *Zeitschrift für katholische Theologie* 86 (1964), pp. 286–303, and A. Röper, *Die Anonymen Christen* (Mainz: Matthias-Grünewald-Verlag, 1963). Rahner himself approved of both Riesenhuber's article and Röper's book in a letter, printed in the English translation of Röper's book, *The Anonymous Christian* (New York: Sheed and Ward, 1966), pp. vi–vii.
63. See K. Rahner, *Theological Investigations* Vol. 16 (London: Darton, Longman & Todd 1979), p. 218.
64. *Ibid.*

65. See J. Dupuis, *Toward a Christian Theology of Religious Pluralism* (Maryknoll, N.Y.: Orbis Books, 1997). For positions even more aberrant than those of Dupuis, see *inter alia* P. F. Knitter, *No Other Name? A Critical Study of Christian Attitudes toward Other Religions* (Maryknoll, N.Y.: Orbis Books, 1985); Idem, *Jesus and the Other Names* (Maryknoll, N.Y.: Orbis Books, 1996); and G. D'Costa, *The Meeting of Religions and the Trinity* (Maryknoll, N.Y.: Orbis Books, 2000). See also the Congregation for the Doctrine of the Faith's *Notification* concerning Dupuis' work (24 January 2001) and the subsequent *Commentary on the Notification* (12 March 2001).
66. Cfr. St Thomas Aquinas, *Summa Theologiae,* III, q. 8, a. 3.
67. Vatican II, *Lumen Gentium,* 16. Cf. Cf. Rm 9: 4–5.
68. Vatican II, *Lumen Gentium,* 16.
69. *Ibid.*. See Ac 17:25–28; Cf. 1 Tm 2:4.
70. See Vatican II, *Lumen Gentium,* 16.
71. Cfr. Eusebius of Caesaria, *Praeparatio Evangelica,* 1, 1 in *PG* 21, 28.
72. See Vatican II, *Lumen Gentium,* 16. See also Rm 1: 21, 25.
73. See Vatican II, *Ad Gentes,* 7; CCC 848; cf. Heb 11:6; 1 Co 9:16.
74. See Pope John Paul II, Encyclical Letter *Redemptoris Missio,* 36.
75. Congregation for the Doctrine of the Faith, *Dominus Jesus,* 22. Cf. Pope Pius XII, Encyclical Letter *Mystici Corporis,* 103.

8

The Church and the World

When political government (regnum) and ecclesiastical authority (sacerdotium) are agreed, the world is well ruled and the Church flourishes and bears fruit. But when they disagree, not only do less important interests fail to prosper, but those of the greatest moment fall into miserable decay.

Ivo of Chartres, *Epistle 238*

The complex and much-discussed relationship between the Church and the world has been the subject and the fruit of long reflection over nearly two thousand years. Despite the fact that the Second Vatican Council devoted one fine document to this issue, it cannot be said that the theme is definitively resolved.[1] In our present discussion, two particular aspects of the theme will be developed, one the relationship between Church and State, and the other between the Church and science. These two themes fall within the description which the Second Vatican Council proposed:

> If by the autonomy of earthly affairs we mean that created things and societies themselves enjoy their own laws and values which must be gradually deciphered, put to use, and regulated by men, then it is entirely right to demand that autonomy. Such is not merely required by modern man, but harmonizes also with the will of the Creator. For by the very circumstance of their having been created, all things

> are endowed with their own stability, truth, goodness, proper laws and order.[2]

This autonomy should be understood as relational, based on the philosophical concept of secondary causality.[3] It should not be taken as a justification for the secular state, which most often turns out to be *secularist*. The idea of a strict separation between Church and State and between religion and science is, in some ways, a product of Enlightenment thought, and as such is now outdated and outmoded as a concept and as a reality. Many theologians within the Church itself have not grasped that the separationist model is now past its prime. The best of the modern world seek rather a much more *holistic* model for the relations between the Church and secular realities, as it does for so many other areas of life. This holism is based on the fact that the human person is created one in his capacity to know.[4] Or, in the words of the poet Alfred Noyes:

> With such a mind,
> We might achieve, not that armed truce of thought
> Between the Faith and Science, reconciled
> Only to pass, and shun each other's gaze,
> But that great golden symphony of thought
> Which, long ago, the Angelic Doctor heard
> Throbbing from hell to heaven, organic truth,
> Wherein each note, in its own grade, rings clear,
> As in a single orchestra, whose chords
> Were chaos, till each filled its own true place
> In the one golden cosmos of the song.[5]

Holism is also fashionable in less reputable forms because of the influence of New Age ideologies. Less reputable because New Age holism is not based on a realist concept, but rather seeks to unite entities arbitrarily. In any case, it is false and detrimental to separate God from human culture and from human activity:

> But if the expression, the independence of temporal affairs, is taken to mean that created things do not depend on God, and that man can use them

> without any reference to their Creator, anyone who acknowledges God will see how false such a meaning is. For without the Creator the creature would disappear. For their part, however, all believers of whatever religion always hear His revealing voice in the discourse of creatures. When God is forgotten, however, the creature itself grows unintelligible.[6]

Without those supernatural means which are to be found in the Church, humanity is unable to achieve fully even its own natural goals, such as harmony, peace and justice. Therefore, human society has need of the Church, a need which is more pressing than ever as evidenced by the problems facing society at the beginning of the third millennium. The idea of a pluralist society in which a philosophical law of the jungle and of minority pressure groups rules the day is unacceptable. The further the nations distance themselves from the Church, the more they fall away into degradation, even at a material level; to be far from the Church is to be separated from Christ who alone can give the grace for human beings to live in harmony with each other and with the whole of creation. One area where this whole question is particularly highlighted is the relationship between Church and State and another is the link between science and religion.

Church and State

The question of Church and State and the problems to which their relation has given rise, are as old as Christianity. In a true sense there was no problem of Church and State before the advent of Christ when, for all practical purposes, the public authority was regarded equally competent in the field of religion as in the secular domain. With the coming of the Catholic Church, however, an essential change was introduced by her Founder, who transferred to her the sphere of religion and the whole moral direction of mankind, independent of the power of the State.

Some development has taken place in this mutual relation between two disparate societies, one derived from nature and created by the social instincts of the human race, the other based on the supernatural order and founded by the Incarnate Son of God. The issues of Church and State have fallen into two broad categories, those which are immutable because flowing from the natural law or determined by divine revelation, and others that are adaptable to different times and ages and which even in the same period may vary according to different circumstances. It is crucial not to separate these issues from the historical context in which they occurred, otherwise the real development in Church and State policy can scarcely be appreciated and, more seriously, the distinction between eternal principles and adaptable norms would be hard to recognize.

The classic statement of Christ on the relation of His kingdom to the civil authority was provoked by officials of religion who had no sympathy with the secular power to which they were subject. The Pharisees sought to trap Jesus by asking Him if it was lawful to render tribute to Caesar; the word tribute comprised all kinds of taxes payable to state officials. The Pharisees and Herodians had long since adjusted their conscience to the payment. However, they now hoped to force Christ to compromise Himself no matter how He answered. If He advised non-payment, as they expected, He would have become liable to Roman punishment. The pseudo-Messiah, Judas the Galilean, had perished for this very cause some twenty years before. Should He have advised payment, He would have lost His Messianic hold on the people for whom Messianism meant complete independence from foreign domination. Instead of falling into the trap set for Him, Jesus asked for a coin with Caesar's image on it, declaring that, since the coin had come from Caesar, justice requires that it be returned to him. 'Pay to Caesar,' He replied, 'what belongs to Caesar, and to God what belongs to God' (Mt 22:21). In other words, civil transactions like the payment of taxes lie on one plane, but the rights of God are on another. There is no inevitable clash provided, as was the case in the relationship of Rome to the Jewish people, that the civil demands did not hinder the exercise of man's duties to God.

One aspect of Christ's reply to the Pharisees that is easy to overlook is His recognition of the rights of civil authority, as distinct from those of the Church. The emperor to whom Christ declared that tribute could be lawfully paid was officially a god. From the first beginnings of the Empire, the deification of Roman rulers became an established practice of the nation. Julius Caesar was proclaimed to be a god. *Divus* was the expression adopted; this title had been given him by senatorial decree, and his worship was put on a full ceremonial basis, with temple, priests, and ritual. The same thing was done for Augustus, Claudius, Vespasian, and Titus. As time went on, this phase of Roman religion grew spontaneously and accounted in great measure for the hostility of Rome to Christianity. The last of the *Divi*, deified in 307 AD, was Romulus, the son of Maxentius, whom Constantine defeated at the Milvian bridge. When Christ, therefore, granted the right of rulers to demand obedience in temporal and secular affairs, He made the most drastic distinction possible between legitimate civil authority and its illegitimate pretensions. Insofar as the Emperor commanded what was due to him as a ruler of state, all the citizens, including Christians, were bound to obey, notwithstanding his abuse of power and even the blasphemous claim to divinity.

In the apostolic Church, Peter implemented Christ's teaching by urging Christians to accept the established form of government and submit to those in authority 'for the sake of the Lord', in order not to bring discredit on His followers: 'Accept the authority of every human institution: the emperor, as the supreme authority, and the governors as commissioned by him to punish criminals and praise those who do good. It is God's will that by your good deeds you should silence the ignorant talk of fools' (1 Pt 2:13–15). St Peter concluded, 'fear God and honour the emperor' (1 Pt 2:17). As with the case of Christ, so here the injunction to be subject to the emperor, takes on added significance when this emperor is identified as Nero, and the motive indicated is the will of God.

The most elaborate exponent of Church and State relations in early Christianity was St Paul. His exhortation to the Romans remains to this day an epitome of the obedience that a Christian owes to the civil rulers:

> Everyone is to obey the governing authorities, because there is no authority except from God and so whatever authorities exist have been appointed by God. So anyone who disobeys an authority is rebelling against God's ordinance; and rebels must expect to receive the condemnation they deserve. Magistrates bring fear not to those who do good, but to those who do evil (Rm 13:1–3).

Yet the ultimate reason for submission is not the physical punishment caused by disobedience. Rather, one 'must be obedient, therefore, not only because of this retribution, but also for conscience's sake' (Rm 13:5). This is also why one should pay taxes, 'because the authorities are all serving God as His agents, even while they are busily occupied with that particular task' (Rm 13:6).

All subsequent theology on the duties of Christian citizens has appealed to this dictum of St Paul, that there exists no authority, including the civil, except from God, and those who possess it have been appointed by God. Nevertheless, later generations have also questioned whether every *de facto* government can be seen as divinely appointed, even when it is tyrannical or anti-religious, as happened during the Roman persecutions, and more recently in Elizabethan England, modern Mexico, or Communist countries.

In the first three centuries of the Christian era, the relation of Church and State was one of incessant conflict, in which the Roman Empire reacted against the Church as its mortal enemy, conscious on the one hand of the latter's inherent power over the hearts and minds of men, but blind to the fact that Christianity was not a political rival and still less a threat to civil authority. Pliny's letter to Trajan (112 AD) describing how he dealt with the Christians in Bithynia furnishes an insight into motives behind the pagan persecution. 'I ask them if they are Christian,' wrote Pliny. 'If they admit it, I repeat the question a second and a third time, threatening capital punishment; if they persist, I sentence them to death. For I do not doubt that, whatever kind of crime it may be to which they have confessed, their pertinacity and inflexible obstinacy should certainly be punished.'[7] The crime for which the Christians were punished was nothing more or less than 'obstinacy' in professing their religious belief against the mandates of civil power.

Nevertheless, all the time they were being persecuted, the Christians protested their loyalty to the government and only pleaded for justice, not to be punished for crimes they did not commit or, as Christ Himself had demanded, to be shown where they had done wrong (cf. Jn 18:23). 'If it is certain,' Tertullian asked, 'that we are the most guilty of men, why do you trust us differently from our fellows, that is, from other criminals?... Christians alone are not allowed to say anything to clear themselves, to defend truth, to save a judge from injustice. That alone is looked for, which public hatred requires: the confession of the name, not the investigation of the charge.' In spite of this manifest injustice, however, 'We call upon God for the welfare of the Emperor, upon God the eternal...whose favour, beyond all others, the Emperor desires.' If this seems incredible to the pagan mind, let them 'examine God's words, our scriptures [and] learn from them that a superfluity of benevolence is enjoined upon us, even so far as to pray for our enemies and to entreat blessings for our persecutors.'[8] Evidently the early Christians distinguished between the spiritual allegiance they owed the Church and the civic loyalty that was due to the State. Where the latter encroached on the former, it could not be obeyed; but within the limits of due authority, the State had a right to obedience and a claim on Christian prayer, that the Lord might direct the rulers in their government and assist their temporal reign.

When, after three centuries of cruel persecution, the State finally gave freedom to the Christian religion, it recognized what the Church had always been teaching, that Christianity is not an enemy of the State but its most powerful ally. The edict of liberation ran:

> When we, Constantine and Licinius, Emperors, met at Milan in conference concerning the welfare and security of the realm, we decided that of the things that are of profit to all mankind, the worship of God ought rightly to be our first and most important care... We therefore announce that, notwithstanding any provisions concerning the Christians in our former instructions, all who choose that religion should be allowed to continue in practising it, without any let or hindrance, and are not to be troubled or molested in any way.[9]

At the same time that Christianity was being legalized, all others are to be allowed the free and unrestricted practice of their religions; 'for it accords with the good order of the realm and the peacefulness of our times that each should have freedom to worship God after his own choice.'[10] The Edict of Milan was thus a political compromise between Licinius, an avowed pagan, and Constantine, who was already a Christian at heart, although he did not immediately profess the faith. Prescinding from its motive, the decree was a practical necessity, a *modus vivendi* for two strong opposing forces. Soon after the edict, Licinius started a pagan reaction, which Constantine repulsed by defeating his rival in 324. Despite being at an advantage as a result, Constantine was still obliged to make concessions to the pagan nobility. However, later proclamations became even more favourable to the Christians, like the prohibition of soothsaying and fortune-telling, the grant of a regular subsidy to the Catholic clergy, their exemption from military and other civil duties, and the state recognition of Sunday as a feast day with civil effects. However, paganism was not yet entirely suppressed.

Within less than a century of the Edict of Milan, Catholicism had become so widely recognized that the civil authorities found in religious unity their strongest support for political stability. With the fall of paganism, Catholic Christianity might have become the religion of the Empire without State intervention, except for the Arian crisis of the fourth century. After its condemnation at the Councils of Nicea and Constantinople, Arianism was finally crushed by a composite decree of the Emperors Gratian, Valentinian II and Theodosius, who made acknowledgment of the Most Holy Trinity a condition of civil liberty:

> We desire all people, whom the benign influence of our clemency rules, to turn to the religion which tradition from Peter to the present day declares to have been delivered to the Romans by blessed Peter the Apostle... This faith is that we should believe that there is one Godhead, Father, Son and Holy Spirit, in an equal Majesty and a holy Trinity. We order those who follow this doctrine to receive the title of Catholic Christians, but others we judge to be mad and raving and worthy of incurring the disgrace of heretical teaching, nor are their assemblies to receive the name of churches. They are to be punished not only by divine retribution but also by our own measures, which we have decided in accordance with divine inspiration.[11]

This imperial edict did more than introduce Catholic orthodoxy as the established religion of the Roman world. It is the first recorded instance when the civil power contemplated the use of physical force in the service of Christianity with consequences that critics of the Church have exploited beyond the objective facts. There is no evidence that the threat of punishment radically 'converted' the heretics against whom the decree was aimed; on the other hand, there is ample evidence that, even without civil intervention, orthodox Christianity would have continued (as it had begun) its conquest of the Mediterranean world simply by preaching the word of God.

More significant from the viewpoint of Church-State relations was another imperial decree in the following century (445 AD) when Valentinian III and Theodosius II recognized the Pope as Head of the Catholic Church. Aside from its value as an early witness of the Petrine primacy, the document shows how carefully even the rulers of the Roman Empire distinguished between the spiritual autonomy of the Papacy and their own function as aids to the Pope in those material forces which he did not enjoy. The emperors stated:

> It is clear that for us and our Empire the only support is in the favour of the Supreme Godhead; to merit this we must assist in the first place the Christian faith and venerable religion. Since therefore the merit of St Peter… the dignity of the City of Rome and the authority of a holy synod have established the primacy of the Apostolic See, let not presumption attempt to carry out anything contrary to the authority of that See. But let whatever the Apostolic See decrees or shall decree, be accepted as law by all.[12]

The emperors intervened to protect papal authority against an episcopal rebel, the Bishop of Arles, who challenged the right of Pope Leo I to decide against him.

In the latter part of the fifth century, the Holy See stated its concept of the relative status of ecclesiastical and civil power which to this day is the most succinct expression of the Church's mind on the subject. It was occasioned by the attitude of the Eastern Emperor, Anastasius I, who presumed to favour the schismatic patriarchs of Constantinople, particularly with regard to the Monophysite heresy condemned by Rome. Pope Gelasius I (492–496), wrote to the Emperor, to point out to him the illegality of his interference in Church affairs. His letter included an exposition of the Gelasian thesis that the spiritual and secular authorities are each independent in their own sphere, with which the other must not interfere:

> There are two powers by which this world is chiefly ruled: the sacred authority of the Popes and the royal power. Of these, the priestly power is much more important, because it has to render account for the kinds of men themselves at the divine tribunal. For you know that although you have the highest place in dignity over the human race, yet you must submit yourself faithfully to those who have charge of divine things, and look to them for the means of your salvation... For if in matters pertaining to the administration of public discipline, the bishops of the Church, knowing that the Empire has been conferred on you by divine instrumentality, are themselves obedient to your laws, lest in purely material affairs contrary opinions may seem to be voiced, with what willingness, I ask you, should you obey those to whom is assigned the administration of divine mysteries?[13]

Here, for the first time, a papal document of universal application spells out the Church's new status in reference to the political power. Until the Edict of Milan, the problem was almost unilateral, how the Church's rights could be protected in the atmosphere of a totalitarian State. A period of flux followed for a century or so after Constantine, in which the hitherto pagan civil authority gradually became Christian and, while emancipating the Church, also assumed (often without being asked) the responsibility of assisting the Church with the might of its secular arm. Depending on their ambition, the emperors sometimes went beyond their legitimate function of auxiliaries to interfere in the internal affairs of ecclesiastical policy, with consequent harm to the Church's spiritual welfare. Gelasius' reprimand of Anastasius was chronologically the beginning of a long line of similar papal reactions. Basically the attitude is not different from Peter's during the persecution of Nero, except that now the Church is in a position to protest against political intrusion, instead of merely exhorting the Christians to bear the injustice with patience. However, as in Peter, so in Gelasius, the sovereign rights of the State are forcefully recognized, even to the point of obedience on the part of ecclesiastics when purely secular interests are involved.

In the tenth century, with the disintegration of Charlemagne's empire and the inroads of the Norsemen, Magyars and Saracens, political and moral values fell into decay and the Church herself was deeply affected by the return to 'semi-barbarism'. When feudalism emerged as a reaction to the crisis, ecclesiastical authority came under the sway of feudal lords and princes. A reforming tendency within the Church had started as a monastic movement in France (Cluny) and in Germany (Lorraine). After the deposition in 1046 of the anti-pope, Sylvester III (created by a Roman Political party), a series of high-minded Pontiffs ascended the papal throne, culminating in the pontificate of St Gregory VII (1073–1085), who had served as secretary and adviser to his five predecessors.

The two principal objects of Gregory's reform were clerical celibacy and lay investiture, in which the latter was a cause of problems in the former. By controlling the elections of bishops, lay princes had been able to name their own creatures or relatives and even to sell bishoprics to the highest bidder. And after a bishop's consecration, they further assumed the power of 'vesting' the prelate ostensibly with temporal assets like property and buildings but actually (as symbolized in the ring and pastoral staff used for investiture) by claiming also to give him ecclesiastical jurisdiction in the diocese. As a result, bishops considered themselves quite independent of the pope. Simony, incontinence and clerical abuses remained unchecked and were fostered by the political overlords.

A year after his election, Pope Gregory held a synod in Rome, which renewed old legislation against simony and violations of celibacy. This was followed by another synod against the custom of lay investiture, with the result that at Worms, in 1076, the Emperor Henry IV forced the bishops to repudiate the authority of the Pope. Gregory thereupon excommunicated two German archbishops and the emperor, and then absolved Henry's subjects from their allegiance, in the first recorded papal deposition of a civil monarch. Addressing St Peter, Gregory declares that since

> as your deputy, God has given me the power of binding and loosing in heaven and earth, therefore, by your power and authority I withdraw from Henry the King, son of Henry the Emperor, who has arisen against the Church with unheard-of insolence, the rule over the whole kingdom of the Germans and over Italy. And I absolve all Christians from the bonds of the oath which they have taken to him or which they shall in the future take; and I forbid anyone to serve him as king... Moreover, since he has scorned to obey as a Christian, and has not come back to God whom he has deserted, I bind him, in your stead, with the chains of the anathema.[14]

Henry made his submission and was absolved at Canossa in 1077; but as soon as he had regained power, he renewed the opposition and was again deposed and excommunicated. However, this time, the Pope went beyond the first sentence. Not only was Henry dethroned but the royal power was granted by the Pope to the Duke Rudolf of Swabia. In concluding the sentence, Gregory prayed that Henry 'be confounded until he makes penance in order that his soul be safe at the day of the Lord'.[15] Henry retaliated by marching into Italy with an army, seizing Rome and setting up an antipope, Clement III. Gregory received protection from the Normans but had to retire to Salerno, where he passed away in 1085 as one of the greatest reformers in the history of the Papacy. His last words were 'I have loved justice and hated iniquity, therefore I die in exile.' Victor III, who succeeded him, excommunicated Clement III and continued the policy of Gregory, which even non-Catholic writers admit was the salvation of the Roman primacy.

A clear high point in the expression of Papal power and its civil consequences is found in Pope Boniface VIII, and his Bull *Unam Sanctam*, issued in 1302.[16] In order to appreciate the full import of Pope Boniface's legislation, one should recall the circumstances under which it was enacted. Political rivalry among the Hapsburgs prevented the coronation of a Western Emperor for half a century in the late 1200s, with the result that during this time the Roman Pontiffs became the acknowledged visible heads of Catholic Christianity to a degree unparalleled in papal history. When Boniface VIII, a professional jurist, ascended the throne of Peter, he decided to embody in a general enactment the legal position of the Roman See, as it had crystallized during the thirteenth century. His instrument was the Bull *Unam Sanctam* which subsequently became part of the Church's Canon Law.

The immediate occasion of the Bull was a long and heated conflict between the Pope and the king of France, Philip IV, called 'The Fair'. Philip insisted on deriving his authority in the tradition of Charlemagne and was reluctant to admit any principle of subordination to the Papacy in secular matters. When the king imposed a heavy taxation on the French clergy without previous agreement with Rome, Boniface took this as an infringement of ecclesiastical rights and after protracted study of the principles involved, published the document that was to sum up the plenitude of papal power over all the Christian community, including France and her king. Some have wrongly considered the *Unam Sanctam* an angry rejoinder of the Pope, composed in a fit of rage. Actually it was the deliberate pronouncement of a synod, headed by the Pope, in which there were (among others) thirty-nine French archbishops and bishops. Nor is it a document which the Holy See has ever retracted. In fact it was solemnly confirmed by the Fifth Lateran Council in 1513; and the very point in its teaching to which exception has been taken is reaffirmed in the Syllabus of Errors of Blessed Pius IX.

After declaring there is only one Holy, Catholic and Apostolic Church, over which Christ placed only one head, 'not two heads as if it were a monster', Boniface explains the relation of the secular power to the spiritual:

> We are taught by the words of the Gospel that in this Church and in its power there are two swords, namely, a spiritual and a temporal... Both are in the power of the Church; the one, indeed, to be wielded for the Church, and the other by the Church. The former by the priest, the latter by the hands of kings and knights, but by the bidding and consent of the priesthood. It is necessary that one sword should be under the other, and that temporal authority be subjected to the spiritual... For, with truth as our witness, it belongs to spiritual power to establish the temporal power and to pass judgement if it has not been good... Hence we declare, affirm, and define and pronounce that *it is altogether necessary for the salvation of every creature to be subject to the Roman Pontiff.*[17]

From the outset, one must distinguish between defined doctrine and ordinary papal teaching. Only the final sentence, as italicized, was solemnly defined and clearly represents traditional Catholic dogma on the Church's necessity for salvation.

However, how can one understand the preceding statements on the subordination of State to Church, that the temporal sword is wielded 'by the bidding and consent of the priesthood'? Those who interpret Boniface to mean that the whole sphere of temporal jurisdiction is directly subject to the Church do the Pope an injustice against which he protested shortly after the Bull was published. In a solemn consistory, Boniface denounced the forgery inserted into the document by followers of Philip the Fair: 'For forty years We have studied law, and We know that there are two powers appointed by God. Who should, then, or can, believe that We entertain, or have entertained, such stupid absurdity? We declare that in no way do We wish to usurp the jurisdiction of the king... And yet, neither the king nor any one else of the faithful can deny that he is subject to Us where a question of sin is involved (*ratione peccati*).'[18] The pope's phrase *ratione peccati,* has since become the standard theological norm to judge when and to what extent the Church may use her spiritual power to intervene in the secular affairs of State. She may do so when, in her judgment, an otherwise temporal affair (like civil legislation) affects the religious interests of the faithful by placing unwarranted burden on their conscience, exposing them to sin or otherwise conflicting with that spiritual welfare over which the Church alone has ultimate jurisdiction by the mandate of her Founder.

Within Eastern Orthodoxy, the Byzantine ideal of mutual cooperation between Church and State has been embraced. This model of Church-State relations has a pedigree going back much further than Byzantium, right to Old Testament theology: 'In Byzantium, Empire and Church were virtually identified in each other. The emperor was also the head of the Church. He considered himself a representative of Christ and—following the Biblical example of Melchizedek, who was king and priest at the same time (Gn 14: 18)—he bore the official title, "king and priest," from the sixth century on.'[19] The Orthodox ideal is therefore that of *symphoneia* or the symphony of the State upholding law and the social good, and the Church conferring spiritual blessing and moral leadership from the Heavenly Kingdom. This was the particular gift of the Byzantine world to the Church as a whole, worked out over one millennium of rise and decline. Both God-ordained orders complemented each other in the East through their distinct but cooperative functions. In so doing they made possible the idea of a Christian commonwealth and indeed, an internationalism of sorts at a higher level of human good. The weak link in this synthesis, however, was and is the security of the State in a fallen world in terms of its vulnerability to corruption. The security of the Kingdom of God and its purity is never in doubt. The Orthodox Churches have been mindful of this tension and how fragile the symphony can be.

Among the changes in religious thought introduced by the Protestant Reformation, few have been more radical or consequential than the negation of the ministerial priesthood and the corresponding denial of a real distinction between the secular and ecclesiastical state. Luther's theories have been rightly considered the watershed which divided Church and State relations into two diverse principles, the Catholic and the Protestant. Some of the modern problems arising in this sphere can be traced to his ideas. Luther first proposed his notion in the appeal he made to the Emperor Charles V and the German nobility in 1520, just three years after his breach with Rome. Luther denied the reality of the distinction between the spiritual and temporal realms in strong terms:

> It is a fiction by which the pope, bishops, priests, and monks are called the 'spiritual estate,' while princes, lords, artisans and peasants are the 'temporal estate'. This is an artful lie and hypocritical invention, but let no one be made afraid of it, because all Christians are truly of the spiritual estate, and there is no difference among them, save of office... For we are all consecrated priests by baptism... Consequently, since we are all priests alike, no man may put himself forward, or take upon himself without our consent and election, to do that which we have all alike power to do... Therefore a priest should be nothing in Christendom but a functionary; as long as he holds his office, he has precedence; if he is deprived of it, he is a peasant or a citizen like the rest. But now they have invented 'indelible characters' and even imagine that a priest can never become a layman; which is all nothing but mere talk and a figment of human invention.

The logical consequence of Luther's attempt to equate the secular and priestly state, was that the Church could not be superior to the State: 'What kind of Christian doctrine is this, that the "temporal power" is not above the "spiritual", and therefore cannot punish it.' And if the temporal is superior, 'it has been ordained by God for the punishment of the bad and the protection of the good. So that we must let it do its duty throughout the whole Christian body, without respect of persons, whether it strikes popes, bishops, priests, monks, nuns, or whoever it may be.'[20] Curiously, however, in some traditionally Protestant countries, like England and Sweden, the Church and State remain linked.

The Council of Trent reacted against this destructive doctrine which literally undermined the whole structure of Christianity. Its condemnations laid the foundation for some subsequent dealings of the Church with civil authority. In particular the Council proclaimed:

> If anyone says that holy ordination is not truly and properly a sacrament instituted by Christ our Lord, or that it is a kind of human invention; or if anyone says that no character is imprinted by ordination, or that he who was once a priest can become a layman again; if anyone says that the orders conferred by the bishops are void without the consent of the people or of secular power, let him be anathema.[21]

Behind Luther's denial of a real distinction between the temporal and ecclesiastical domain lay the denial that Christ established a visible Church, vested with His authority and delegated by Him as a perfect society with divine rights to carry out its spiritual aims. His motives, we know, were dictated by the pressing need for protection from the secular rulers of Germany. The price he paid was to deny any superiority of Church over State. The full implications of Lutheran iconoclasm touches every aspect of Church and State relationship. Only civil laws have binding power on the citizens, since the State has a right to pass judgment on ecclesiastical legislation, but not *vice versa*. Civil officials may determine if churchmen are serving the common interest, and punish or depose them as they please; but the Church has no rights except those conceded by the State. Indeed, civil coercion can deprive any ecclesiastic, even the Pope, not only of the exercise of his ministry but the very title to his sacred office, which he pretends to have received from God.

Reformed teaching had an effect on subsequent generations including our own. John Dewey found in Protestant thought the origins of the modern secularist concept of

Church and State: 'The lesson of the two and a half centuries lying between the Protestant revolt and the formation of the [American] nation was well learned as respected the necessity of maintaining the integrity of the State against all divisive ecclesiastical divisions.' Oblivious of the spirit that was moving them, 'many of our ancestors would have been somewhat shocked to realize the full logic of their own attitude with respect to the subordinating of churches to the State—falsely termed the separation of Church and State.'[22] Fortunately for the Church and the good of society not every non-Catholic political philosopher, either accepted Luther's principles or followed them as rigidly to their logical conclusion as did Dewey.

A bright interlude in the frequent conflict of ecclesiastical and civil authority was the collaborative effort of Pope and king in the sixteenth century in favour of the native tribes found in the New World. With the discovery of the Americas arose the problem of the pagan races now subject to the rule of European Christians. Some of the colonists contended that the Indians were little better than animals, as they did not observe the precepts of the natural law. One evidence cited was the practice of human sacrifice among the Aztecs of Mexico: so there was no injustice in treating them as slaves, for which they were naturally fitted. Against this view, the missionaries preached and protested that the Indians were rational human beings capable of conversion to the true faith. They appealed to the Bull of Pope Alexander VI, issued six months after the discovery of America (4 May 1493) and commanding the colonists, 'with God's grace to bring the natives to the Catholic faith'. When this proved ineffective, Pope Paul III promulgated his celebrated Brief, *Pastorale Officium*, dated 29 May 1537, forbidding the enslavement of the Indians and threatening the severest penalties against those who disobeyed. Directing this letter to the Archbishop of Toledo, to whose jurisdiction the Indians belonged, the Pope acknowledged that, by a general law, Charles V had forbidden slavery among West or East Indians. He had therefore taken their freedom and property under his protection; but apparently without success, hence the need for papal intervention. The Pontiff declared:

> These Indians, although they live outside the bosom of the Church, nevertheless have not been, nor are they to be deprived of their freedom or of ownership of their possessions, since they are human beings, capable of faith and salvation. They are not to be destroyed by slavery, but invited to life by preaching and example. Furthermore, desiring to repress the shameful deeds of such wicked men, to ensure that the Indians are not alienated by injury and injustice, so that they find it more difficult to embrace the faith of Christ... We enjoin that you very strictly forbid all and sundry of whatever dignity, position, condition, rank or excellence, to bring the aforementioned Indians into slavery in any way or dare to deprive them of their possessions in any manner under pain, if they do so, of thereby incurring automatic *latae sententiae* excommunication, from which they can be absolved only by Ourselves or the Roman Pontiff reigning at that time, except if they are at the point of death and have previously made amends.[23]

A week later (2 June 1537), the Pope followed the previous declaration with a solemn Bull entitled *Sublimis Deus*, addressed to Christendom at large, forbidding absolutely the slavery of all Indians, even in regions not yet discovered:

> By our Apostolic Authority we decree and declare by these present letters that the same Indians and all other peoples—even though they are outside the faith—... should not be deprived of their liberty... Rather they are to be able to use and enjoy this liberty and this ownership of property freely and licitly, and are not to be reduced to slavery.[24]

The Spanish kings gave full support to the papal injunctions, notably with the 'New Laws' of 1542 which forbade slavery and added civil penalties to the ecclesiastical sanctions against the offenders. A sidelight of this collaboration between Spain and the Holy See to protect the natives is the contrary policy pursued in North America, except in Mexico and Spanish (or Portuguese) territories, where English colonizers lacked the restraining hands of the Church's legislation.

On 8 December 1864, two important documents touching on Church and State relations were issued at Rome: one, an Encyclical of Pius IX on naturalism and communism, and the other a Syllabus of errors. The Syllabus is a digest of errors condemned on various occasions by the Pope. It contains 80 propositions arranged under ten headings. Nearly half of the errors condemned by the Syllabus deal, at least implicitly, with the subject of Church and State. Among the false notions regarding the Church and her rights are found radical principles of liberalism, ultimately derived from Enlightenment ideas. One such error proposed: 'The Church is not a true and perfect society, enjoying full liberty, nor does she possess any permanent rights conferred exclusively upon her by her divine Founder. Rather, the civil power is to determine what are the Church's rights and the limitation within which these rights may be exercised.'[25] Furthermore, these liberal errors denied that the Church had an inherent and legitimate right to possess property.[26]

Following on from a denial of the Church's nature as a perfect society, modern liberals also refuse her rights to use the means she needs to fulfil the purpose of her existence, which is the sanctification and salvation of people. Among these, the most imperative is Christian education under the Church's auspices. One particular error stated: 'The civil authority can intervene in matters which pertain to religion, morals and spiritual discipline. Hence it can decide concerning the instructions which the clergy of the Church issue, as part of their duty, for the regulations of consciences.'[27] Consistent with the Protestant laicization of matrimony was a type of naturalism separating the marital contract and its responsibilities from ecclesiastical jurisdiction. Another error condemned in the Syllabus encourages civil divorce: 'The bond of matrimony is not indissoluble by the natural law, and in various cases the civil authority may grant divorces properly so-called.'[28]

The prophetic realism of the Papal Syllabus was seen in secularist France, once the principles of secularism had taken root. In 1880, compulsory Sunday rest was abolished. Even the money was secularized, and the motto *Dieu protégé la France* was removed from 5-franc pieces. A series of enactments named after their principal author, the *Lois Ferry,* secularized primary education during the period 1880–1886. By a law of 20 March 1880, the Jesuits were ordered to leave their residences within three months and their schools within five months. A second law required all religious congregations to apply for State authorization under pain of expulsion. In 1884 divorce was re-introduced. Prayers were discontinued at the opening of parliamentary sessions. The hospitals of Paris were laicized in 1885. In 1889, exemption of seminarians from military service was withdrawn. After a brief lull in the religious struggle, a new law of the Congregations was passed in 1901, which forced practically all religious orders and congregations of both sexes to leave France. It was this concept of 'separation' of Church and State which Blessed Pius IX condemned in the now famous 55th error of the Syllabus, that 'The Church should be separated from the State and the State from the Church.'[29]

As later Pontiffs were to explain, there is a type of separation which the Church does not deprecate absolutely, and is willing to accept with reservation, provided the basic rights of Catholic citizens are respected and the practice of their religion is not restrained. The phrase 'separation of Church and State' is derived from a letter written by Thomas Jefferson to a group identifying themselves as the Danbury Baptists. In that letter, quoting the First Amendment of the United States Constitution, he stated: 'I contemplate with sovereign reverence that act of the whole American people which declared that their legislature should make no law respecting an establishment of religion, or prohibiting the free exercise thereof, thus building a wall of separation between Church and State.'[30]

The extensive writings of Leo XIII on the relation of Church and State corroborate the foregoing traditional teaching of the Church, as seen in the foregoing survey, with one exception. By the end of the nineteenth century, non-Catholic governments became the rule in many countries of Europe and the two Americas, and created the logical need for some principles of action to guide Catholic citizens in their attitude towards the civil authorities. Circumstances differed widely, as between countries like France where the State was openly anti-Catholic and the United States where religious freedom was granted to all the people, with no preferential treatment to any group. Nevertheless, the basic issue was the same and substantially revolved around the Catholic attitude towards separation of Church and State.

The most radical concept of Church and State separation which Leo XIII had to combat was the French anti-clericalism previously denounced by Gregory XVI and Pius IX. Speaking of the 'vast conspiracy that certain men have formed for the annihilation of Christianity in France,' the Pope denounced their vaunted separation of Church and State as 'equivalent to the separation of human laws from Christian and divine legislation. [For] as soon as the State refuses to give to God what belongs to God, by a necessary consequent it refuses to give to citizens what they as men have a right to receive; since, whether agreeable or not, it cannot be denied that man's rights spring from his duty towards God... Therefore Catholics cannot be too careful in defending themselves against such a separation.'[31] This is more correctly a separation of the State from the Church, rather than *vice versa,* and implies an impossible dichotomy between secular and religious authority, as though it were possible to operate civil society with full justice to its citizens without a foundation in the moral law. Any separation built on this premise is a practical denial of the Church's right to existence and reduces her function to something less than useless. It is simply another name for political atheism.

The most elaborate exposition of Church and State relationship published by Leo XIII was his Encyclical, *Immortale Dei,* issued in 1885. This was a defence of traditional teaching and also a guide for handling current problems. He proposed the best situation, where States are governed by the principles of the Gospels, and by Christian philosophy.[32] He quoted as 'the immutable law' of religious history, the axiom of Ivo of Chartres, that 'when civil power and the priesthood are in agreement, the world is well governed and the Church flourishes and develops. But when they disagree, not only smaller interests suffer but even things of greatest moment fall into miserable decay.'[33] For centuries civil governments had been built on a Christian foundation with consequent benefits to themselves and posterity that only a prejudiced mind will deny. Then came the 'that harmful and deplorable passion for innovation which was aroused in the sixteenth century' and 'threw first of all into confusion the Christian religion, and next, by natural sequence, invaded the precincts of philosophy'.[34] This is the acknowledged source of modern apostasy from God or at least of indifference towards the true religion. The Church, wrote Pope Leo XIII, does not 'condemn those rulers who for the sake of securing some greater good, or of hindering some great evil, allow in practice that these various forms of religion have a place in the State. In fact, the Church is more careful not to have any one forced to embrace the Catholic faith against his will, for, as St Augustine wisely reminds us, "Man cannot believe except of his own free will."'[35]

In 1902, Pope Leo XIII wrote to congratulate the bishops of the United States on the steady growth of the Church in that country. He assigned three causes: the providence of God, the energy of the American people and the religious liberty which the country enjoys. In contrast with the sad 'changes and tendencies in nearly all nations that were Catholic for centuries, the state of your churches, in their flourishing vigour, gives Us great pleasure and joy to behold. True, you are shown no special favour by the civil government, but on the other hand your lawgivers are certainly entitled to praise because they do not restrain you in your just liberty.'[36]

The Church and State principles of Leo XIII were subsequently successfully embodied in the Constitution of the Irish Free State. Pope Leo's norms (sometimes *verbatim*) were incorporated into this document that is correct from the viewpoint of Catholic theology and yet sufficiently concessive to allow for freedom of worship and the belief of other religious bodies. The preamble of the Constitution is an unqualified profession of the Christian faith:

> In the Name of the Most Holy Trinity, from Whom is all authority and to Whom, as our final end, all actions both of men and State must be referred, We, the people of Eire, humbly acknowledging all our obligations to our Divine Lord Jesus Christ, Who sustained our fathers through centuries of trial, gratefully remembering their heroic and unremitting struggle to regain the rightful independence of our Nation... do hereby adopt, and give ourselves this Constitution.[37]

Specifically, the Christian concept of the family is fully recognized as 'the necessary basis of social order and is indispensable to the welfare of the Nation and the State.' Accordingly, 'the State recognizes that by her life within the home, woman gives to the State a support without which the common good cannot be achieved.'[38] The Constitution provides for the defence of marriage, decreeing that 'no law shall be enacted for the grant of a dissolution of marriage, (and) no person whose marriage has been dissolved under the civil law of any other State but is a subsisting valid marriage...shall be capable of contracting a valid marriage...during the lifetime of the other party to the marriage so dissolved.'[39] A most significant portion of the Irish Constitution deals with the status of the Catholic Church, along with other religious bodies within the juridical limits of the Irish Free State. On the one hand, 'the State recognizes the special position of the Holy Catholic Apostolic and Roman Church as the guardian of the faith professed by the great majority of the citizens.' However, 'the State also recognizes the Church of Ireland, the Presbyterian Church in Ireland, the Methodist Church in Ireland, and Religious Society of Friends in Ireland, as well as the Jewish Congregations and the other religious denominations existing in Ireland at the date of the coming into operation of this Constitution.' Nor shall the State 'impose any disabilities or make any discrimination on the ground of religious profession, belief or status'.[40]

In the twentieth century, some aspects of Church and State relations had evolved, and received corresponding attention in ecclesiastical circles. First, there was a need to stem the problems arising from a secularist separation of Church and State, exemplified in the French model at the turn of the century. The second need was a reemphasis of the divine limitation of State authority, in protest against the most tyrannical usurpation in human history in the wake of Nazism and Communism. The third issue was a clarification of the Church's attitude towards non-Catholics in a region where Catholics have a dominant voice in the civil government.

Pope St Pius X clearly spelt out the dangers of a secularist separation of Church and State in the context of the French model of the time:

> That the State must be separated from the Church is an absolutely false thesis, a most pernicious error. Based, as it is, on the principle that the State must not recognize any religious cult, it is in the first place guilty of a great injustice to God; for the Creator of man is also the Founder of human societies, and preserves their existence as He preserves our own. We owe Him, therefore, not only a private cult, but a public and social worship to honour Him. Besides, this thesis is an obvious negation of the

> supernatural order. It limits the action of the State to the pursuit of public prosperity during this life only, which is but the proximate object of political societies; and it occupies itself in no fashion (on the plea that this is foreign to it) with their ultimate object which is man's eternal happiness after this short life shall have run its course. But as the present order of things is temporary and subordinated to the conquest of man's supreme and absolute welfare, it follows that the civil power must not only place no obstacle in the way of this conquest, but must aid us in effecting it. The same thesis also upsets the order providentially established by God in the world, which demands a harmonious agreement between the two societies. Both of them, the civil and the religious society, although each exercises in its own sphere its authority over them. It follows necessarily that there are many things belonging to them in common in which both societies must have relations with one another. Remove the agreement between Church and State, and the result will be that from these common matters will spring the seeds of disputes which will become acute on both sides; it will become more difficult to see where the truth lies, and great confusion is certain to arise. Finally, this thesis inflicts great injury on society itself, for it cannot either prosper or last long when due place is not left for religion, which is the supreme rule and the sovereign mistress in all questions touching the rights and the duties of men.[41]

While Communist strategy against the Church has varied with local conditions, the general sequence is practically uniform: a violent hostility to the Holy See, with the Vatican invariably represented as an 'alien power' whose influence is inconsistent with the totalitarian concept of State sovereignty; then a tendency to discord local hierarchy by accusing it of various political crimes of subservience to the Vatican—hence the processes against Cardinal Mindszenty in Hungary, Cardinal Stepinac in Yugoslavia, the confinement of all Czechoslovak and some Polish bishops, the cruel persecution endured by Christians in Cuba and China; and finally, an effort to create pro-Communist currents among the clergy and the faithful, willing to cooperate with the regime, as in the creation of a sympathetic 'hierarchy'.

From the beginning of his pontificate and all through his reign, Pius XII solemnly protested against this inversion of the divine law. It is nothing short of blasphemy 'to divorce civil authority from every kind of dependence upon the Supreme Being, First Cause and Absolute Master of man and of society and from every restraint of a Higher Law derived from God as its primary Source'.[42] After the imprisonment of Cardinal Mindszenty, the Pope insisted on the Church's knowledge of her function. 'She does not meddle in problems purely political and economic, nor does she pass judgment on the usefulness or harm of one form of government or another.' However, a 'totalitarian and anti-religious state would be like a church silent when it should speak, a church that would weaken the law of God, adapting it to the desire of human wills... a church that does not resist oppression of the conscience and does not watch over the legitimate rights and the just liberty of the people.' Can the Pope be silent, 'when the rights of educating children are taken from the parents, when the State arrogates to itself the power of suppressing dioceses, of deposing bishops, when a priest is punished with imprisonment for not violating the seal of confession?... Is all this, perhaps, an illegitimate interference with the political powers of the State?'[43] It becomes interference only on the arrogant assumption that the State is bound by no law, human or divine, except its own arbitrary will; and when faced with a Church that demands respect for the rights of conscience, not to say its revealed commission from God, she becomes an enemy of society either to be forced into submission or crushed for insubordination.

In 1953, Pope Pius XII stated to a convention of Catholic jurists, that 'no human authority, no state, no community of nations can give a positive command to teach or do what is contrary to religious truth or moral good'.[44] The following year, he also stated firmly that even if Church and State were separated, the power of the Church cannot be restricted solely to the religious sphere, but touches on all the matters of the natural law.[45] The Pope also faced broader issue of religious liberty, declaring that, over the centuries, the Church's efforts to remain free of the civil power were 'always directed to safeguarding the freedom of religious convictions'. The stock objection is that the Church is interested in freedom of religion, but only for herself. This, protested the Pope, is not true. 'Let no one object that the Church scorns the personal convictions of those who do not think as she does… On the contrary, she believes that their convictions constitute a reason, though not always the principle one, for tolerance.' She would be unfaithful to the mandate of her Founder to 'hide the fact that on principle she considers collaboration [of Church and State] normal and regards unity of the people in the true religion and unanimity of action between herself and the State as an ideal'. This being granted, 'she also knows that for some time events have been developing in a different direction, namely, toward the multiplicity of beliefs and conceptions of life in the same national community'.[46]

Pope John Paul II, who had suffered directly under the totalitarian systems of the twentieth centuries, issued a timely warning about them. 'The root of modern totalitarianism' he remarked 'is to be found in the denial of the transcendent dignity of the human person who, as the visible image of the invisible God, is therefore by his very nature the subject of rights which no one may violate—no individual, group, class, nation or State. Not even the majority of a social body may violate these rights, by going against the minority, by isolating, oppressing, or exploiting it, or by attempting to annihilate it.' The Pope added that 'the culture and praxis of totalitarianism also involve a rejection of the Church. The State or the party which claims to be able to lead history towards perfect goodness, and which sets itself above all values, cannot tolerate the affirmation of an *objective criterion of good and evil* beyond the will of those in power, since such a criterion, in given circumstances, could be used to judge their actions. This explains why totalitarianism attempts to destroy the Church, or at least to reduce her to submission, making her an instrument of its own ideological apparatus.'[47]

The thought of Joseph Ratzinger, later Pope Benedict XVI merits special attention. Joseph Ratzinger proposed that Christ's words 'Render unto to Caesar what belongs to Caesar, and to God what belongs to God' (Mt 22:21) opened up a new era in the history of the relationship between politics and religion. Until then the general rule was that state was recognized as the bearer of a supreme sacrality. This equation of the state's claim on man with the sacral claim of the universal divine will was cut in two by the saying of Jesus. Ratzinger indicated that this separation of the authority of the state and sacral authority, the new dualism that this contains, represents the origin and the permanent foundation of the western idea of freedom. Henceforth, there are two societies related to each other but not identical with each other, neither of which have this character of totality. The state is no longer itself the bearer of a religious authority that reaches into the ultimate depths of conscience, but for its moral basis refers beyond itself to another community. This community in its turn, the Church, understands itself as a final moral authority which however depends on voluntary adherence and is entitled only to spiritual but not to civil penalties, precisely because it does not have the status the state has of being accepted by all as something given in advance. Thus each of these communities is circumscribed in its radius, and on the balance of this relation depends freedom. Where the Church itself becomes the state freedom becomes lost. However, when the Church is done away with as a public and publicly relevant authority, then too freedom is extinguished.[48]

In the face of the 'dictatorship of relativism' which threatens to obscure the unchanging truth about man's nature, his destiny and his ultimate good, Pope Benedict XVI has developed his thought on Church State relations.[49] He has insisted that the Church cannot be relegated to the private sphere:

> Religion, in other words, is not a problem for legislators to solve, but a vital contributor to the national conversation. In this light, I cannot but voice my concern at the increasing marginalization of religion, particularly of Christianity, that is taking place in some quarters, even in nations which place a great emphasis on tolerance. There are those who would advocate that the voice of religion be silenced, or at least relegated to the purely private sphere. There are those who argue that the public celebration of festivals such as Christmas should be discouraged, in the questionable belief that it might somehow offend those of other religions or none. And there are those who argue—paradoxically with the intention of eliminating discrimination—that Christians in public roles should be required at times to act against their conscience. These are worrying signs of a failure to appreciate not only the rights of believers to freedom of conscience and freedom of religion, but also the legitimate role of religion in the public square.[50]

Concerning different forms of political system, St Thomas Aquinas had taught that the best regime is one in which 'all are eligible to govern', and in which 'the rules are chosen by all'. Partial democracy is preferred since, 'in so far as the rulers can be chosen from the people, ...the people have the right to choose their rulers'.[51] Thus Aquinas advocated a mixed regime:

> The best form of government is in a state or kingdom, wherein one is given the power to preside over all; while under him are others having governing powers: and yet a government of this kind is shared by all, both because all are eligible to govern, and because the rules are chosen by all. For this is the best form of polity, being partly kingdom, since there

> is one at the head of all; partly aristocracy, in so far as a number of persons are set in authority; partly democracy, namely government by the people.[52]

Elsewhere, after describing what is meant by monarchy, aristocracy and democracy, St Thomas says, 'Finally, there is a form of government made up of all these, and which is the best.'[53]

The monarchy was classified by Pope Pius VI as the best form of government (*praestantioris monarchici regiminis forma*).[54] When speaking of the various types of government, Leo XIII made it quite clear that 'each of them is good, provided it lead straight to its end—that is to say, to the common good for which social authority is constituted; and finally, it may be added that, from a relative point of view, such and such a form of government may be preferable because of being better adapted to the character and customs of such or such a nation.'[55] In particular to be rejected is the revolutionary error of hostility against the monarchy and aristocracy, on the principle that they are essentially incompatible with human dignity and the normal order of things. This error was condemned by Pope Saint Pius X, when he censured the thesis of *Le Sillon*, that 'only democracy will inaugurate the reign of perfect justice', and he adds: 'Is this not an injury to the other forms of government, which are thus reduced to the category of impotent governments, acceptable only for lack of something better?'[56]

On the one hand, the Church values the democratic system inasmuch as it ensures the participation of citizens in making political choices, guarantees to the governed the possibility both of electing and holding accountable those who govern them, and of replacing them through peaceful means when appropriate. At the same time, as history demonstrates, 'a democracy without values easily turns into open or thinly disguised totalitarianism'.[57] It is precisely the cultural relativism existing today, evident in the conceptualization and defence of an ethical pluralism, which sanctions the decadence and disintegration of reason and the principles of the natural moral law. While some people say that such ethical pluralism is the very condition for democracy, in reality it brings about totalitarianism.[58]

The Catholic doctrine concerning Church and State which we have proposed clearly excludes the error of *antinomianism*, (from the Greek αντι, 'against' and νομος, 'law'). This is the false notion that Christians are exempt from the obligations of moral and civil law. For the antinomians the only source of authority to which Christians are ultimately answerable is God, embodied in the teachings of Jesus, and so government and sometimes established churches do not, or should not, have power over them or other people. The term was apparently coined by Luther to stigmatize Johannes Agricola and his followers, indicating an interpretation of the antithesis between law and gospel, recurrent from the earliest times. Anabaptists, Mennonites and Quakers have sometimes been accused of antinomianism.

Nevertheless, even in mainstream Christian tradition, a limit has been placed on civil government. Following St Paul's injunction that we must obey God rather than men (cf. Ac 5:29), citizens are obliged in conscience not to follow the directives of civil authorities when they are contrary to the demands of the moral order.[59] When citizens are under the oppression of a public authority which oversteps its competence, it is legitimate for them to defend their own rights and those of their fellow citizens against the abuse of this authority within the limits of the natural law and the Law of the Gospel.[60] Christian tradition maintains that, in an extreme case, armed resistance to oppression by political authority is only legitimate, if all the following conditions are met. First, that there is certain, grave, and prolonged violation of fundamental rights. Second, that all other means of redress have been exhausted. Third, that such resistance will not provoke worse disorders, and there is a well-founded hope of success. Fourth, that it is impossible reasonably to foresee any better solution.[61] The classic case is that of *tyrannicide*, or the killing of a tyrant, and specifically, the killing of a tyrant by a private person for the common good. Technically, there are two classes of tyrants: a tyrant by usurpation (*tyrannus in titulo*), a ruler who has illegitimately seized power; and a tyrant by oppression (*tyrannus in regimine*), a ruler who wields power unjustly, oppressively, and arbitrarily. Tyrannicide has had support from various philosophers and theologians through the centuries, including the ancient Greeks and Romans, most notably Cicero; from Catholics, most notably John of Salisbury (d. 1180) Jean Petit (d. 1411), and Suarez (d. 1617); and from Protestants, most notably, Luther, Melanchthon, Zwingli, and Calvin. St Thomas Aquinas gave the most substantial argument for tyrannicide, basing his position on his arguments for just war and capital punishment, and: 'He who kills a tyrant (i.e. a usurper) to free his country is praised and rewarded.'[62]

Our conclusion is that the relation between Church and State should not be reduced to separation. If the practical solution of this relation in recent times in the West has often been expressed in this way, that does not mean that separation is an ideal but rather a *modus vivendi* for Catholics and other Christians living in a secular and pluralist State.[63] The Second Vatican Council is nuanced in its position for it affirms that 'the political community and the Church are autonomous and independent of each other in their own fields'.[64] However, these fields often meet and interact. Thus, this secular and pluralist State cannot be exalted as an ideal, for many reasons. First, a State can never be neutral towards the Christian Faith; it is either essentially in favour or against. For the Lord Himself has said: 'Anyone who is not with me is against me, and anyone who does not gather in with me throws away' (Mt 12:30). Jesus also remarked: 'Anyone who is not against us is for us' (Mk 9:40). Therefore, neutrality to Christ and His Church is not possible. Next, in practice the secular State never fully respects the natural law, composed as it is of politicians and legislators who are fallen. Third, the secular State is either totalitarian or pluralistic. If it is totalitarian, it oppresses its people; if it is pluralistic, it is a contradiction, because it is an attempt to reconcile the irreconcilable. A further problem with those theological currents which uphold a secular State separate from the Church and opposed to her, is the whole concept of the secular. Those theologians often forget what the Second Vatican Council affirmed, namely that 'even in secular affairs there is no human activity which can be withdrawn from God's dominion'.[65] The same Council held high the ideal of ceaselessly and efficaciously seeking for the return of all humanity and all its goods under Christ the Head in the unity of His Spirit.[66] Moreover, Vatican II also condemned and rejected that 'ominous doctrine which attempts to build a society with no regard whatever for religion, and which attacks and destroys the religious liberty of its citizens'.[67]

What can be accepted in the concept of the secular State is the technical competence of those who manage the political and economic apparatus, which is a discipline separate from theology, but which should nevertheless be guided by those human and ethical principles which are enlightened by natural law and by Divine Revelation. Separation is never a real good, because it brings about a division within the human person and within society. Instead, just as a scientist can be both a scientist and a Catholic, and the two aspects of life are united in his one person, so also the politician who is a Christian will live his or her life as a unity; any other approach bespeaks schizophrenia.

The Church and Science

There are various ways of conceiving the relation between science and religion. The first is that of conflict, espoused for example by secularism which maintains that the Church is opposed to science as exemplified in the Galileo affair. Under this position falls that of scientific materialism on the one hand, and biblical fundamentalism on the other. A second type of relation is that of identity, where one sphere is subsumed into the other: this does not respect the specificity of either science or faith. A third approach is that of independence, whereby science and theology can be considered as separate domains, or different languages and functions, but without real contact. A fourth way proposes dialogue, involving frontier issues like the beginning of the universe, or the meaning of design. In a fifth model, some thinkers also conceive of the relations between science and faith in terms of integration, adopting natural theology, the theology of nature or else a systematic synthesis. In any case, harmony between faith and science preceded discord.

Inherent in the Christian doctrine of creation is the belief that God freely chose to create the universe. He was not in any way constrained either to create or not to create it in the way that He did. It is therefore not a necessary universe in the sense that it had to be created or could not have been created otherwise. There is therefore no possibility of investigating the universe by pure thought or by *a priori* reasoning. We can only hope to understand it by studying it and by making experiments. Thus the mindset of the Christian doctrine of creation encouraged the experimental method, essential for the development of science. All ancient cultures held a cyclic view of the world, and this was one of the beliefs that hindered the development of science. This cyclic pessimism was decisively broken by the belief in the unique Incarnation of Christ; thereafter time and history were seen as linear, with a beginning and an end.

The two characteristics of the Western intellectual tradition that make science possible are the insistence on logical coherence and experimental verification. These are already present in a qualitative way among the Greeks, and the vital contribution of the Middle Ages was to refine these conditions into a more effective union. This was done principally by insisting on the quantitative precision that can be attained by using mathematics in the formulation of the theories, and then verifying them not by observation alone, but by precise measurements.

That science suffered stillbirths in many cultures and that these stillbirths can be linked with world-pictures inadequate for the stimulation of scientific growth implies that, since science is now a self-sustaining enterprise, the conditions for its growth must be found in the relatively recent past. In fact, the period of the viable birth of science can be regarded as 1250–1650 in Europe. Pierre Duhem's monumental work, *Le système du monde*, first showed the medieval period was not a dark age for science but rather its very cradle.[68] The accepted view had been, for three hundred years prior to Duhem, that the Renaissance was the important period for the rise of modern science. This derived 'partly from the reformer's scorn for medieval Catholicism and partly from the hostility of the leaders of the French Enlightenment to anything Christian'.[69] Instead, it is emphatically not 'a freak happening of history that science was born in a Europe that was living through its centuries of faith'.[70]

Stanley Jaki explains how the idea of the beginning of the cosmos, which is so much part of Christian tradition, stands in sharp contrast to the scene outside of Christianity where many world religions and world-pictures had great difficulty in maintaining that the world actually began. Even for many people today, the world is eternal in the sense that it simply *is*.[71] The world was often regarded as eternal in seven principal ancient cultures: Chinese, Hindu, Meso-American, Egyptian, Babylonian, Greek and Arabic.[72] From the cosmic imprisonment represented by all these world pictures, Christianity was to bring liberation. For in the Christian vision, time is linear, and each moment is unique and irreversible. This simple truth is anchored in the doctrine that Christ died once and for all, as St Augustine poignantly taught.[73] The doctrine of creation with time is the pivot upon which hang all the other articles of the Christian creed:

> Whenever the meaning of creation in time is weakened, let alone eliminated, the meaning of all other tenets of the Christian creed become weakened or eliminated. Those tenets—Fall, Incarnation, redemption, the growth of the Kingdom of God,

> eschatology, final judgement—presuppose not only creation but also a creation in time because all those tenets refer to events in time which alone can constitute that sequence which is salvation history.[74]

It is indeed from Christian faith that one acquires an understanding of the beginning of the universe, for 'physics in no way contains a proof of the temporal beginning of the universe. The method of physics always means an inference from one observable state to another.'[75]

A fundamental historical question is why science only came to its viable birth during the high Middle Ages. Modern experimental science was rendered possible as a result of the Christian philosophical atmosphere of that period, fostered by the Church. Although a talent for science was certainly present in the ancient world (for example in the design and construction of the Egyptian pyramids), nevertheless the philosophical and psychological climate was hostile to a self-sustaining scientific process. Thus science suffered stillbirths in the cultures of ancient China, India, Egypt, Babylonia. It also failed to come to fruition among the Maya, Incas, and Aztecs of the pre-Columbian Americas. Even though ancient Greece came closer to achieving a continuous scientific enterprise than any other ancient culture, science was not born there either. Science did not come to birth among the medieval Muslim heirs to Aristotle. These stillbirths in science can be linked with the doctrine concerning original sin.[76] The weakening of the intellect was the cause of false visions of the cosmos, involving eternal cycles and a necessary universe. The psychological climate of such ancient cultures was often either hopelessness or complacency, and in either case there was a failure to arrive at a belief in the existence of God the Creator, and an inability to produce a self-sustaining scientific enterprise.[77]

If science suffered only stillbirths in ancient cultures, this implies that it arrived more recently at its unique viable birth. The beginning of science as a fully fledged enterprise can be said to have taken place in relation to two important definitions of the Magisterium of the Church. The first was the definition at the Fourth Lateran Council, in the year 1215, that the universe was created out of nothing at the beginning of time. The second magisterial statement was at local level, enunciated by Bishop Stephen Tempier of Paris who, on 7 March 1277 condemned 219 Aristotelian propositions, so outlawing the deterministic and necessitarian views of the creation. These statements of the teaching authority of the Church expressed an atmosphere in which faith in God the Creator had penetrated the medieval culture and given rise to philosophical consequences. The cosmos was seen as contingent in its *existence* and thus dependent on a divine choice which called it into being; the universe is also contingent in its *nature* and so God was free to create this particular form of world among an infinity of other possibilities. Thus the cosmos cannot be a necessary form of existence and so has to be approached by *a posteriori* investigation. The universe is also rational and so a coherent discourse can be made about it. Indeed the contingency and rationality of the cosmos are like two pillars supporting the Christian vision of the cosmos:

> The contingency of the universe obviates an *a priori* discourse about it, while its rationality makes it accessible to the mind though only in an *a posteriori* manner...; the rise of science needed the broad and persistent sharing by the whole population, that is, an entire culture, of a very specific body of doctrines relating the universe to a universal and absolute intelligibility embodied in the tenet about a personal God, the Creator of all.[78]

Therefore it was not chance that the first physicist was John Buridan, professor at the Sorbonne around the year 1330, just after the time of the two above-mentioned statements of the Church's teaching office. Buridan's vision of the universe was steeped in the Christian doctrine of the creation; in particular, he rejected the Aristotelian idea of a cosmos existing from all eternity. He developed the idea of impetus in which God was seen as responsible for the initial setting in motion of heavenly bodies, which then remained in motion without the necessity of a direct action on the part of God. This was different from Aristotle's approach, in which the motion of heavenly bodies had no beginning and would also have no end. Buridan's work was continued by his disciple, Nicholas Oresme, around the year 1370; impetus theory anticipated Newton's first law of motion.[79]

The doctrine that God created the universe out of nothing and that the universe had a beginning was later to be reiterated at the First Vatican Council, against the errors of materialism and pantheism which enjoyed a new vogue at that time. In addition, Vatican I stated the absolute freedom of God to create, and made clear, against fideism, the possibility of arriving at God's existence through a rational reflection upon creation. As Jaki states: 'The council, in line with a tradition almost two millennia old, could but insist on the very foundation of that relation which is man's ability to see the reasonability of revelation, which in turn is inconceivable if man is not able to infer from the world surrounding him the existence of its Creator.'[80] Natural theology is crucial as 'the highest and deepest form of the exercise of a mind which, precisely because it knows truth, can be known to reflect, however modestly, the infinite rationality of an absolutely truthful God.'[81] It is precisely the inability of many scientists to trace the grandeur of the Creator in His works that leads to an antiscientific ideology, from the atheistic posturings of R. Dawkins in the biological sphere to those of S. Hawking in cosmology. The best way to unmask the thought of non-believing scientists is to show how the basis for their reasoning cannot be proven scientifically. In an unjustified way they leave the realm of their own scientific disciplines and make *a priori* philosophical deductions against Christian belief. One example of this is the pervasive chance or chaos ideology used to 'explain' the coming into being of the material universe, of life and of the human person.[82]

In the Middle Ages, ideas about the created universe had developed which were greatly conducive to scientific enterprise. The philosophical vision of the Christian Middle Ages perceived the cosmos as demythologized, free from the capricious whims of pantheistic voluntarism reified in pagan deities. This world vision included the idea that the cosmos is good, and therefore attractive to study. Also the universe was considered to be single entity with inner coherence and order, and not a gigantic animal which would behave in an arbitrary fashion, as was often believed in antiquity. The unity of the universe offers a challenge to investigators to search for the connections in nature and make them explicit. Further, the cosmos was seen to be rational and consistent, so that what was investigated one day would also hold true the next. This encouraged repetition and verification of experiments. The world picture also involved the tenet that cosmic order is accessible to the human mind, and needs to be investigated experimentally, not just by pure thought. The world was considered to be endowed with its own laws which could be tested and verified; it was not magical or divine. In addition to these ideas, medieval Christendom also was imbued with the concept that it was worthwhile to share knowledge for the common good. Finally the cosmos was seen as beautiful, and therefore investigation of it gave a participation in such beauty which elevated the mind and heart of the believing scientist to the Creator.

During this fertile medieval period of scientific growth, there was a harmonious relationship between science and Christianity, and indeed many of the earliest scientists were devout believers. Pope Sylvester II (950–1003), born Gerbert d'Aurillac, was a prolific scholar of the tenth century. He introduced Arab knowledge of arithmetic and astronomy to Europe. Gerbert, as a scientist, was said to be way ahead of his time. He wrote a series of works dealing with matters of the quadrivium. He had learned the non-zero Hindu-Arabic digits in Spain, and could do calculations in his head that were extremely difficult for people thinking in terms of the Roman numerals. In Rheims, he constructed a hydraulic organ that excelled all previously known instruments, where the air had to be pumped manually. Gerbert reintroduced the abacus into Europe, and in a letter of 984, he asked Lupitus of Barcelona for a translation of an Arabic astronomical treatise. Gerbert may have been the author of a description of the astrolabe that was edited by Hermannus Contractus some fifty years later.[83] St Hildegard of Bingen (1078–1179), was known for her pioneering work in the biological, medical and ecological areas. She used the curative powers of natural objects for healing, and wrote treatises about natural history and medicinal uses of plants, animals, trees and stones.

Another key medieval figure was Robert Grosseteste (1168–1253), who is regarded as the founder of experimental science in general. Grosseteste was a widely-read man who made extensive contributions to many areas of human knowledge. He was one of the first Chancellors of the University of Oxford, and did much to establish the nascent university. He was also Bishop of Lincoln, the diocese in which Oxford used to be situated. His work on experimental science owed much to Plato, who taught that the pure forms behind the appearances of things are mathematical in nature; thus our theories must be themselves mathematical, and so the results of our measurements must be expressed in numbers. Grosseteste elaborated his theory of the scientific method in some detail, though he did not himself carry out many experiments. He recommended the method of analysis and synthesis; namely that the problem is first resolved into its simplest parts and when these are understood the results can be combined to give the explanation of the whole. The observations and experiments may themselves suggest hypotheses and then theories, and these in turn may be verified or disproved by comparison with further observations and measurements. He first applied his method to the phenomena of light. He believed that light is the most fundamental form, the first principle of motion, so that the laws of light must lie at the basis of scientific explanation. God created light, and from that all things came. Light itself follows geometrical rules, in the way it is propagated, reflected and refracted, and is the means whereby higher bodies act on lower. Motion is therefore also geometrical. He studied the rainbow and his criticisms of the formulations of Aristotle and Seneca were useful steps along the road to an adequate explanation. For all his emphasis on mathematics, he was clear that mathematical entities have no objective reality; they are simply abstractions from material bodies. Implicit in the work of Grosseteste and others is the insistence on quantitative measurement, and this in turn derives from the Biblical insistence on the rationality of the Creator, who disposed everything in number, weight and measure (cfr. Ws 11:20). Saint Albert the Great (1206–1280), also criticized Aristotle on some crucial ideas, and was renowned for his investigations in the natural sciences; he was an authority on physics, geography, astronomy, mineralogy, chemistry, zoology and physiology.

Other unknown early scientists worked on such areas as the development of clocks. Before the rise of science, human activity followed biological time and solar time, regulated by the natural succession of night and day. In contrast scientific time requires high numerical accuracy. Monasteries needed to have a way of measuring time with reasonable accuracy so as to regularize the hours of prayer, work and study and while they followed biological time at first, gradually they developed sand and water clocks. By the twelfth century, highly sophisticated mechanical clocks had been built, and these produced a profound effect on civil society as well. At the heart of all scientific activity lies the measurement of time.

Even after the Middle Ages, many scientists were convinced members of the Church. One example is Niels Stensen (1638–1686), a convert to Catholicism, and later a bishop, who was a pioneer in several sciences. During the early 1660s, at the University of Leiden, he distinguished glands from the lymph nodes according to their function, and found a series of glands furnishing fluid to each of the body cavities. Stensen discovered hitherto unknown glands in the nose and the mouth, and also identified passages, known as the Stenonian ducts running between the nose and the palate. Another particular area of interest concerned solid objects enclosed in other solid objects, namely shells and fossils, crystals and minerals. He made original discoveries regarding crystal growth, and the laws which govern crystallography, leading to the formulation of *Steno's law of constant angles,* which states that the angles between corresponding faces on crystals are the same for all specimens of the same mineral. Niels Stensen was beatified by Pope John Paul II on 23rd October 1988.

The Galileo affair, which took place after science had been born in a Christian setting, is sometimes used to obscure the many examples of harmonious and fruitful collaboration between the Church and science. Many books, even written by non-Catholics, now concede that the Galileo affair cannot be reduced to 'the standard caricature of the merely-blinkered Church against the noble scientist'.[84] In fact, Galileo himself was an example of a devout Christian and a great scientist. Moreover, even in the Galileo case 'the agreements between religion and science are more numerous and above all more important than the incomprehension which led to the bitter and painful conflict that continued in the course of the following centuries'.[85] It is true that in the Galileo affair, as in other misunderstandings, a healing of memories is needed. What can be learned from the Galileo situation is the necessity to delineate with increasing clarity the respective fields of competence, methods and value of the conclusions of science and theology, according to their respective nature. In particular, the Holy Scriptures do not teach us scientific details about the physical world but rather the fact that it was created.[86]

Church authorities have often expressed the essential and basic harmony between science and religion. Over one hundred years ago, the First Vatican Council put it this way: 'Truth cannot contradict truth.'[87] In 1936, Pope Pius XI enunciated what must be the first principle of relations between science and religion when he wrote 'science as a true understanding of reality can never contradict the truths of the Christian faith'.[88] At the Second Vatican Council, some basic principles of the relations between the Church and science were enunciated:

> Therefore if methodical investigation within every branch of learning is carried out in a genuinely scientific manner and in accord with moral norms, it never truly conflicts with faith, for earthly matters and the concerns of faith derive from the same God. Indeed whoever labours to penetrate the secrets of reality with a humble and steady mind, even though he is unaware of the fact, is nevertheless being led by the hand of God, who holds all things in existence, and gives them their identity.[89]

Some years later, at the celebration of the fiftieth anniversary of the Pontifical Academy of Sciences, Pope John Paul II stated that 'there is no contradiction between science and religion'.[90]

While science and religion enjoy their own fields of competence, there can be fruitful collaboration between them. Scientific discovery uncovers more and more of the material cosmos, both in the realm of the very small atomic world and the very large astrophysical universe. More and more can be seen and is understood in the biological sphere. The complexity, beauty and intricacy of the universe thus unveiled are a stimulus towards adoration of the Creator who made this cosmos, and who guides it in His Providence. Scientific progress has helped to exorcise superstition, another service for which religion is grateful. At the same time, religion can assist science not to close its eyes to a larger canvas. At this present time, it can guide scientists and technologists to use their discoveries for the real good of mankind. Such guidance is needed so that the right decisions are made regarding the applications of advances in genetics, and other matters which touch the beginning and end of human life, so that the immense value of human life is always respected and never manipulated or damaged. Religion can assist in the sharing of scientific progress with all sectors of the community, especially with those who are less fortunate. Science and technology have brought untold benefits to mankind, for which we should be thankful and which we must use for the best. In Christ's words: 'When someone is given a great deal, a great deal will be demanded of that person; when someone is entrusted with a great deal, of that person even more will be expected' (Lk 12:48). Much has been entrusted to humanity through scientific growth, and thus more will be expected in loving response to the Creator.

The effect of faith on Christian culture is a clear way in which the Church and science are related. If not understood correctly, the specifically European nature of the cultural matrix discussed, might seem to imply the superiority of European culture. In fact, the cultural matrix in which science came to birth depended much more upon the Gospel than on a Europe which had to shed its pagan ways and superstitions which would have been detrimental to scientific progress. There is a tendency to forget how Europe was radically changed by the power of the Christian mystery. Of course, the European cultural matrix in which science was born cannot be considered in isolation, as Arabic learning formed part of the inherited corpus of European science. All cultures (including that of Europe) must lose something in the encounter with Christian Revelation, but the gain is infinitely greater. By analogy with the individual who converts to the Christian faith and may have to renounce some of his old pagan ways if these are in discord with the Gospel, so also cultures have to shed their bondage to what contradicts the Christian faith, but in doing so will embrace a progress which is both human and divine. Clearly, those elements in a culture which are consistent with the Gospel will be kept and perfected. Thus, in Europe, the Greek thought of Aristotle was Christianised: some elements were corrected, some were perfected, and this process was influential in the formation of the cradle of science, which the Church nurtured.

The impact of the Church's faith upon culture is especially illustrated in the one viable birth of science. Faith, although primarily connected with eternal life has a real effect on the here and now. This vision has its basis in the scriptures where Christ says to His followers that setting their hearts first on God's Kingdom will have beneficial effects not only in heaven, but also here upon earth: 'Set your hearts on His Kingdom first, and on His righteousness and all these other things will be yours as well' (Mt 6:33). The followers of Christ are promised something of a reward in this life (despite persecutions) as well as a reward in the life to come: 'And everyone who has left houses, brothers, sisters, father, mother, children or land for the sake of My Name will be repaid a hundred times over and also inherit eternal life' (Mt 19:29).[91] This conversion to Christianity has had material as well as spiritual effects, for 'even in the secular history of mankind the Gospel has acted as a leaven in the interests of liberty and progress'.[92] Thus Christian faith, although primarily connected with eternal life, has a real effect on the here and now. One specific 'reward' which Christian faith in God the Creator has brought about is a reinforcement of the realist vision of the universe which was germane to the unique rise of science. The healing power of Christ has changed human society for the better, and scientific progress is but one example of the advance in human culture, as a fruit of divine Providence. In the course of history many scientists were devout Christians, and not agnostics or atheists as the secular media would have one believe.[93]

Nevertheless, there are those who would claim that the scientific progress stimulated by Christianity has in fact brought in its wake many problems and much evil.[94] If Christianity is responsible for the unique birth of science, is it not also to be blamed for the technological ills which beset the world of today? A distinction needs to be made here between scientific discovery and its technological application. Now the reason why there is a moral crisis concerning technological application of various products of science (for example, discoveries in nuclear physics and in bio-engineering) is that while the philosophical framework conducive to scientific discovery has been handed on as an implicit (and often subconscious) body of principles, nevertheless because Western society is no longer (in many parts) explicitly Christian, it lacks the courage and the apparatus to tackle such moral questions. The application of science therefore rests upon purely political or economic criteria which can only be described as utilitarian, without proper regard for the good of the human person and his environment.

A few vaguely Christian ideals have therefore been inherited by a secularized and secularizing society where there is a lack of radical Christian culture and vision to back up the vague ideals. Agnostics feel frustrated because they are unable to link up the implicit cultural principles with a synthetic Christian vision, and some Christians feel inadequate because they do not see the way forward very clearly. Progress lies in seeing that since science grew up in a Christian milieu, its applications were, at first, put to use according to a Christian ethic arising from Christian faith in God the Creator who had left these moral laws imprinted upon creation. It is of course true that man has the power to read the natural law written upon his heart, even aside from Revelation, but because of the Fall, the will of man is adversely affected in making moral decisions. Furthermore, Revelation does not merely reinforce the natural law, but shows a more perfect way. Christ reveals to mankind perfect Man as well as true God; through the Incarnation and Redemption, grace is given to guide man towards this ideal revealed by and in Christ. Hence the need for a specifically Christian morality to provide criteria which guide mankind away from purely greedy or destructive applications of science. Since they do not contain their own explanation within their own fields, science, language and history all need to be referred to metaphysics, before any dialogue between faith and science can be made or before any consistent ethical discourse can be pursued.

Even if one holds the thesis that modern science came to birth as a result of the effect on culture of Christian belief in God the Creator, one can hold this as a *strong* or a *weak* position.[95] The *strong* approach makes belief in God the Creator the key condition for the viable birth of science. The *weak* position would maintain that belief in God the Creator may not have been a necessary condition, but was indirectly responsible for aiding the rise of science among a number of other factors. Against the weak position, which maintains that social, political and economic factors were also responsible for the rise of science, the holder of the strong position could still argue that all these other factors were themselves a function of Christian belief. The strong position seems to me very much more in keeping with the scriptural notion of God Who acts in history in a personal way and Who has become incarnate. Those who stress too strong an autonomy for history and creation risk deism or a mechanistic relation between God and the cosmos.

Also in the ecological sphere, the Church has been a pioneer in the promotion of a balanced care for the environment.[96] The conclusion here is that since the Church has had such an important role in generating modern science and in helping the modern state to evolve, both realities as well as other temporal structures can only be considered in an intimate relation with the same Church. However, only by viewing these earthly realities in the light of the Kingdom can their true value be appreciated. The relation between the Church and the Kingdom will form the subject of the next and final chapter.

Notes

1. Vatican II, *Gaudium et Spes*.
2. *Ibid.*, 36.
3. Secondary causality is a way of expressing that the creature has an active part in producing its proper actions. Accordingly God communicated His goodness to His creatures in such a way that one being can communicate to

another the good it has received. The entire order of secondary causes, as well as their power, comes from God. See St Thomas Aquinas, *Summa Contra Gentiles,* Book 3a, Chapters 69–71. See also, Idem, *Compendium of Theology,* part I, Chapter 136.

4. See Pope John Paul II, *Discourse to the Congress promoted by the Vatican Observatory on the occasion of the tercentenary of Newton's Principia* (26 September 1987) in *OR* 127/231 (27 September 1987), p. 5: 'l'uomo è creato *uno* nelle sue diverse facoltà di conoscere il reale: siano esse analitiche o sintetiche, induttive o deduttive, sperimentale o intuitive.'
5. A. Noyes, *The Torch–Bearers,* Vol. 3, *The Last Voyage* (Edinburgh & London: William Blackwood and Sons, 1930), pp. 70–71.
6. Vatican II, *Gaudium et Spes,* 36.
7. C. Plinius Secundus Minor, *Epistola ad Trajanum,* n.96. See also J. Hardon, manuscript *Christ to Catholicism,* chapter XII 'Principles of Church and State in Historical Perspective' which provided material for some of the following points.
8. Tertullian, *Apologeticus adversus gentes pro christianis,* chapter 2, 1 and 3; chapter 30, 1; chapter 31, 1–2 in *CCL* 1, 87; 1, 141–142.
9. *Edict of Milan* in Lactantius, *De Mortibus Persecutorum,* in *PL* 7, 267–270.
10. *Ibid.*
11. T. Mommsen, *Codex Theodosianus* (Berlin: 1905), Vol. I, part 2, p. 833.
12. Valentinian III, *Novella 17* (July 8, 445), in *PL* 54, 636–637.
13. Pope Gelasius I, *Epistula ad Anastasium,* in *PL* 56, 633.
14. Pope St Gregory VII, in P. Jaffe (ed), *Monumenta Gregoriana* (Berlin: 1865), p. 223, (sentence dated Feb.22, 1076).
15. *Ibid.,* p. 401 (sentence dated 7 March 1080).
16. The Bull was mentioned in another context in chapter seven, pp. 193–194 above.
17. Pope Boniface VIII, Bull *Unam Sanctam* (18 November 1302) in DS 873.
18. Text found in H. Finke, *Aus den Tagen Bonifaz VIII* (Münster: 1902), p. 156. The spurious phrase was: 'We wish you (the king) to know that you hold your kingdom from Us,' adding that anyone who denied the proposition was a heretic.

19. J. Ratzinger, 'The Spiritual Roots of Europe: Yesterday, Today, and Tomorrow' in M. Pera & J. Ratzinger, *Without Roots. Europe, Relativism, Christianity, Islam.* See also E. von Ivanka, *Rhomäerreich und Gottesvolk* (Freiburg-Munich: K. Alber, 1968).
20. M. Luther, *Open Letter to the Christian Nobility of the German Nation*, I, in *Dr. Martin Luthers Werke*, vol. 6 (Weimar: Hermann Boehlaus Nachfolger, 1909), pp. 405–415.
21. Council of Trent, Session XXIII, Doctrine concerning the Sacrament of Orders, *Canons on the Sacrament of Orders*, 3, 4 and 7 in DS 1773, 1774, 1777.
22. J. Dewey, *Characters and Events* (London: Allen & Unwin, 1929), volume II, pp. 507–508.
23. Pope Paul III, Brief *Pastorale Officium* as found in C. Mirbt, *Quellen Zur Geschichte des Papstums* (Tubingen: Mohr, 1901), p. 270.
24. Pope Paul III, Bull *Sublimis Deus*, in J. S. Panzer, *The Popes and Slavery* (New York: Alba House, 1996), pp. 79–81.
25. Pope Bl Pius IX, *Syllabus*, 19 in DS 2919.
26. Pope Bl Pius IX, *Syllabus*, 26 in DS 2926.
27. Pope Bl Pius IX, *Syllabus*, 44 in DS 2944.
28. Pope Bl Pius IX, *Syllabus*, 67 in DS 2967.
29. Pope Bl Pius IX, *Syllabus*, 55 in DS 2955.
30. T. Jefferson, *Letter to the Danbury Baptists* (1 January 1802), as found in the US Library of Congress.
31. Pope Leo XIII, Encyclical Letter *Au Milieu des Sollicitudes*, 28.
32. Leo XIII, Encyclical *Immortale Dei* (1 Nov 1885), 2, 3.
33. Leo XIII, Encyclical *Immortale Dei*, 22. See Ivo of Chartres, *Letter 238 to Pope Paschal II*, in *PL* 162, 246.
34. Leo XIII, Encyclical *Immortale Dei*, 23.
35. *Ibid.*, 36.
36. Leo XIII, *Letter to the American Bishops* (15 Apr 1902), in *Acta Sanctae Sedis*, vol. XXIV.
37. *The Constitution of Eire* (Adopted 29 December 1937), (Dublin: Government Publication Office, 1945), preamble.
38. *Ibid.*, Article 41, section 2, n. 1.
39. *Ibid.*, Article 41, section 3, nn. 2–3.

40. *Ibid.*, Article 44, section 1, nn. 2–3.
41. Pope St Pius X, Encyclical *Vehementer Nos* (11 February 1906), 3.
42. Pope Pius XII, Encyclical *Summi Pontificatus* (Oct. 20, 1939), 52.
43. Pope Pius XII, *Discourse* as found in *L'Osservatore Romano* (21 February 1949).
44. Pope Pius XII, *Discourse to a convention of Catholic jurists,* in *L'Osservatore Romano* (7 December 1953).
45. Pope Pius XII, *Allocution to the Sacred College and to the Bishops* (2 November 1954) in *AAS* 46 (1954), p. 671.
46. Pope Pius XII, *Discourse at the International Congress of Historical Studies,* in *L'Osservatore Romano,* (8 September 1955).
47. Pope John Paul II, Encyclical Letter *Centesimus Annus,* 44, 45.
48. Cf. J. Ratzinger, *Church, Ecumenism and Politics: New Essays in Ecclesiology* (NY: Crossroad, 1988), pp. 160-162.
49. For the idea of the 'dictatorship of relativism' see, for example Pope Benedict XVI, *Homily at Bellahouston Park, Glasgow* (16 September 2010).
50. Pope Benedict XVI, *Address to the representatives of British society, Westminster Hall,* (17 September 2010).
51. St Thomas Aquinas, *Summa Theologiae,* I–II, q. 105, a. 1.
52. *Ibid.*
53. St Thomas Aquinas, *Summa Theologiae,* I–II, q. 95, a. 4. Aquinas also lists oligarchy (government by a few rich and powerful men), as one form of government.
54. Pope Pius VI, *Allocution to the Consistory of June 17, 1793* in *La Paix Intérieure des nations,* Enseignements pontificaux, présentation et tables par les moines de Solesmes (Paris: Desclee & Cie, 1962), p. 8.
55. Pope Leo XIII, Encyclical *Au milieu des sollicitudes,* 14.
56. Pope St Pius X, *Notre charge apostolique* (25 August 1910 in *AAS* 2 (1910), p. 618.
57. Pope John Paul II, Encyclical Letter *Centesimus Annus,* 46.
58. Congregation for the Doctrine of the Faith, *Doctrinal Note on some questions regarding the participation of Catholics in political life* (24 November 2002), 2. Cf. Pope John Paul II, Encyclical

Letter *Centesimus annus,* 46; Encyclical Letter *Veritatis splendor,* 101; *Discourse to the Italian Parliament,* 5 (November 2002).

59. See *CCC* 2256.
60. See Vatican II, *Gaudium et Spes,* 74.5. Cf. also *CCC* 2242.
61. See *CCC* 2243.
62. St Thomas Aquinas, *In II Sententiarum,* d. 44, q. 2, a. 2: 'Ad quintum dicendum, quod tullius loquitur in casu illo quando aliquis dominium sibi per violentiam surripit, nolentibus subditis, vel etiam ad consensum coactis, et quando non est recursus ad superiorem, per quem judicium de invasore possit fieri: tunc enim qui ad liberationem patriae tyrannum occidit, laudatur, et praemium accipit.' A tyrant by usurpation has illegitimately seized power and, therefore, is a criminal. When there are no other means available of ridding the community of the tyrant, the community may kill him. According to St Thomas, the legitimate authority may condemn him to death using the normal course of law. However, if the normal course of law is not available (due to the actions of the tyrant), then the legitimate authority can proceed 'informally' to condemn the tyrant and even grant individuals a mandate to execute the tyrant. A private citizen who takes the life of a tyrant acts with public authority in the same way that a soldier does in war. The key conditions for a justifiable act of tyrannicide in this case include that the killing be necessary to end the usurpation and restore legitimate authority; that there is no higher authority available that is able and willing to depose the usurper; and that there is no probability that the tyrannicide will result in even greater evil than allowing the usurper to remain in power. A tyrant by oppression is one who has come to power legitimately, but rules unjustly, oppressively, and arbitrarily. Here the community must confront the tyrant, and if necessary, depose him, formally or informally, according to the course of law available. In most circumstances, a private citizen morally cannot kill a tyrant by oppression, because the tyrant came to power through a legitimate means and thereby the community must depose him. If the community does depose the tyrant, according to St Thomas, he becomes now a tyrant by usurpation and thereby may be eliminated by an act of justifiable tyrannicide in accord

with the above norms. However, if the tyrant by oppression attacks the citizen, jeopardizes the welfare of the community with the intent leading it to destruction or killing the citizens, or commits other evils, then a private citizen can morally commit an act of justifiable tyrannicide. Moreover, if because of the tyrant's rule, a nation cannot defend itself, is on the course of destruction, and has no lawful means to depose or to condemn the tyrant, then a citizen may commit an act of justifiable tyrannicide. Interestingly, many modern political philosophers would posit that a leader who abuses power and has become tyrannical *ipso facto* loses legitimacy and becomes an usurper.

63. See Benedict XVI, *Christmas Address to the Roman Curia* (22 December 2005), where he remarked how Vatican II sought 'to give a new definition to the relationship between the Church and the modern State that would make room impartially for citizens of various religions and ideologies, merely assuming responsibility for an orderly and tolerant coexistence among them and for the freedom to practise their own religion.'
64. Vatican II, *Gaudium et Spes*, 76.3.
65. Vatican II, *Lumen Gentium*, 36.
66. Cf. Vatican II, *Lumen Gentium*, 13.2.
67. Vatican II, *Lumen Gentium*, 36.
68. See P. Duhem, *Le système du monde. Histoire des doctrines cosmologiques de Platon à Copernic*. 10 vols. (Paris: Hermann, 1913–1959).
69. S. L. Jaki, 'On Whose Side is History?' in *National Review* (23 August 1985), pp. 43–44.
70. S. L. Jaki, 'The Role of Faith in Physics' in *Zygon* 2 (1967), p. 195.
71. One exponent of this present-day yet very ancient notion of an eternal self-sufficient universe is S. W. Hawking who in his *Brief History of Time* (London: Bantam Press, 1988), p. 141 states: 'if the universe is really completely self-contained, having no boundary or edge, it would have neither beginning nor end: it would simply be. What place, then, for a creator?'

72. See S. L. Jaki, *Science and Creation* (Edinburgh: Scottish Academic Press, 1974), chapters 1–6 and 9.
73. See St Augustine *The City of God* Book 12, Chapter 13 n.2 in *PL* 41, 362: 'For once Christ died for our sins; and rising from the dead, He dies no more. "Death has no more power over Him" (Rom 6:9).' Jaki cites this passage in *Science and Creation*, p. 179.
74. S. L. Jaki, 'From Scientific Cosmology to a Created Universe' in *Irish Astronomical Journal* 15 (1982), p. 259.
75. S. L. Jaki, *God and the Cosmologists* (Washington, D.C.: Regnery Gateway, 1989), p. 81.
76. See S. L. Jaki, *The Savior of Science* (Washington, D.C.: Regnery Gateway, 1988), pp. 21–22.
77. See *Ibid*, p. 42.
78. S. L. Jaki, *The Road of Science and the Ways to God* (Edinburgh: Scottish Academic Press, 1978), pp. 38, 33.
79. See Jaki, *The Savior of Science*, pp. 46–54.
80. S. L. Jaki, *Cosmos and Creator* (Edinburgh: Scottish Academic Press, 1980), pp. 84–85. See also Vatican I, *Dei Filius*, cap. 1, 'De Deo rerum omnium creatore,' in DS 3002 and cap. 2, 'De revelatione,' in DS 3004.
81. S. L. Jaki, *Bible and Science* (Front Royal, Va.: Christendom Press, 1996), p. 139.
82. S. L. Jaki, *The Purpose of It All* (Edinburgh: Scottish Academic Press, 1990); Idem, *Patterns and Principles and Other Essays* (Bryn Mawr, Pennsylvania: Intercollegiate Studies Institute, 1995).
83. See Gerbertus Auriliacensis, *De numerorum divisione* in *PL* 139, 85–92; Idem, *De geometria* in *PL* 139, 93–152; Idem, *De sphaerae construtione* in *PL* 139, 155–156. See also H. Pratt Lattin, *The peasant boy who became pope; story of Gerbert* (New York: H. Schuman, 1951); Idem, *The letters of Gerbert, with his papal privileges as Sylvester II*. Translated with an introduction by H. Pratt Lattin (New York: Columbia University Press, 1961).
84. C. Southgate et al, *God, Humanity and the Cosmos* (Harrisburg, Pa: Trinity Press International, 1999), p. 30.

85. Pope John Paul II, *Discourse to the Plenary Session of the Pontifical Academy of Sciences to commemorate the centenary of the birth of Albert Einstein*, (10 November 1979). Referring in a note to the life and works of Galileo, the Pastoral Constitution of Vatican II, *Gaudium et Spes*, 36.1 stated: 'We cannot but deplore certain attitudes (not unknown among Christians) deriving from a short-sighted view of the rightful autonomy of science; they have occasioned conflict and controversy and have misled many into opposing faith and science.'

86. See Pope John Paul II, *Discourse to the Plenary Session of the Pontifical Academy of Sciences*, (31 October 1992), paragraphs 6 and 12. In particular, the Pope cited the adage of Cardinal Baronius: 'Spiritui Sancto mentem fuisse nos docere quomodo ad caelum eatur, non quomodo caelum gradiatur.' (The Holy Spirit wishes to teach us how to go to heaven, but not how the heavens go).

87. Vatican I, Dogmatic Constitution *Dei Filius* on the Catholic Faith, chapter IV in *DS* 3017.

88. Pius XI, Motu Proprio *In multis solaciis* in *AAS* 28(1936), p. 421.

89. Vatican II, *Gaudium et Spes*, 36. Cf. Vatican I, *Dogmatic Constitution on the Catholic Faith*, Chapter III, in DS 3004–3005.

90. Pope John Paul II, *Discourse on the occasion of the Fiftieth Anniversary of the Pontifical Academy of Sciences*, 28 October 1986, 3.

91. Cf. Mk 10:29–30; Lk 18:29–30; 1 Tim 4:8. See also Vatican II, *Gaudium et Spes*, 38.2: 'Constituted Lord by His Resurrection and given all authority in heaven and on earth, Christ is now at work in the hearts of all men by the power of His Spirit; not only does He arouse in them a desire for the world to come but He quickens, purifies and strengthens the generous aspirations of mankind to make life more humane and conquer the earth for this purpose.'

92. Vatican II, *Ad Gentes Divinitus*, 8.

93. See K. A. Kneller, *Christianity and the Leaders of Modern Science. A Contribution to the History of Culture during the Nineteenth Century*, with an Introductory Essay by S. L. Jaki (Port Huron, MI: Real-View Books, 1995). This book dispels

the myth that scientists had abandoned religious convictions by the nineteenth century.

94. See, for example, the classic article of Lynn White which was the basis for a critique of Christianity by ecologists, who claimed that the Judaeo-Christian idea of man's sovereignty over nature brought about an aggressive abuse of the environment. L. White, 'The Historical Roots of Our Ecological Crisis' in *Science* 155 (1967), pp. 1203–1207.

95. This distinction is found in G. B. Deason in his article 'The Protestant Reformation and the Rise of Modern Science,' in *Scottish Journal of Theology* 38 (1985), p. 221. He uses the terms with respect to the Reformation and the rise of modern science; I am adopting them with regard to the medieval Christian matrix.

96. See P. Haffner, *Towards a Theology of the Environment* (Leominster: Gracewing, 2008).

9

The Church and the Kingdom

It is the kingdoms of the world that are to be raised to the Kingdom of God; not the Kingdom of God degraded to the level of the kingdoms of this world. If I sacrifice the perfect Divine Plan in one detail, I do not save the world; and I lose myself.

R. H. Benson, *Christ in the Church*

Old Testament prefiguration

The Kingdom of God is prefigured and prophesied in the Old Testament. After his victory over the Midianites, Gideon addressed these words to the Israelites living in the region of Shechem: 'The Lord must rule over you' (Jg 8:23). Two tendencies, monarchical and antimonarchical, characterize the period of Israel's formation as a politically united and established people. The prophet Samuel reconciled the demand for a profane monarchy with the prerogatives of God's absolute kingship. He anointed the kings given to Israel as a sign of their religious role, besides their political one. David was the king who symbolized this reconciliation of aspects and roles, and became the anointed *par excellence,* a figure of the future Messiah and King of the new people, Jesus Christ. The God of Israel is a King in the religious sense, even when those who rule the people in His name are the political heads. The idea of God as King and Lord of all, inasmuch as He is the Creator, appears in the historical and prophetic books of the Bible, as well as in the psalms. This transcendent and universal kingship was first expressed in the covenant with Israel: 'Therefore, if you hearken to my voice and keep my covenant, you shall be my special possession, dearer to me than all other people, though all the earth is mine. You shall be to Me a kingdom of priests, a holy nation' (Ex 19:5–6). Progressively, there was a growing hope in Israel for a messianic King, an ideal sovereign, about whom Isaiah writes that 'his dominion is vast and forever peaceful, from David's throne, and over his kingdom, which he confirms and sustains by judgment and justice, both now and forever' (Is 9:6).

After the exile and the Babylonian captivity, the vision of a 'messianic' king takes on even more clearly the sense of a direct kingship on God's part. Almost as if to overcome all the disappointments which the people experienced with their political sovereigns, Israel's hope, nourished by the prophets, turns toward a universal kingdom in which God Himself will be the King: 'The Lord shall become king over the whole earth; on that day the Lord shall be the only one, and His name the only one' (Zc 14:9). The eschatological dimension of God's kingdom is accentuated more and more as the time of Christ's coming approaches. In particular, the Book of Daniel emphasizes this aspect of the future age in the visions which it describes:

> As the visions during the night continued, I saw one like a son of man coming on the clouds of heaven; when he reached the Ancient One and was presented before him, he received dominion, glory and kingship; nations and peoples of every language serve him. His dominion is an everlasting dominion that shall not be taken away; his kingship shall not be destroyed. (Da 7:13–14)

The wisdom literature of the Old Testament also expresses the idea of Kingdom: 'The just... shall judge nations and rule over peoples, and the Lord shall be their King forever' (Ws 3:1, 8).[1]

New Testament fulfilment

Christ was foretold in the Old Covenant and awaited as the Messiah-King with Whom the Kingdom of God is identified. In the New Covenant, Christ identifies the Kingdom of God with His own Person and His own mission. He not only proclaims the fact that with Him the kingdom of God is in the world, but He teaches that one should give up everything which is humanly most valuable 'for the kingdom of God' (cf. Lk 18:29–30), and at another point, to leave all this 'for the sake of My name' (cf. Mt 19:29) or 'for My sake and for the sake of the Gospel' (Mk 10:29). The kingdom of God is thus identified with the kingdom of Christ. It is present in Him and is realized in Him. It passes from Him, on His own initiative, to the Church in the person of Peter and the apostles, and through them to all those who will believe in Him: 'I confer a kingdom on you, just as My Father has conferred one on Me' (Lk 22:29). It is a kingdom which consists in the spread of Christ Himself through the world, through human history, as a new life which comes from Him and is communicated to believers in virtue of the Holy Spirit, the Paraclete, whom He sends (cf. Jn 1:16; 7:38–39; 15:26; 16:7).

The messianic kingdom realized by Christ in the world is revealed and shows its precise and definitive meaning in the context of His Passion and Death on the Cross. During Christ's entrance into Jerusalem an event occurred, which He had planned and which Matthew presents as a fulfilment of a prophetic prediction made by Zechariah about the 'king who comes to you riding on an ass, and on a colt, the foal of a beast of burden' (Zech 9:9; Mt 21:5). In the prophet's mind, in Jesus' intention and in the evangelist's interpretation, the ass signifies meekness and humility. Jesus was the meek and humble King who entered the city of David, where He fulfilled the prophecies about the true messianic kingship by His own Sacrifice.

Various New Testament parables furnish pictures of the Kingdom. In chapter thirteen of St Matthew's Gospel, the

Christian is offered eight special images of the Kingdom and its growth in the world. First, the parable of the Sower, and the four sorts of soil (Mt 13:3–23). This illustrates the obstacles presented to the message of the Kingdom. The soil in which this seed is sown represents the hearts of men and women, which are differently qualified and disposed, and accordingly the success of the Word is different. The second example is the parable of the Wheat and the Weeds (Mt 13:24–43). This indicates there would be a mixture of good and bad in the Kingdom on earth, in the Church on earth, true and false prophets, which would continue till the great separation between them on the Day of Judgment. The parable of the Fishing Net thrown into the Sea (Mt 13:47–50), indicates the universality of Christ's call into the Kingdom, and at the same time the Judgement to come. The fishers' net catches all kinds of fish, good and worthless, and it is only when the fishing is over, and the net has been pulled to the shore, that the selection can take place. The truth which the parable teaches is that in the Kingdom of God, as realized on earth, there would be good and bad members, and that the separation between them is reserved for the end at the Final Judgment. It thus forewarns the disciples against scandal resulting from the presence of evil in the Kingdom, and reminds them that the establishment of the Kingdom of God will not result in the disappearance of evil from the world. The disciples, therefore, must not expect a sudden, miraculous transformation of the world, which would make it resemble heaven, and must not be scandalized when persecution comes, from the coexistence of the Kingdom and of evil.

The parable of the Mustard Seed (Mt 13:31–32) illustrates the small beginning of Christ's Kingdom, its gradual and imperceptible growth, both in the individual and in the world at large, ultimately reaching vast proportions, leavening cultures, institutions, philosophies, and governments. In the life of the individual Christian, the Kingdom may start small but it should grow up to fill our entire life, on earth and in eternity. A similar parable is that of the

Yeast in the Dough (Mt 13:33; cf. 16:11–12). The woman in the parable takes three measures of flour, an amount sufficient to feed about fifty people. Three measures of flour are the same measure that we hear about in Genesis, when Sarah provides bread at Abraham's request for the three angelic visitors at the Oak of Mamre. Thus in the minds of the hearers of the parable, the number suggests that a special revelation of God is taking place. Yeast is a powerful agent of change. A lump of dough left to itself remains just what it is. However, when the yeast is added to it, a transformation takes place which produces rich and wholesome bread when baked. The Kingdom of God produces a transformation in those who receive the new life which Jesus Christ offers. The yeast works quietly and yet powerfully.

The parable of the Treasure hidden in the Field (Mt 13:44) is one of those at the lakeside reproduced by Saint Matthew in which different aspects of the Kingdom of Heaven are brought out by Our Lord. This parable is followed by that of the pearl of great price and that of the fishing net and forms with those a group of parables found only in the Gospel of Saint Matthew. The two parables of the hidden treasure and of the pearl of great price are closely related and teach the same lesson, namely the supreme value of the Kingdom of Heaven, for which all else must be sacrificed without any hesitation. The lesson comes over so clearly that Our Lord does not give an explanation of these two parables to the disciples. Christ does not intend us to imitate the manner in which the finder gets possession of the treasure. The sole point which Our Lord intends here is the eagerness of the man who is willing to sell everything he owns in order to get the treasure, the latter being supposed naturally to be of much greater value. Jesus Christ is the true Treasure; in Him there is an abundance of all that which is rich and useful and glorious. The Field in which this treasure is hidden is the Church, with her teaching and sacraments. The parable of the Pearl of Great Price (Mt 13:45–46) resembles that of the treasure. Both parables have some common and some different elements. In both cases, it is about something precious: a treasure and a pearl. In both cases there is a finding of the object desired, and in both cases the person goes and sells all he owns so as to be able to buy the precious item. In the first parable, the discovery seems by chance. In the second, the discovery is the result of the effort of seeking. Here we see two basic aspects of the Kingdom of God. The Kingdom exists, it is hidden in life, waiting for those who will find it; the Kingdom is the result of a seeking process. These are the two basic dimensions of Christian life: gratitude of love that welcomes us and comes to meet us, and the faithful observance that brings us to meet God.

Finally, in the parable of the Householder (Mt 13:51–52), Jesus directs the Apostles to follow the instructions He had given them for the benefit of others. He compares them to a good householder, who *brings forth out of his treasure things new and old*. The scribe is compared to 'a householder'. The Greek word translated as householder means 'the master of the house'. Master implies great authority as well as responsibility over his house. The master of the house has the final say in deciding what is best for his household. This parable therefore alludes to the authority entrusted by Christ to His Apostles in teaching, governing and sanctifying His Church as the seed of the Kingdom.

Christ's Kingship is clarified during the questioning Jesus underwent before the judgment seat of Pilate. The accusations made against Jesus were that 'He misleads the people; He opposes the payment of taxes to Caesar and maintains that He is the Messiah, a king' (Lk 23:2). Therefore, Pilate asked Christ if He was a king. Jesus replied: 'Mine is not a kingdom of this world; if My kingdom were of this world, My men would have fought to prevent my being surrendered to the Jews. As it is, My kingdom does not belong here.' The evangelist states: 'So Pilate said to Him, "Then you are a king?" Jesus answered, "You say I am a king. For this I was born and for this I came into the world, to testify to the truth. Everyone who belongs to the truth listens to My voice"' (Jn 18:36–37).

This declaration concludes all the ancient prophecies which flow through Israel's history and which become a fact and a revelation in Christ. The words of Jesus enable us to grasp the flashes of light which streak through the mystery condensed in the three terms: kingdom of God, messianic kingdom, People of God called together in the Church. Along this path of prophetic and messianic light, we can better understand and repeat, with clearer comprehension of the words, the prayer Jesus taught us (Mt 6:10): 'Thy kingdom come'. It is the kingdom of the Father, which entered the world with Christ; it is the messianic kingdom which develops through the work of the Holy Spirit in man and in the world, in order to return to the heart of the Father in the glory of heaven.[2]

This Kingdom of God, begun with Christ's Death and Resurrection, must be further extended by the Church, until it has been brought into perfection by Christ at the end of time. Jesus gathered disciples to be the seed and the beginning of His Kingdom on earth, and Jesus sent the Holy Spirit to guide them. The Christian does this by living the way Christ lived, by thinking the way Christ thought and by promoting peace and justice. This can be accomplished by discerning how the Holy Spirit is calling one to act in the concrete circumstances of one's life. The Church on earth prays, asking God for what is necessary to cooperate with the coming of His Kingdom. Jesus continues to call all people to come together around Him and to spread His Kingdom across the entire world. However, the ultimate triumph of Christ's Kingdom will not come about until Christ's return to earth at the end of time. During Christ's second coming, He will judge the living and the dead. Only those who are judged to be righteous and just will reign with Christ forever. Christ's second coming will also mark the absolute defeat of all evil powers, including Satan. Until then, the coming of the Kingdom will continue to be attacked by evil powers as Christians wait with hope for the second coming of their Saviour. This is why

Christians pray to hasten Christ's return by saying to him 'Marana tha!' which means 'Come, Lord Jesus!'

The phrase 'Kingdom of God' occurs 122 times in the New Testament as a whole; 99 of these passages are found in the three Synoptic Gospels, and 90 of these 99 texts report words of Jesus Himself. In the Gospel of John, and the rest of the New Testament writings, the term plays only a small role.[3] The Kingdom of God or Reign of God (Greek: Βασιλεία τοῦ Θεοῦ) is a foundational concept as a central theme of Jesus of Nazareth's message in the synoptic Gospels. The phrase is defined almost entirely by parable, as has just been outlined. In the synoptic Gospels (which were written in Greek), Mark and Luke adopt the Greek term 'Basileia tou Theou', commonly translated in English as 'Kingdom of God', while Matthew prefers the Greek expression 'Basileia tōn Ouranōn' (Βασιλεία τῶν Ουρανῶν) which has been translated as 'Kingdom of Heaven'. Biblical scholars speculate that the Matthean text adopted the Greek word for 'heaven' instead of the Greek word for 'God' because, unlike Mark and Luke, it was written by a Jew for a Jewish audience so, in keeping with their custom, avoided using God's name as an act of piety. In Matthew, 'heaven' stands for 'God'. The basis for these terms being equivalent is found in the apocalyptic literature of Daniel 2:44 where 'the "God of heaven" will set up a "kingdom" which will never be destroyed'. The term 'kingdom' is a translation of the Greek expression *basileia* which in turn is a translation of the words *malkuth* (Hebrew) and *malkutha* (Aramaic). These words do not define kingdom by territory but by dominion. Jesus said of the Kingdom of God that one cannot say, 'Look here it is!' or 'There it is!' (Lk 17:21).[4] The Greek word *basileia* can be rendered in English as 'kingship', 'kingdom' or 'reign'.

The Church cannot be reduced to an earthly dimension but is at one and the same time, earthly and heavenly.[5] The Church, while on earth journeys in a foreign land away from the Lord, and is living in exile. It seeks and experiences those things which are above, where Christ is seated at the right-hand of God, where the life of the Church is hidden with Christ in God until it appears in glory with her Spouse (cf. Col 3: 1–4).[6] It is part of the very mystery of the Church that her end is already present in a hidden way during her pilgrimage on earth. The Church's homeland (πολίτευμα) is in heaven (Ph 3:20), and the Jerusalem above is our mother (Ga 4:26).

Communion of saints

The communion of saints to which the Creed refers has two closely linked meanings. First, it signifies communion in holy things (*sancta*), above all the Holy Eucharist, by which 'the unity of believers, who form one body in Christ, is both represented and brought about'.[7] The acclamation *Sancta sanctis*! ('God's holy gifts for God's holy people!') is proclaimed by the celebrant in most Eastern liturgies during the elevation of the holy Gifts before the distribution of Communion. The term 'communion of saints' refers also to the communion of 'holy persons' (*sancti*) in Christ who 'died for all', so that what each one does or suffers in and for Christ bears fruit for all.[8]

At the present time some of Christ's people are pilgrims on earth. Others have died and are being purified, while still others are already in glory, contemplating God the Holy Trinity in full light.[9] All of the Church militant, the suffering Church and the triumphant Church in varying degrees and in different ways share in the same bond of love towards God and each other, and all sing the one hymn of glory to God. All, indeed, who are of Christ and who have His Spirit form one Church and in Christ form one communion.[10] The impact of the saints in heaven upon the Church on earth is not only by way of example, or that we merely cherish the memory of those in heaven. Rather, devotion to the saints strengthens communion within the whole Church in the power of the Holy Spirit: 'Exactly as Christian communion among our fellow pilgrims brings us closer to Christ, so our communion with the saints joins us to Christ, from Whom as from its fountain and Head issues all grace, and the life of the People of God itself.'[11] The saints in heaven intercede actively for the Church on its pilgrim way here on earth: 'So it is that the union of the wayfarers with the brethren who sleep in the peace of Christ is in no way interrupted, but on the contrary, according to the constant faith of the Church, this union is reinforced by an exchange of spiritual goods.'[12]

There exists also a communion with the Holy Souls still awaiting their final purification. The communion of the whole Mystical Body of Jesus Christ also implies a charitable concern to pray for the deceased, 'because it is a holy and a wholesome thought to pray for the dead that they may be loosed from their sins' (cf. 2 M 12:45). The Holy Sacrifice of the Mass offered for the dead helps them, and 'our prayer for them is capable not only of helping them, but also of making their intercession for us effective'.[13]

This communion of saints which reveals the features of the Kingdom is somewhat hidden to the eye of modern man, caught up as he is in the tangible and empirical realities of the cosmos:

> For many, the life of the Kingdom of God seems too demanding, a weak competitor in relation to the dazzling fascinations offered by the world of material wealth and pleasure. For nearly two thousand years, throngs have rejected God's call in Christ to the kind of discipleship we have been describing. But this does not disprove the validity of that call; it simply testifies to the fact that it relates to a truth which the world is still unwilling to accept. Jesus, therefore, stands before the church not as a quaint symbol of its past, but as a daring sign of the future toward which all reality yearns.[14]

The concept of kingdom has been understood and interpreted in various ways throughout the history of the Church. Among the Church Fathers, there were several interpretations of this term. The first dimension is the Christological one. Origen called Jesus the *autobasileia,* or the Kingdom in person. Thus the Kingdom is not a thing, it is not a domain governed like worldly kingdoms; rather, Jesus Himself is the Kingdom. The Kingdom is so inseparable from Christ that, in a certain sense, it is identified with Him.[15]

A second way of looking at the significance of the Kingdom of God, is the mystical interpretation. It locates the Kingdom of God within man. Origen also developed this approach when, in his treatise on prayer, he observes:

> Those who pray for the coming of the Kingdom of God pray without any doubt concerning the Kingdom of God that they contain in themselves, and they pray that this Kingdom might bear fruit and attain its fullness. For in every holy man it is God who reigns... So if we want God to reign in us, then sin must not be allowed in any way to take hold in our mortal body... Rather, let God stroll at leisure in us as in a spiritual paradise and rule in us alone with his Christ.[16]

Thus, the Kingdom is located in man's inner being, and grows and radiates outward from that inner space.

A third dimension of the interpretation of the Kingdom of God is one that may be termed ecclesial: the Kingdom of God and the Church are related in different ways and brought into varying degrees of proximity. This last approach gradually became the dominant one.[17] Thereafter, for many of the Fathers of the Church, the medieval Doctors and even the reformers, the Church and the Kingdom were practically identified. However, over the last two centuries there has been a tendency to distinguish between the Church and the Kingdom in various ways.

Nowadays the Kingdom is often treated theologically, but not always in a way consonant with the mind of the Church. Some ideas about salvation and mission are 'anthropocentric' in the reductive sense of the word, inasmuch as they are focused solely on man's earthly needs. In this view, the Kingdom tends to become a completely human and secularized reality; what counts are programs and struggles for a liberation which is socio-economic, political and even cultural, but within a horizon that is closed to God. This view easily dissolves into yet another ideology of purely earthly progress. The kingdom of God, however, is not of this world, nor does it derive from the world (Jn 18:36).[18] Any analysis of the relationship between the Kingdom of God, the Kingdom of Christ, and the Church, must avoid one-sided solutions, as is the case with those conceptions which exclusively emphasize the Kingdom and which describe themselves as kingdom-centred. They stress the image of a Church which is not concerned about herself, but which is totally concerned with bearing witness to and serving the kingdom. It is a 'Church for others,' just as Christ is the 'man for others'. Together with positive aspects, these conceptions often reveal negative aspects as well. First, they are silent about Christ: the kingdom of which they speak is 'theocentrically' based, since, according to them, Christ cannot be understood by those who lack Christian faith, whereas different peoples, cultures, and religions are capable of finding common ground in the one divine reality, by whatever name it is called. For the same reason, they put great stress on the mystery of creation, which is reflected in the diversity of cultures and beliefs, but they are silent about the mystery of Redemption. Furthermore, the Kingdom, as they understand it, ends up either leaving very little room for the Church or else undervaluing the Church in reaction to a presumed ecclesiocentrism of the past and because they consider the Church herself only an ambiguous sign.[19] These theses are contrary to Catholic faith because they deny the unicity of the relationship which Christ and the Church have with the Kingdom of God.

The meaning of the expressions Kingdom of heaven, Kingdom of God, and Kingdom of Christ in Sacred Scripture and the Fathers of the Church, as well as in the documents of the Magisterium, is not always exactly the same, nor is their relationship to the Church, which is a mystery that cannot be totally contained by a human concept. Therefore, there can be various theological explanations of these terms. However, none of these possible explanations can deny or empty in any way the intimate connection between Christ, the Kingdom, and the Church.[20] In fact, the kingdom of God which we know from revelation, cannot be detached either from Christ or from the Church.

> If the kingdom is separated from Jesus, it is no longer the kingdom of God which He revealed. The result is a distortion of the meaning of the kingdom, which runs the risk of being transformed into a purely human or ideological goal and a distortion of the identity of Christ, who no longer appears as the Lord to Whom everything must one day be subjected (cf. 1 Co 15:27). Likewise, one may not separate the kingdom from the Church. It is true that the Church is not an end unto herself, since she is ordered toward the kingdom of God, of which she is the seed, sign and instrument. Yet, while remaining distinct from Christ and the kingdom, the Church is indissolubly united to both.[21]

Here on earth, the Church is the initial budding forth of that Kingdom, its seed and beginning.[22] While it slowly grows, 'the Church strains toward the completed Kingdom and, with all its strength, hopes and desires to be united in glory with its King'.[23] The birth of the Church and the coming of the Kingdom are simultaneous. The Church is the Kingdom already present in mystery.[24] It is clear that the final destiny of the Church and the Kingdom must be one and the same. The inseparable relationship between Christ and the Kingdom does not eliminate the fact that the Kingdom of God, even considered in its historical phase, is not completely identified with the Church in her visible and social reality. The action of Christ and the Spirit happens also outside the Church's visible boundaries.[25]

Can one consider the Church to be the sacrament of the Kingdom? If one were to use this term, it is clear that it is in an analogical way, like when it is used to designate the Church as sacrament of Christ.[26] This idea expresses the relation between the Kingdom understood in its full significance as fulfilment on the one hand, and the Church on its pilgrim way, on the other. The term sacrament renders the fact that the Church is the reality of the Kingdom present here in mystery. The Church is not purely a sign (*sacramentum tantum*), but contains the reality signified and present in the sign (*res et sacramentum*) as a reality of the Kingdom.[27] The concept of Church cannot be limited only to her earthly and temporal existence, and, at the same the time, the idea of Kingdom includes a presence here and now in mystery.

The Church and the Kingdom find their most perfect fulfilment in Mary, Mother of God. In Our Lady the Church can be seen already realized as the Kingdom. The fact that the Church renders the Kingdom present in mystery is clear from the fact that Mary is the tabernacle of the Holy Spirit, the model of faith, and the Mother of the Word Incarnate. In Mary, the Church has already reached that perfection in which she is without spot or wrinkle (Ep 5:27). The distance between the pilgrim Church and the fulfilment of the Kingdom has been bridged by Mary assumed into heaven, who already anticipates and experiences the beatific vision of all the blessed in heaven. Therefore, the Mother of God is the first fruits and image of the Church which will experience her fulfilment in the world to come.[28]

The triumph of the Church

In recent years, at least since the Second Vatican Council, there has been a tendency to ignore the glorious aspect of the Church, her link with those members who have already arrived at the end of their pilgrimage. The problem arises with the application of kenotic theology to the Church. The Greek word kénōsis (κένωσις) signifies an 'emptying', from kenós (κενός), meaning 'empty'. The expression has been employed mainly in a Christological context, deriving from St Paul's letter to the Philippians: 'Jesus emptied (ἐκένωσε) Himself, taking the form of a slave' (Ph 2:7). The kenosis theory states that Jesus gave up some of His divine attributes while He was a man here on earth. These attributes were omniscience, omnipresence, and omnipotence. Christ did this voluntarily so that He could function as a man in order to fulfil the work of redemption. This view was first introduced in the late eighteenth century in Germany with Gottfried Thomasius (1802–1875), a Lutheran theologian. However, the letter to the Philippians does not teach that Jesus gave up any of His divine attributes and in fact does not treat those attributes; He did not give up the divine attributes nor their use. That He still possessed His divinity may be seen, for example, in the Transfiguration. Christ only exercised the divine attributes as directed by the Holy Spirit for the purpose of His Messianic and Redemptive mission. Therefore, kenosis speaks of His humility that moved Him, according to the will of the Father, to leave His majestic state in heaven and enter into the humble position of human nature.

A further danger emerges when kenotic theology is applied to the Church, in opposed to the so-called triumphalism of the past. In recent years, the kenotic aspect of the Church has been over-stressed at the expense of her present participation in the glorious Risen Christ. It is true, however, that before Christ's Second Coming the Church must pass through a final trial that will shake the faith of many believers (cf. Lk 18:8; Mt 24:12). The persecution that accompanies her pilgrimage on earth will unveil the 'mystery of iniquity' in the form of a religious deception offering men an apparent solution to their problems at the price of apostasy from the truth. The supreme religious deception is that of the Antichrist, a pseudo-messianism by which man glorifies himself in place of God and of His Messiah come in the flesh.[29] The Antichrist's fraud already begins to take shape in the world every time the claim is made to achieve within history that messianic hope which can only be realized beyond history through the eschatological judgement.

The Church has rejected false notions of the coming Kingdom under the name of *millenarianism*. This involves a thousand-year reign of Christ on earth prior to the Universal Judgment. The error is also known as *chiliasm*, from the Greek *chiliasmos*, meaning 'a thousand years'. The essence of this teaching is as follows. Before the end of the world, Christ will once again return to earth, defeat the Antichrist, resurrect only the righteous, and establish a kingdom on earth in which the righteous, as a reward for their struggles and sufferings, will reign with Him for a period of thousand years, enjoying all the good things of temporal life. After this, another resurrection will follow in which the rest of the people will be raised from the dead. Then the Universal Judgment will take place, and God will reward the righteous and punish the sinners. The defenders of this teaching base their arguments on the vision of the Apostle John in the book of Revelation (Jn 20:4–8). Millenaristic views in antiquity were spread chiefly among heretics. For example, the Gnostic Cerinthus, who flourished towards the end of the first century, proclaimed a splendid kingdom of Christ on earth which He would establish with the risen saints upon His second coming, and pictured the pleasures of this one thousand years in vivid sensual detail.[30] However, unfortunately also the Catholic bishop Papias of Hierapolis, a disciple of St John, appeared as an advocate of millenarianism. In his writings, as recounted by Eusebius, Papias asserted that the resurrection of the dead would be followed by one thousand years of a visible glorious earthly kingdom of Christ.[31] According to St Irenaeus, Papias taught that the saints too would enjoy a superabundance of earthly pleasures.[32] In 381 AD, the First Council of Constantinople condemned the heresy of Apollinaris of Laodicea concerning the thousand-year Kingdom of Christ.[33] To put a stop to further attempts at introducing this error, the Fathers of the Council inserted into the Creed these words about Christ: 'His Kingdom will have no end.'

The most powerful adversary of millenarianism was Origen of Alexandria. Because of the Neo-Platonism on which his doctrines were founded and of his spiritual-allegorical method of explaining the Holy Scriptures, he could not side with the millenarians. He combatted them expressly, and, owing to the great influence which his writings exerted on theology especially in Oriental countries, millenarianism gradually disappeared from the panorama of Oriental Christendom. In the Middle Ages, forms of millenarianism were taken up again by Joachim of Fiore and the spiritual Franciscans. Later, the Protestantism of the sixteenth century ushered in a new epoch of millenarian doctrines. Protestant fanatics of the earlier years, particularly the Anabaptists, dreamed of a new, golden age under the sceptre of Christ, after the overthrow of the Papacy and secular empires. It is important to understand that the twentieth chapter of the book of Revelation does not introduce any new teaching about the end of the world and the Second Coming of Christ. Its purpose is to summarize the battle between the Church and the devil which permeates the whole history of mankind. The devil is defeated twice: first spiritually, by the redemptive Death of the Saviour, and at the end of the world, completely and finally, when he will be thrown into the lake of fire. Even mitigated forms of millenarianism which appeared in the middle of last century are unacceptable and these systems cannot safely be taught.[34]

Similarly to be rejected are utopian views of the Kingdom. Utopia refers to an imaginary, ideal civilization, which may range from a city to a world, regarded by some as attainable in the future of this present world.[35] Excluded by the Christian vision is the view, common to Marxism and other materialistic philosophies, that man, through his own efforts, will be able to set up his own earthly paradise in the here and now. Communism claims to inaugurate a new era and a new civilization which is the result of blind evolutionary forces culminating in a humanity without God. It involves a collectivist mentality in the utopia of a classless society.[36] Communism, more emphatically than similar movements in the past, conceals in itself a false messianic ideal. A pseudo-ideal of justice, of equality and fraternity in labour impregnates all its doctrine and activity with a deceptive mysticism, which communicates a zealous and contagious enthusiasm to the multitudes entrapped by delusive promises. This is especially true in an age like ours, when unusual misery has resulted from the unequal distribution of the goods of this world.[37] Also false is the notion, prevalent in materialistic Western thought, that a scientific utopia can be created, whereby advanced science and technology will allow utopian living standards; for example, the absence of death and suffering, and changes in human nature and the human condition. In many ways, utopianism is but a representation of gnosticism in modern guise.[38]

The Church will enter the glory of the kingdom only through a final Passover, when she will follow her Lord in His Death and Resurrection. The Kingdom will be fulfilled, not by a historic triumph of the Church through a smooth progressive ascendancy, but only by God's victory over the final unleashing of evil, which will cause His Bride to come down from heaven (cf. Rev 13:8; 20:7–10; 21:2–4). God's triumph over the revolt of evil will take the form of the Last Judgement after the final cosmic upheaval of this passing world (Cf. Rev 20:12; 2 P 3:12–13).[39]

The Church will therefore receive its final perfection only in the glory of heaven, at the time of Christ's glorious return. Until that day, the Church progresses on her pilgrimage amidst this world's persecutions and God's consolations.[40] Here below she knows that she is still in exile far from the Lord, and longs for the full coming of the Kingdom, when she will be united in glory with her King. The Church, and through her the world, will not be perfected in glory without great trials. Just as there was a special outpouring of divine grace to welcome our Lord's first coming, so it will be at His second advent. We do not know how near that may be, but the wheels of His chariot are speeding on. Only then will all the just from the time of Adam, from Abel, the just one, to the last of the elect, be gathered together in the universal Church in the Father's presence.[41]

The union between the Church on earth and the Church in heaven is brought about in the most special way in the sacred Liturgy, where the power of the Holy Spirit acts upon us through sacramental signs. The Eucharist gives a real foretaste of the eschatological fulfilment for which every human being and all creation are destined (cf. Rm 8:19ff.). While man is created for that true and eternal happiness which only God's love can give, his wounded freedom would go astray were it not already able to experience something of that future fulfilment. That fulfilment and goal is Christ Himself, the Lord who conquered sin and death, and who is present in His Body and Blood in the Eucharistic sacrifice. Even though we remain 'aliens and exiles' in this world (1 Pt 2:11), the Eucharistic banquet, by revealing its powerful eschatological dimension, comes to the aid of our freedom as we continue our journey. Every Eucharistic celebration accomplishes sacramentally the eschatological gathering of the People of God. So, the Eucharistic banquet is a real foretaste of the final banquet foretold by the prophets (cf. Is 25:6–9) and described in the New Testament as 'the marriage-feast of the Lamb' (Rev 19:7–9), to be celebrated in the joy of the communion of saints.[42] Then, with combined rejoicing we celebrate together the praise of the divine majesty; then all those from every tribe and tongue and people and nation who have been redeemed by the Blood of Christ and gathered together into one Church, with one song of praise magnify the one and triune God. Celebrating the Eucharistic sacrifice therefore, we are most closely united to the Church in heaven in communion with and venerating the memory first of all of the glorious ever-Virgin Mary, of Blessed Joseph and the blessed apostles and martyrs and of all the saints.[43]

Notes

1. See Pope John Paul II, *Discourse at General Audience* (7 August 1991).
2. See Pope John Paul II, *Discourse at General Audience* (4 September 1991).
3. See Pope Benedict XVI, *Jesus of Nazareth* (New York: Doubleday, 2007), pp. 47–48.
4. According to C. H. Dodd, the common translation of 'malkuth' with 'basileia' in Greek and hence 'kingdom' in English is therefore problematic; a translation with 'kingship,' 'kingly rule,' 'reign' or 'sovereignty' should be preferred. See C. H. Dodd, *The Parables of the Kingdom*, (London: Fontana, 1961), p. 29.
5. See International Theological Commission, *Selected Themes in Ecclesiology* (1985), 10.1.
6. See Vatican II, *Lumen Gentium*, 6.
7. Vatican II, *Lumen Gentium*, 3.
8. See *CCC* 948, 960–961.
9. See Vatican II, *Lumen Gentium*, 49; cf. Mt 25:31; 1 Co 15:26–27.
10. See Vatican II, *Lumen Gentium*, 49; cf. Ep 4:16.
11. Vatican II, *Lumen Gentium*, 50.
12. Vatican II, *Lumen Gentium*, 49
13. *CCC* 958.
14. P. D. Hanson, 'The Identity and Purpose of the Church' in *Theology Today* 43(1985), p. 351.
15. Cf. Origen, *In Matthaeum Homilia*, 14, 7 in *PG* 13, 1197; Tertullian, *Adversus Marcionem*, IV, 33, 8 in *CCL* 1, 634.
16. Origen, *On Prayer*, 25 in *PG* 11, 495–498.
17. See Pope Benedict XVI, *Jesus of Nazareth*, pp. 49–54.
18. See Pope John Paul II, Encyclical Letter *Redemptoris Missio*, 17.
19. *Ibid.*
20. See Congregation for the Doctrine of the Faith, *Dominus Iesus*, 18.
21. Pope John Paul II, Encyclical Letter *Redemptoris Missio*, 18; cf. Idem, Apostolic Exhortation *Ecclesia in Asia*, 17.

22. See Vatican II, *Lumen Gentium*, 5.
23. *Ibid.*
24. See International Theological Commission, *Selected Themes in Ecclesiology*, 10.2. See Vatican II, *Lumen Gentium*, 3: 'The Church, or, in other words, the kingdom of Christ now present in mystery, grows visibly through the power of God in the world.'
25. See Pope John Paul II, Encyclical Letter *Redemptoris Missio*, 18.
26. See Vatican II, *Lumen Gentium*, 1.
27. See International Theological Commission, *Selected Themes in Ecclesiology*, 10.3.
28. See International Theological Commission, *Selected Themes in Ecclesiology*, 10.4. See also Vatican II, *Lumen Gentium*, 65, 68.
29. See 2 Th 2:4–12; 1 Th 5:2–3; 2 Jn 7; 1 Jn 2:18, 22. See also R. H. Benson, *Lord of the World* (Teddington: The Echo Library, 2005). The scene depicted in *Lord of the World* is one where creeping secularism and godless humanism have triumphed over religion and traditional morality. It is a world where philosophical relativism has triumphed over objectivity; a world where, in the name of tolerance, religious doctrine is not tolerated. It is a world where euthanasia is practiced widely and religion hardly practiced at all. The lord of this nightmare world is a benign-looking politician intent on power in the name of 'peace', and intent on the destruction of religion in the name of 'truth'. In such a world, only a small and shrinking Church stands resolutely against the demonic 'Lord of the World.' See also V. Solovëv, *I tre dialoghi—Il racconto dell'Anticristo*, (Torino: Marietti Editori, 1975).
30. See Eusebius, *Ecclesiastical History*, 3, 28 in *PG* 20, 273–276.
31. See Eusebius, *Ecclesiastical History*, 3, 39 in *PG* 20, 299–300.
32. See St Irenaeus, *Adversus Haereses*, Book 5, chapter 33, 3 in *SC* 153, 414–415. Irenaeus recounts how Papias described the days in which vines will grow, each with 10,000 branches, and on each branch 10,000 twigs, and on each twig 10,000 shoots, and in each shoot 10,000 clusters, and on each cluster 10,000 grapes, and each grape will produce 216 gallons (25 metretas) of wine.

33. See Constantinople I, *Symbolum Constantinopolitanum* in DS 150. See also St Basil of Caesarea, *Epistle 263*, 4 in *PG* 32, 980; St Epiphanius, *Panarion*, LXX, 36 in *PG* 62, 696; St Jerome, *Commentary on Isaiah*, 18 in *PL* 24, 627.
34. Holy Office, *Decree* (1941) in DS 3839.
35. The word *utopia* derives from the Greek: οὐ (no), and τόπος, place, meaning 'no place' or 'a place that does not exist'.
36. See Pope Pius XI, Encyclical Letter *Divini Redemptoris*, 12, 13.
37. See *Ibid.*, 8.
38. See C. Gnere, *Le radice dell'utopia. L'incompatibilità tra utopia e giudizio cristiano* (Chieti: Solanelli, 2006), pp. 71–75.
39. See *CCC* 677.
40. See St Augustine, *The City of God*, Book 18, chapter 51, 2 in *PL* 41, 614.
41. See Vatican II, *Lumen Gentium*, 2. See also St Gregory the Great, *Homiliae in Evangelia* 19, 1 in *PL* 76, 1154.
42. See Pope Benedict XVI, Apostolic Exhortation *Sacramentum Caritatis*, 30–31.
43. Vatican II, *Lumen Gentium*, 50.

Select Bibliography

Balthasar, H. U. von, *The Office of Peter and the Structure of the Church*. San Francisco: Ignatius Press, 1986.

Daniélou, J., *L'Eglise face au monde*. Paris : La Palatine, 1966.

Daniélou, J., *Pourquoi l'Eglise?* Paris: Fayard, 1972.

Dulles, A., *Models of the Church*. London: The Catholic Book Club, 1978.

Garuti, A., *Il mistero della Chiesa: manuale di ecclesiologia*. Roma: Pontificio Ateneo Antonianum, 2004.

Hardon, J. A., *Holiness in the church*. Bardstown, KY: Eternal Life, 2000.

Jaki, S. L., *Les tendances nouvelles de l'ecclésiologie*. Rome: Herder and Herder, 1957.

Jaki, S. L., *The Keys of the Kingdom*. Chicago, Ill: Franciscan Herald Press, 1986.

Jaki, S. L., *And on this Rock. The Witness of One Land and Two Covenants*. Manassas, Va: Trinity Communications, 1987[2].

Journet, C., *Theology of the Church*. San Francisco: Ignatius Press, 2004.

Journet, C., *The Church of the Word Incarnate*. London: Sheed and Ward, 1955.

Knox, R., *Enthusiasm. A Chapter in the History of Religion*. Oxford: Clarendon Press, 1977.

La Soujeole, B.-D. de, *Introduction au mystère de l'Église*. Paris: Parole et Silence, 2006.

Lubac, H. de, *Catholicism. Christ and the Common Destiny of Man*. London: Burns & Oates, 1962.

Mersch, E., *The Theology of the Mystical Body*. St Louis: Herder, 1958.

Mondin, B., *Le nuove ecclesiologie*. Roma: Edizioni Paoline, 1980.

Mondin, B., *La Chiesa primizia del Regno*. Bologna: EDB, 1986.

Nicolas, J. H., *La Chiesa e i Sacramenti*, vol. II of *Sintesi Dogmatica. Dalla Trinità alla Trinità*. Città del Vaticano: LEV, 1992.

Ratzinger, J., *Church, ecumenism and politics*. New York: Crossroad, 1987.

Ratzinger, J., *Called to Communion. Understanding the Church Today*. San Francisco: Ignatius Press, 1996.

Ratzinger, J. and Pera, M., *Without Roots. The West, Relativism, Christianity, Islam*. New York: Basic Books, 2006.

Ratzinger, J., *Journey to Easter: Spiritual Reflections for the Lenten Season*. Chestnut Ridge, NY: The Crossroad Publishing Company, 2006.

Ratzinger, J., Benedetto XVI, *New Outpourings of the Spirit*. San Francisco: Ignatius Press, 2007.

Pope Benedict XVI, *Christ and His Church: Seeing the Face of Jesus in the Church of the Apostles*. London: Catholic Truth Society, 2007.

Ratzinger, J., Benedict XVI, *A Turning Point for Europe?* San Francisco: Ignatius Press, 2010.

Schnackenburg, R., *The Church in the New Testament*. London: Burns & Oates, 1974.

Scola, A., *Chi è la Chiesa?: una chiave antropologica e sacramentale per l'ecclesiologia*. Brescia: Queriniana, 2005.

Semmelroth, O., *Die Kirche als Ursakrament*. Frankfurt: Knech, 1953.

Tanner, N. P., *The Church and the world: Gaudium et spes, Inter mirifica*. New York: Paulist Press, 2005.

Teuffenbach, A. von, *Die Bedeutung des subsistit in (LG 8). Zum Selbstverständnis der katholischen Kirche*. München: Herbert Utz Verlag, 2002.

Index

D

Q

R

U

V

W

X

Z

From GRACEWING

By the same author

Mystery of Creation

In practically the only recent book in English to give a global picture of the theology of creation, Paul Haffner explores God's masterpiece, the spiritual and material cosmos, from the angels to man and woman centred in Christ. Mystery of Creation touches many well–worn areas of interest in Christian faith and experience, including creation out of nothing, the beginning of the world, man and woman , and original sin.

Many topics of current concern are treated, like the world of spirits, the evolution of the universe and of life, the problem of evil, and the place of animals. Not only does the book take at new look at scientific, ecological and women's issues, it also shows how this universe is our home and yet is a prelude to the New Creation: the best is yet to come!

'The work achieves its aim admirably, accessibly presenting the principal issues at the heart of this foundational treatise in Christian dogmatics.'

Fr Paul O'Callaghan, Dean of Theology,
Santa Croce University, Rome

ISBN 978 0 85244 316 3

The Sacramental Mystery

The seven sacraments lie at the centre of Christian life and experience, for here God the Holy Trinity touches human lives and hearts. This book is one of the few at the present time to offer a global synthesis of the main themes in the sacramental mystery in which the human and divine, the material and the spiritual realms are intimately intertwined. Paul Haffner outlines how the sacraments are the chief means in the Church through which God's people are reconciled to the Father, through His Son, by the power of the Holy Spirit. The treatise illustrates classical issues like the conditions for the validity and the efficacy of the sacraments, as well as the minister, recipient and effects of these sacred mysteries; it deals with particular topics like the necessity of Baptism, the sacrificial character of the Eucharist, and the nature of Marriage. As he examines each sacrament in turn, the work also explores how new ecumenical questions affect Christian sacramental understanding.

'I warmly commend this work on the subject of sacramental theology.'

Archbishop Csaba Ternyák,
Secretary of the Vatican Congregation for the Clergy

ISBN 978 0 85244 476 4

The Mystery of Reason

The Mystery of Reason investigates the enterprise of human thought searching for God. People have always found stepping–stones to God's existence carved in the world and in the human condition. This book examines the classical proofs of God's existence, and affirms their continued validity. It shows that human thought can connect with God and with other aspects of religious experience. Moreover, it depicts how Christian faith is reasonable, and is neither blind nor naked. Without reason, belief would degenerate into fundamentalism; but without faith, human thought can remain stranded on the reef of its own self–sufficiency. The book closes by proposing that the human mind must be in partnership with the human heart in any quest for God.

'This fine work may be seen as a response to the Papal encyclical *Fides et Ratio*. It is an exploration of the relationship between faith and reason, and in so doing it makes use of a variety of approaches including philosophy, theology and contemplation. It is wholly faithful to the vision of the Church.'

Dr Pravin Thevathasan

ISBN 978 0 85244 538 9

The Mystery of Mary

The Blessed Virgin Mary stands at the heart of the Christian tradition. She holds a unique place in the Church's theology, doctrine and devotion, commensurate with her unique position in human history as the Mother of God. In this book, Paul Haffner offers a clear and structured overview of theology and doctrine concerning Mary, within an historical perspective. He outlines the basic scheme of what constitutes Mariology, set in the context of other forms of theological enquiry, and, working through the contribution of Holy Scripture—in the Old Testament forms of prefiguration and the New Testament witness—he proceeds to examine each of the fundamental doctrines that the Church teaches about Our Lady. From the Immaculate Conception to Mary's continuing Motherhood in the Church as Mediatrix of all graces, the reader will find here a sure and steady guide, faithful to tradition and offering a realist perspective, not reducing the concrete aspects of Mary's gifts and privileges to mere symbols on the one hand, and not confusing doctrine and devotionalism on the other.

'In one comprehensive volume Father Haffner has successfully brought together the major strands of Mariology, both in their historical and doctrinal dimensions. He has once again brought his particular gift of clarity to bear on this important theological discipline as he has done earlier in his texts on the sacraments, fundamental theology and theological anthropology.'

Thomas D. Williams, Dean of Theology,
Regina Apostolorum University, Rome

ISBN 978 0 85244 650 8

Towards a Theology of the Environment

Pope Benedict XVI declared at the beginning of his Pontificate that external deserts in the world are growing, because the internal deserts have become so vast. Therefore the earth's treasures no longer serve to build God's garden for all to live in, but they have been made to serve the powers of exploitation and destruction. This book is a theological investigation of the environment, and takes in scientific, biblical, moral and spiritual themes, all addressed by recent Church teaching on the subject. The starting point is a detailed analysis of the various problems assailing the environment at present. Then a distinction is made between the science of ecology and the ideological overtones which are often associated with this area. Next, an overview of Christian teaching on ecology is present as an antidote to both New Age pseudo-mysticism and political ideology. A Christian theology of the environment is then formulated which has consequences for our moral life and our prayer.

'The author largely succeeds in respect to the lofty goals he set for this deeply thoughtful work. A Christian theology of the environment is well formulated here, one that can have considerable impact on Christianity (the largest of the world religions) but also on other religions, governments and society as a whole.'

Thomas D. Watts, Faculty Member,
University of Texas

ISBN: 978 0 85244 368 2

Creation and scientific creativity
A study in the thought of S. L. Jaki

Father Stanley Jaki (1924-2009) was one of the greatest thinkers of the twentieth century and his contribution to Catholic thought and culture has been profound, especially regarding the relationship between science and religion. Jaki highlighted the Christian origins of the modern natural sciences. He showed that the concept of the cosmos as both contingent and rational, together with the acceptance that God could work through secondary causes, provided the unique environment for the natural sciences to flourish, from the Middle Ages onwards. He explored the crucial role played by belief in creation out of nothing and in time, reinforced by faith in the Incarnation, in enabling this birth of science. This book contains the first systematic treatment of the ideas of the late Stanley Jaki, and is the only complete work, with an entire bibliography, approved by him during his lifetime.

'Haffner's work offers an excellent synthesis of Jaki's thought, with an elegant and fluid style.'

Mgr Mariano Artigas, Dean of Philosophy, University of Navarra

ISBN 978 085244 454 2

Style Manual for Essays and Theses

How often have you struggled over your creative writing or over an academic text and found that you needed help with the style and layout? Many students and scholars find difficulty in organizing their method for producing short papers, dissertations or even books. Here at last is a guide, originally developed for philosophy and theology students, but not exclusively so, which accompanies the would-be writer through the maze of style and method. One consistent approach is followed, in which method is viewed as a means rather than as an end, so that the student should be able to see the wood for the trees. This manual will come to your aid especially if you want to figure out footnotes, end notes, and bibliographies, so as to make your essay or thesis both readable and professional.

'Comprehensive, yet succinct and easy to use, Fr Haffner's style manual is an essential aid for students who want to write well and a boon to teachers who long to read better papers.'

Elizabeth Lev, Professor of Art History
Duquesne University

ISBN 978 085244 743 7

CPSIA information can be obtained
at www.ICGtesting.com
Printed in the USA
LVHW101310200123
737519LV00006B/161